"*Spiritual Junk Food* . . . is an eye-opening book—one that should be required reading for Christian parents and educators everywhere. *Spiritual Junk Food* provides a great service by detailing how a watered-down, psychologized version of Christianity is being presented to students in place of the real thing. The yellow brick road of pop Christianity is paved with good intentions, but as Mickels and McKeever point out so convincingly, it leads in the wrong direction."

—William K. Kilpatrick, Ph.D
Author of *Psychological Seduction* and
Why Johnny Can't Tell Right from Wrong

"*Spiritual Junk Food* . . . is a documented but sad story of how pop psychological concepts have infiltrated Christian religion programs for young people. A kind of feel-good subjective faith is replacing the real thing. Come on, Christians, after years of this sentimental slop, let's wake up!

—Paul Vitz
Professor of Psychology, New York University
Author of *Psychology As a Religion*

D1409484

Printed in the United States of America

Published by WinePress Publishing, PO Box 1406, Mukilteo, WA 98275.

Unless otherwise noted all scriptures are taken from the New American Standard Bible, © 1960, 1963, 1968, 1971, 1972, 1973, 1975, 1977 by The Lockman Foundation. Used by permission.

Verses marked KJV are taken from the King James Version of the Bible.

ISBN 1-57921-169-0
Library of Congress Catalog Card Number: 98-83240

Doug, Shannon, and Scott McKeever; and
Stan, Erik, Aaron, and Elisa Mickels—
we dedicate this book to you.

Acknowledgments

We would like to give a heartfelt and sincere thanks to Paul Beck, pastor of Calvary Bible Church in Huntsville, Alabama, and Gary Small, pastor of Liberty Fundamental Baptist Church in Bellingham, Washington. We are not only indebted to them for their commitment to preach the sufficiency and inerrancy of Scripture, but for their example to uncompromisingly stand in defense of the gospel. The time they spent critiquing our manuscript and then discussing and sharing their insights with us is appreciated more than words can express.

There are many who have given generously of their time and energy and have encouraged us along the way more than we are sure they realize.

We would like to say a special thank you to Lisa Beck, Annetta Small, Eileen Sobjack, Leslie Kelly, Joni Park, Jana Gates, Diane Williams, Heidi and Jerry Watson, Susan Horsmon, Debi Schleimer, Mary Ann Filippini, Sandy Thomas, Ann Giarde, Nancy Galbraith, Linda Nathan, Carol Ann Mickels, Helen Steele, and Debbie Schuitema. We appreciate you.

We would also like to thank John Stormer, author of *None Dare Call It Treason* and *None Dare Call It Education,* for his willingness to share his literary expertise with us.

Finally, we would like to give a special thanks to our husbands, Doug McKeever and Stan Mickels, because if we did not have their support, this book would never have been written.

Contents

Preface xi

Chapter 1:
    But I Don't Like Licorice! 15
Chapter 2:
    Gimmicks, Fads, and Mind Games 31
Chapter 3:
    It *Is* a Duck 41
Chapter 4:
    More Child Abuse in the Classroom 59
Chapter 5:
    Judge Not! Tolerating Tolerance 79
Chapter 6:
    A Pseudo and Reckless Faith 95
Chapter 7:
    Idolatry of Self-Worship 111
Chapter 8:
    Encounter in the Trees 131
Chapter 9:
    Tweaking Scripture 147

Chapter 10:
   Youth Ministry: A Biblical Model? 163
Chapter 11:
   Raising Up Daniels 181

Appendix A:
   Music for the Sensual or the Sacred? 193
Appendix B:
   The Gospel According to St. Bernard? 199
Appendix C:
   Evaluating Curricula Used in the Church 227

Endnotes 233
Index 251
About the Authors 255

Preface

Our story began approximately fifteen years ago when our paths met as we came face to face with the cultural war, each in our own respective school districts. We plunged tirelessly forward in the battle on the local, state, and national fronts, immersing ourselves in writings that revealed the philosophies and goals of secular humanist writers impacting the education of millions of children in this nation.

It quickly became apparent to us that the public education system had become a vehicle to promote ideas contrary to traditional thought and behavior. Children had become a captive audience for experimentation and indoctrination. They were being programmed for politically correct thinking through non-academic social programs, such as sex education, drug abuse courses, death education, and self-esteem programs—all of which were taking valuable time away from instruction in reading, writing, math, history, and science.

We experienced firsthand the radical transformation taking place in the American education system and discovered that the systematic change in educational philosophy had more to do with the evaluation and manipulation of children's values and behavior than it had to do with teaching children to read, write, and compute. What has been referred to as the "old basics"—reading, writing, and arithmetic—were being replaced with the new basics—self-esteem, teamwork, group learning, and tolerance. The new basics dealt with assessing feelings and attitudes instead of acquiring knowledge. *Group encounters, sensitivity training, values clarification, decision making, critical thinking, role-playing,* and *peer teaching* became buzzwords in public school classsrooms across the nation.

This cultural battle in the public schools has been about ideas that have helped contribute to the moral and spiritual decline of our nation—ideas and values that secular humanists have been promoting with great fervency. Their adamant goal to proselytize others to humanism and their open contempt for the Christian faith is evident in the following quote taken from *Humanist* magazine (Jan./Feb. 1983), in an article titled "A Religion for a New Age."

> I am convinced that the battle for human-kind's future must be waged and won in the public school classroom by teachers who correctly perceive their role as the proselytizers of a new faith. . . .
>
> These teachers must embody the same selfless dedication as the most rabid fundamentalist preachers, for they will be ministers of another sort, utilizing a classroom instead of a pulpit to convey humanist values in whatever subjects they teach, regardless of the education level—preschool day care or large state university.
>
> The classroom must and will become an arena of conflict between the old and the new—the rotting corpse of Christianity, together with all its adjacent evils and misery, and the new faith of Humanism, resplendent in its promise of a world in which the never-realized Christian ideal of "love thy neighbor" will finally be achieved.

In order to accomplish their aggressive humanistic goals, teaching methods and techniques were put in place in our nation's schools to capture the hearts and minds of children.

Parents who have been battling in the public schools discovered firsthand the zeal with which many teachers and administrators embraced these humanistic philosophies and teaching methods. In times past, Christian parents could send their children to school knowing that their children would be taught to respect and obey their parents. Today, however, children are being subjected to new educational practices that, in far too many cases, challenge the morals, beliefs, and values of their parents.

There have been many books written on the influences of secular humanism on public education and the subsequent decline of American education. It is not the scope of this book to elaborate upon the crisis in the public school, but rather to show how humanistic philosophies and the teaching methods responsible for this crisis in education have found their way into the church. The writers of the anti-Christian *Humanist Manifesto* acknowledged that, in order to deceive Christians into secular-humanist thought, "the distinction between the sacred and the secular can no longer be maintained."[1] In other words, the particular features that mark the difference between Christianity and humanism must be destroyed.

Tragically, however, not many in the church are talking about this perverse invasion of the secular into the sacred. In fact, once we exposed the harmful philosophies and teaching techniques being foisted upon unsuspecting children, we discovered that the same response given to us by parents, teachers, and administrators in the public schools was given by many Christians in the church. The response was one of denial. We were told: "That may be happening somewhere else, but not in my school, not in my church!"

We fervently hope that this invasion is not happening in your church, but we have personally seen it in our mainstream churches. Even if this subversive aggression is not happening in your church, when other churches fall victim to deception, the entire Body of Christ is affected. Using leaven as a symbol of impurity, Scripture warns, "A little leaven leavens the whole lump of dough" (Gal. 5:9).

We must pay attention and be on guard! We must diligently protect what God has entrusted to us, for these are urgent, critical times. It is crucial that we get back to the basics of our faith as found in the infallible, inerrant Word of God. We do not pretend to have all the answers. We do, however, recognize the pressing need to raise the questions and to initiate the discussion addressing the concerns that are identified in this book.

This is a wake-up call to the Christian church to protect Christian children from the assault on their faith. Christians today must be like the Bereans, Christians of the early church, who scrutinized everything the apostle Paul taught by diligently examining the Scriptures (see Acts 17:11). Our desire should be the same as David's, the Psalmist, who said, "Lead me in Thy Truth and teach me" (Ps. 25:5). After determining the truth, church leaders and all who are followers of Jesus Christ must be bold and willing to take tough stands in order to stop this infiltration of the world's foolishness into the church.

The late Abraham Kuyper (1837–1920), a Dutch theologian, is often quoted when a defense of the Christian faith requires a stand. "When principles that run against your deepest convictions begin to win the day, then battle is your calling, and peace has become sin; you must, at the price of dearest peace, lay your convictions bare before friend and enemy, with all the fire of your faith." A distinguished biblical expositor, the late Dr. Martyn Lloyd-Jones, talks about how we are to take our stand. His words eloquently expressed our prayer for all Christians during these often confusing and turbulent times.

> May He enable us together to stand as a rock in the raging seas all around us. We must, of course, never pride ourselves on our stand, or become self-righteous or small-minded persons. But in humility and obedience, let us follow the apostolic exhortations, always coming to know more deeply our glorious God, remembering that He has redeemed us, and aware of what a glorious faith it is to which He has called us to bear witness. Here let us take our stand.[2]

Chapter 1

But I Don't Like Licorice!

. . . your faith should not rest on the wisdom of men, but on the power of God.

—1 Cor. 2:5

Frustration mixed with disbelief overwhelmed us as one of our teenage daughters described the trust-walk activity done in her church youth group that evening. "You did what?" was our cry of alarm.

Consequently, that very night many of the books written by humanistic authors that we had read in order to understand and then refute curricula being promoted in the public school were once again pulled from our bookshelves. Two books that contained the trust walk were *Carl Rogers on Encounter Groups* and *Teaching Human Beings: 101 Subversive Activities for the Classroom.*

We first discovered this exercise many years ago in a controversial drug education program. Needless to say, we were shocked to find it now being used with youth in our local church. It immediately became an urgent matter for us to warn our children about the dangers of participating in a trust-walk activity—or any other humanistic, psychological mind game.

It took precedent over everything else in which we were currently involved.

Almost simultaneously, a curriculum entitled *The Gospel According to St. Bernard* arrived on our church secretary's desk. Because of our fifteen years of experience with public school curricula, the secretary, disturbed by the curriculum's title, asked if we would preview the video series and accompanying material. Upon critiquing "Bernie's gospel," we were deeply distressed. Not only was Jesus presented as a sinner, but there were activities in which the children were to role-play the devil and tattle on their parents. We could hardly believe it.

It was precisely because of those two personal experiences in our own churches that we were compelled to investigate what else was happening under the guise of Christian education.

Reshaping Values and Attitudes

We discovered that we did not have to look any further than our local Christian bookstore to find the latest fads for Christian youth. The amount of Christian youth curricula saturated with the same activities that have been used for years in controversial, nonacademic, public school curricula was shocking. Many of you will probably recognize at least one of the following:

- Here's Looking at You Two
- Quest
- KNOW
- Positive Action
- Pumsey
- FLASH
- Tribes
- Circles

Those curricula are filled in one form or another with situational ethics; moral dilemmas; role-playing; open-ended, privacy-invading questions; self-esteem; and values clarification. Senior researcher at the Hoover Institution, Thomas Sowell, makes the following disturbing observation about such curricula:

> A variety of courses and programs, under an even wider variety of names, have been set up in schools across the country to change the values, behavior, and beliefs of American youngsters from what they have been taught by their families. . . . These ambitious attempts to reshape the attitudes and consciousness of a generation are as pervasive as they are little known, partly because they have kept a low profile, but more often because they are called by other, high-sounding names— "values clarification," "decision-making," "affective education," "Quest," "drug prevention," "sex education," "gifted and talented" programs, and many other imaginative titles. The particular door through which such programs enter the school curriculum is far less important than what they do after the have gained entrance.[1]

Over ten years ago, the extent of this national public school travesty was published in the book *Child Abuse in the Classroom* by Eagle Forum President and conservative leader Phyllis Schlafly. This eye-opening book contains the official transcripts from grieving parents who testified before the US Department of Education on what was being done in the name of education. From Seattle to Pittsburgh, parents told of how their children had been emotionally, morally, and intellectually abused by psychological and behavioral experiments during classroom hours, when parents thought their children were being taught basic knowledge and skills.

It was not only parents who noticed this radical change in the direction of education in America. In 1978, US Senator and former educator Samuel I. Hayakawa warned the Senate that our nation's schools had become vehicles for a "heresy that rejects the idea of education as the acquisition of knowledge and skills, . . . [and instead] regards the fundamental task of education as therapy."[2]

The result of this disturbing move away from the basics of education can be summed up by the words of an observant

Washington State college professor, who, with remorse in his voice, said, "Today, students can all tell you how they feel, . . . but they can't give you any facts." Why? Because our schools have been busy educating the senses and emotions of the child instead of concentrating on his intellect. Likewise, Christian youth groups that find themselves moving away from the disciplined study of God's Word will suffer the same fate.

We asked ourselves, Why would Christian leaders want to copy the ideas used in the public school to instruct Christian youth? Author and pastor John MacArthur Jr. has identified this overt dependency on worldly methods in his hard-hitting book *Our Sufficiency in Christ*. He warns that "authentic, Christ-centered, sound doctrine is being abandoned for popular market-driven concepts and methods."[3] From all outward appearances, God's Word is no longer considered sufficient to teach Christian youth about God!

Spiritual Malpractice

If Jesus and his disciples walked the earth today, they would never encourage young children to role-play the devil. They also would not teach a biblical truth by simulating for children the excitement of sinning. Neither would they lead teens blindfolded into the woods to hug trees, nor instruct teens to feed each other licorice in order to experience the "sweetness" of Christ's forgiveness. Yet those astounding nontraditional activities, along with their corresponding humanistic philosophies, have become the popular approach embraced by the leading publishers of contemporary Christian youth material.

In order to justify the use of those unconventional methods and activities, Youth Specialties (Zondervan) accuses the church of indoctrinating youth by trying to preach its point of view louder than the rest of the world. In contrast, the stated alternative of Youth Specialties is to discourage teachers from being too preachy, by refraining themselves from correcting a student even "if what they say is opposed to the teachings of the Bible . . ." or, worse yet, even if "those comments . . . seem like heresy."[4]

In defense of their nontraditional position, they say teenagers need to feel secure about what they are thinking "no matter how unpopular or 'wild' their ideas might be." In other words, the message being given to teens is that there are no right or wrong answers. And unknown to parents, under the new rules of this classroom, Christian youth may be participating in activities that only add to the moral confusion that already exists.

Zondervan is guilty of making skeptics out of our teens by telling them that "each of them should be questioning their belief in God independently of their parents' faith." Although Zondervan defends that as the stretching of the students' minds, it actually undermines the faith and authority of the parents. Zondervan is encouraging teens to doubt and question biblical truth, which sounds similar to the eighteenth-century humanists, who believed that in order to arrive at truth one must question and doubt everything. How many parents use this stretching of the mind with their own children? To be sure, this is not what Christian parents would expect from a Christian publisher.

In contemporary youth curricula the teacher's role is also changing. In the traditional Sunday school or Christian classroom, the teacher was the authority figure expected to teach and transmit biblical truth to the next generation. But just as in the public school, the teacher has a new title and job description. Teachers are now becoming *facilitators* who direct and encourage group discussion. According to Youth Specialties the teacher is to discourage the group from assuming he or she is the authority on the subject. Why? Because if the teacher is reduced to the same level as students, "They will pay more attention to what you have to say."[5]

The endorsement of humanistic learning theories by leading Christian publishers is also relegating the Bible to the back of the class. According to Group Publishing, Inc., reading the Word of God is not considered one of the more potent forms of learning. Instead, Group Publishing unabashedly claims that it is man's personal experiences that will prove the most successful in teaching both adults and youth in the church. Hence, in their own words:

> Learning methods such as listening to lectures and sermons have their place. And reading the Word is essential. But we've tended to place all our hopes in these *passive methods*. And we've almost completely ignored the *more potent forms of learning*.[6]

The more potent forms of learning include personal experiences, contrived experiences, games, simulations, role-plays, . . . motion pictures, and television.[7] In other words, everything other than hearing and reading the Word of God is more potent! Thus, instead of depending on the sufficiency of Scripture "inspired by God and profitable for teaching" (2 Tim. 3:16), publishers are relying on the reasoning of man that places *self* in the driver's seat. This lack of absolute confidence in the power of the Word of God causes one to wonder what role the Bible will play in the days ahead. Will the Bible eventually be completely diregarded as Christian publishers advance the idea that truth can be discovered in personal and/or contrived experiences? To the contrary, experience cannot be a litmus test for truth, because man's experiences can lead to wrong conclusions. Biblical truth, on the other hand, is never wrong.

Joseph and Mary—Soap Opera Stars?

Zondervan's Youth Specialties is not alone in straying from the use of traditionally sound teaching methods in the church. Gospel Light, another publisher of youth material, claims they "believe it's a sin to bore a young person with the gospel."[8] So, in spite of their admission that most young people are biblically illiterate, they have resorted to presenting the gospel in "creative ways"—primarily unorthodox activities, including role-playing Matthew 1:18–25 as if it were happening on a daytime soap opera.[9] Teens are supposed to role-play, soap-opera style, Joseph receiving news that Mary, his wife-to-be, has already conceived a child.

Besides also depending on value clarification strategies, Gospel Light recommends illustrating an idea or theme by using a video clip from a movie, such as the *Dead Poet's Society* or *Indiana Jones and the Last Crusade,* which they say are "powerful ways to bring the Word of God into focus for this media-raised generation."[10] But it is a far stretch of the imagination to think that after students have watched the final scene of *Raiders of the Lost Ark* they will see "what a lot of people think about when it comes to the end of the world."[11] Or, likewise, to think a worthwhile discussion on the Book of Revelation will follow after viewing a Steven Spielberg video clip. Is not this publisher perverting the gospel and just giving back to Christian youth what the world has already given them? But, more importantly, for anyone to suggest the gospel is boring, and thus recommend it should share center stage with Hollywood productions, reveals a lack of belief in the power of the gospel of Jesus Christ.

As you seriously reflect on the humanistic philosophies and activities unfolding throughout the pages of this book, we ask you to prayerfully consider: Are these the philosophies and activities of a vibrant Spirit-led church, or are they the activities of a church that is losing its way?

More Moral Confusion

Upon reading *Trust Builders* by Denny Rydberg, national president of Young Life, we were surprised to discover that the book draws from many of the same unusual activities developed and popularized by secular humanists. Although Rydberg asserts that all the activities in his book are intended to help youth leaders bring their members closer to one another and closer to God, the activities will do otherwise. For instance, as you read the following exercise, consider the emotional impact of placing Christian friends in a moral dilemma requiring them to choose from two negative, unacceptable choices.

> You and your best friend are abducted by terrorists. They tell you that one of you must die. You both get to decide who it

will be—you or your friend. How will you and your friend decide what to do?[12]

To be sure, if an activity like this took place in a public school today, concerned parents would show up at their child's school insisting that this activity has nothing to do with academic learning and that the school has no business playing mind games with their child. Likewise, Christians should ask why it is being used on our youth in the church?

Whadaya Want on *Your* Tombstone?

Humanist educators in the early seventies developed a values clarification strategy to help students see their lives more clearly from the perspective of their imagined deaths. In order to achieve that, teachers instructed students to write out their own obituaries as they would appear in the school newspaper that day, or "as they would like it to appear in the school or town newspaper if they were to die three years hence." The authors recognized the sensitivity of the subject matter and warned the teacher to "try not to generate a lot of anxiety about this exercise. . . . Give some comfort to the few students who will be very resistant."[13]

One would never expect this controversial death-education activity to find its way into the church, but it has. However, the Christian version is worse! The activity found in a curriculum published by David C. Cook, yet another leading publisher of Christian youth material, takes Christian youth to the graveyard. The youth leader is instructed to "Insist on intense silence and have students dwell on one, solemn thought: When you're dead, what do you want people to say about you? What do you want on your tombstone?"

If they are not able to go to a cemetery, "bring the cemetery to the student" the exercise says, by cutting out individual tombstones, personalized with their own names. Instructions include dimming the lights in the room, and as the students enter, "encourage them to be quiet and reflective, and to ponder the question: What do you want your tombstone to say when you die?"

If the above emotional trauma is not enough, a variation is provided with an adult volunteer dressed in black, wearing a black hood, holding a hockey stick, silently pointing students to the graveyard where they can see their names on gravestones. The activity states that if the volunteer says anything at all it should be questions like: "What would they say at your eulogy if you died today?" and "Would you have any regrets if you died on the spot right now?"[14]

The authors of "Whadaya Want on Your Tombstone?" claim their series will challenge students to take their faith to the extreme and they should "Be prepared for an intense ride." However, we warn youth pastors and parents, this is one intense ride you do not want your youth to take.

Simulating Sinning

It is bad enough that contemporary youth curricula suggest taking youth to a graveyard to help them imagine their own death, or propose having youth decide whether it will be their friend or themselves who will live or die. But incredibly, Christian youth may actively take part in an exercise that simulates sinning! According to the lesson "Steal the Jewels" by Group, in order to teach children ages four through twelve avoidance of temptation, the teachers need to simulate for the children the excitement of temptation.

Youth are instructed to stand in a circle about ten feet across. After one child is chosen to be "It," marbles representing jewels are placed in a bandanna at his feet. The object of the game is for the remaining children to steal the jewels from the child who is "It" without getting caught (touched and frozen). Hence, the act of stealing goes from a simulated temptation to a simulated sin. However, in real life, sinning is serious and should never be taken lightly. It should never be presented to young children as exciting—and we should not have them practice it to ensure they discover that excitement! Ask any parent with young children, "Does the flesh of your child need reinforcement in doing what comes naturally?"

Tragically, the Sunday school lesson acknowledges that some children may have trouble bringing themselves to steal the jewels. In other words, there may be children in the class who take seriously the commandment that states unequivocally, "Thou shalt not steal." In an attempt to make such a child feel more comfortable about the simulated temptation, the teacher is instructed to "hint that they can all go for the bandanna at once." Under this kind of group pressure, in spite of a child's reluctance, he or she will more than likely go against the still, small voice telling him or her not to even entertain such ideas.

It should come as no surprise that the simulation is also followed by encounter group questions, like: "How did it feel to steal the jewels? How are those feelings like when you're tempted to do something wrong that you know is wrong? How is playing this game like giving in to temptation?"[15] The directions for the teacher state that when "kids give 'wrong' answers, don't correct them."[16] In essence, they are suggesting the acceptance of error is permissable in the church!

Instead of Christian authors and publishers depending on active learning (teaching by experience) to help "students internalize the truth as it unfolds" or "discover the truth for themselves," they need to get into the Word of God.[17] It is the Spirit of God and not the teaching methods of humanist educator John Dewey that will impact a child's life for eternity. Furthermore, the Christian response to sin and temptation could not be more clear than the very words of Jesus Himself on how we are to pray: "Lead us not into temptation, but deliver us from evil . . ." (Matt. 6:13). Keeping those words in mind, Christian parents need to protect their children from the spiritual confusion created by those who would use the simulation of sinning or the excitement of temptation as a teaching tool.

Hug a Tree

In the Book of Romans the apostle Paul warns us about those who would exchange the truth of God for a lie by worshipping and serving the creature rather than the Creator (see Rom. 1:25).

24

In other words, we are to worship God the Creator, *not* His creation. To do otherwise is to bring the seeds of pantheism into the church. Yet, in spite of this warning, Group is carelessly marketing a Sunday school curriculum that sounds more like material written for members of the radical environmental group Greenpeace than the children of Christian parents!

Claiming that Christian youth must learn to "think green," they are introduced to a "green" activity to learn stewardship of God's creation. With that objective, blindfolded children gather outside in the midst of trees to hug and feel them with their hands. Then, after everyone has had a chance to hug a tree, the teacher is instructed to proceed with touchy-feely questions, such as: "How did it *feel* to hug a tree? . . . How did you *feel* when you recognized the tree you hugged?" (emphasis added).[18] Suggesting to Christian youth that hugging a tree is going to bring about a positive human response is more than absurd and raises many questions about the kind of material being published by "Christian" publishing houses.

It is interesting to note that this ridiculous philosophy was the foundation for an outrageous experience for business owner Daniele Malpeli. Mr. Malpeli was actually cited for abusing a tree by chaining his bicycle to it in front of his delicatessen in Manhattan. The Manhattan city park commissioner suggested to the deli owner that "were he to apologize to the tree, he might receive amnesty from the environmental control board, which in such cases usually levies a $1,000 fine."[19] Therefore, in order to avoid further insult, the deli owner succumbed to the terms and agreed to literally hug a tree.

Consequently, to engage in the "green" activity will condition youth in the church to accept, like Mr. Malpeli, a philosophy that is at odds with biblical truth. As both the activity and above true story prove, the further we drift from truth, the more we are confronted with the foolishness of man. When unorthodox teachings are accepted and tolerated, we should not be surprised by the unorthodox activities that are sure to follow. Conversely, a theologically sound understanding of stewardship must recognize the biblical parameter that nature is not sacred and that the worship of a single, all-powerful God transcends His creation—and excludes the hugging of trees.

The Licorice Trick

What does licorice have to do with teaching children how to be set free from our sins? According to Group, the following activity of tying licorice strips around children's thumbs to represent sin is the new, contemporary way of imparting biblical truth to a fast-food generation stimulated by movies and videos games. The untraditional licorice activity is based on Group's stated philosophy:

> Traditional church curriculum, which often centers around *Bible memorization* (verses they can't even read) and exercises such as crossword puzzles and various fill-in-the-blank activities, is extremely *threatening* and *embarrassing* to functionally illiterate people. And in such situations, they usually opt to not attend Sunday school or other Bible-learning activities where the potential for embarrassment is high.[20] (emphasis added)

In other words, according to Group, to be traditional is to be outdated and no longer relevant for today's Christian youth, particularly when dealing with a society of nonreaders. However, we should question developers of Christian youth material who suggest or even imply that memorization of the Word of God is ever outdated, threatening, or embarrassing.

In the licorice activity, the teacher is instructed to mention four sins we've all done, such as, ". . . when you didn't tell the truth . . . when you were mean to someone . . . when you took something that wasn't yours . . . when you didn't obey your parents . . ." Each child should end up with four licorice strips tied in a knot around his or her thumbs. The children are told not to move their thumbs or break the licorice while the following questions are discussed: "How does it feel to be all tied up? What if you had to stay tied up like that all day? What do we need to do to be set free from our sins?"[21]

The teacher then tells the class that Jesus came to find lost people and save them, and that by accepting Jesus' free gift of forgiveness they can be saved too. Then, on the count of three, the children are told they can break out of their licorice ropes while the teacher leads kids in cheering. But before the class is allowed to eat any of their licorice, they must break off little pieces to feed each other. Once again, questions follow: "How is feeding each other like giving and receiving forgiveness? Why is it important to forgive other people?"

The teacher concludes the activity by saying: "Jesus is loving and forgiving, and He wants us to be loving and forgiving, too. And remember; Forgiveness is sweet—just like licorice—so share it."[22] To the contrary, dumbing down Scripture to suit what Group describes as an entertainment-learning culture serves to not only minimize the seriousness of sin and the biblical account of the forgiveness of a Holy God, but misses the mark entirely—particularly if, unknown to the teacher, one of the children happens to dislike licorice.

The Foolishness of Man

As evidenced by the preceding activities, publishers and developers of Christian youth material are unashamedly accepting the same worldly philosophies and secular teaching methods being promoted by the radical contemporary gurus of public education. The president of Group Publishing, Inc., Thom Schultz, blatantly states that the churches "can benefit from listening to the best thinkers in education today."[23]

In fact, on the back cover of his book, *Why Nobody Learns Much of Anything at Church: And How to Fix It,* Schultz states: ". . . we are all victims of an old approach to teaching and learning . . . programmed to repeat the mistakes of the past." Admitting that he plans to help "launch a new revolution" in the church, he boasts that his book contains the "cutting edge secular education models to help any church reinvent its approach to learning." One cannot help but wonder how men and women of the past became people of God without these latest educational fads to assist them!

This controversial experimental philosophy of learning that supports the removal of textbooks from the public school classroom and deemphasizes and even ridicules competition, traditional lecture-style teaching, and memorization has caused an uproar from parents crying out for a return to the basics. Many Christians, however, are unaware that leading contemporary Christian publishers and authors have also embraced these same radical educational theories and practices and are foisting them upon unsuspecting youth in the church. Just as these educational practices have backfired in our nation's schools, we predict that using them in the church will produce the same disastrous results.

Christian parents must not underestimate the far-reaching impact of ideas as has been noted and expounded upon by the late Richard Weaver (1910–1963), author of the book *Ideas Have Consequences* (University of Chicago Press, 1948). To be sure, there will be consequences when major Christian publishers mass market across the nation books and curricula filled with secular philosophies and teaching methods. Therefore, be aware! Even though a youth group, etc., is not using any of the curricula or material we mention, nonetheless, the potential for their ideas and philosophies reaching into churches is enormous.

No human game or exercise can even come close to teaching youth the attributes of God. To attempt to teach the sacred with the use of humanistic mind games while embracing trends and fads that the world has been using for the past thirty years or more, is to dethrone our God and insult His Holy Being. One must ask, Why would a Christian teacher try to come up with a man-made gimmick as a teaching tool when we have the Bible inspired by God? Because secular humanists attempt to live independently of God, they have nothing else to rely on but the latest trends and techniques.

The church must guard with fervor against becoming reliant on worldly trends and theories under the assumption that they can impart biblical truth. Any attempt to combine the secular and the sacred will result in a dumbed-down Christian unable to fully grasp or understand the power of God and His Word. All the wisdom of man is foolishness to God (see 1 Cor. 3:19). The previously mentioned gimmicks will not lead youth to a deeper relationship with Christ. To the contrary, youth leaders who participate in these worldly fads will be responsible for dumbing down the youth in the church and replacing a solid foundation in Christ with the foolishness of the world. In fact, lessons and activities that employ worldly methods and trends in an attempt to teach biblical truths are nothing more than spiritual junk food leading Christian youth toward spiritual malnutrition.

Chapter 2

Gimmicks, Fads, and Mind Games

Guard what has been entrusted to you, avoiding worldly and
empty chatter and the opposing argument of what is falsely
called "knowledge"—which some have professed and thus
gone astray from the faith.

—1 Tim. 6:20–21

Although it is not the purpose of this book to explore the worldly
theories of the psychologists who have contributed to the modern trends in education, some background must be laid concerning the undeniable impact of the theories of Dr. Abraham
Maslow and Dr. Carl Rogers, the acknowledged cofounders of
humanistic psychology. These men stand out as major contribu-
tors to the trends toward the psychotherapeutic classrooms in
the public schools, trends that tragically have found their way
into the church.

Even though the background information in chapters 2 and
3 is detailed and particular, it is important information in order to help understand and identify the perverse invasion of
the secular into the sacred. Christians need to be aware that
the theories of both Maslow and Rogers are unscriptural because they place "man and his needs at the center of the universe rather than God."[1]

Abraham Maslow hypothesized that human needs are ar-
ranged in a hierarchy. This is known as Maslow's Pyramid.

According to him, an individual must satisfy the higher-order needs—safety and security, love and belonging, and self-esteem— before he can be self-fulfilled, i.e., *self-actualized*.[2] The by-product of this process is the false belief that each individual has within himself the ability to discover the truth within. Many of the activities for contemporary youth curricula described in this book are based on Maslow's Pyramid.

Martin and Deidre Bobgan, authors and founders of PsychoHeresy Awareness Ministries, argue that Maslow's hierarchy of needs, along with many other need structures developed by contemporary psychologists, "operate as though God doesn't even exist."[3] Jay Adams, biblical counselor and noted author, also explains that, according to Maslow's theory, "to love God and to love other people (the sum of the commandments and, for that matter, the entire Scriptures) is not possible for a person until all his other needs have been met."[4] Adams adds:

> God or man is loved *in order to satisfy the needs of the one doing the loving*. One wonders how that kind of love can be equated with *agape* love—love in which a person reaches out to another with no thought of himself. Be that as it may, notice that the important thing to remember is that, according to this movement, unless one first gets his strokes, he cannot stroke another person. And whenever he strokes another, he is in reality only stroking himself.[5]

Carl Rogers is known for developing a nondirective technique of psychotherapy. The technique puts the psychologist in the role of listener as he guides the client to turn inward and seek the solutions to his own problems. Rogers later adapted this technique to a group setting, which popularly became known as an encounter group. This same psychotherapy technique found its way into the public school classroom during the late 1960s, via drug- and sex-education programs and other non-academic curricula. These curricula that frequently dealt with contemporary social issues encouraged students to "turn inward" and explore their feelings, values, and beliefs.

According to Adams, Christians should reject Rogerian counseling because the fundamental presupposition of the Rogerian method of psychotherapy is that the solution to man's problems lies in man himself, thus man is autonomous and has no need of God. Another Rogerian presupposition is that people in sin must be accepted and not criticized or admonished, no matter what they do.[6] Morality is not important. Both of those presuppositions are contrary to Scripture and must be rejected.

A Failed Experiment

As the psychotherapy approach to education in the public school classrooms across this nation gained momentum, disturbing trends in education began to develop. Perhaps the most obvious was the decline in national test scores, as disciplined study in academics, reading, writing, and computation were replaced with touchy, feel-good activities that taught children to love themselves and trust others in an attempt to meet their "felt needs." There had been a major shift "in emphasis on the part of curricula developers and educators from cognitive academic learning to the psychological development and social adjustment of the child in the affective domain, that is, his feelings, attitudes, and opinions."[7] Maslow saw in this academic decline a loss of respect for knowledge and the discipline of learning. Being Jewish, Maslow had "a long ethnic tradition of scholarship and professional attainment,"[8] so he grieved for his undergraduates who became more interested in encountering than in pursuing knowledge.

Another disturbing trend of the psychotherapeutic classroom was to redefine the loving and protective relationship between children and their parents. The new underlying presumption was that a child should be autonomous from his parents. The child was to become his own authority as he turned inward to determine which values and morals he would embrace and which course of action he would pursue. As the child took center stage, teachers took on the new role of facilitators and parents frequently abdicated their responsibility to teach and give direction. Surprisingly, Carl Rogers and his wife did not use the nondirective approach to parent their own children. Tacitly, they knew the dangers of raising their children without strong and persistent directives. It wasn't until their parental responsibilities had been met that Carl Rogers, under the influence of his own students, began to "argue that every home and classrooom ought to become the locus of nonstop, nondirective psychotherapy."[9]

Both Maslow and Rogers retracted their theories, but unfortunately this fact is little known. Maslow asserts in the preface for the posthumous edition of his book *Motivation and Personality* that "self-actualization should very definitely never have been applied to children."[10] Even Carl Rogers, who wanted and promoted therapeutic classrooms, saw one experiment after another fail. He wrote about this failed series of experiments in the section "A Pattern of Failure" in *Freedom to Learn for the '80s,* his final book on education.[11] Also, in 1981 at the convention of the Association for Humanistic Psychology, Rogers told those in attendance, "I hope Rogerian therapy goes down the drain."[12]

Dr. W. R. Coulson, who worked with Maslow and Rogers at the Western Behavioral Sciences Institute in the 1960s, was directly involved in the experiments to adapt humanistic therapeutic principles—active listening, "I" messages, and unconditional acceptance—to the classroom. Coulson, however, was one of the first to recognize that therapeutic classrooms were negatively affecting children. He is now trying to undo the damage of the therapeutic classrooms he helped to create. He travels around the country warning parents, teachers, administrators, and legislators.

Group Think

When we first became involved in reading and evaluating nonacademic curricula in our local public school districts, we discovered that teaching children the importance of the group was an integral part of preparing them to feel comfortable about encountering (i.e., openly expressing themselves). We also discovered that while parents were teaching their sons and daughters at home the importance of resisting the temptation to go along with the crowd, or the group, curricula in public school was subtly reinforcing the importance of acceptance by their peers.

We came across the activity "You're One of the Bunch" and thought it was a peculiar exercise for first graders—in, of all places, a drug-education program. According to the lesson plan, the teacher is to explain that "the whole class will work together to assemble one giant-sized puzzle with a special message. . . . Distribute a puzzle piece to each student. Place the puzzle outline on the floor and assemble the students around the outline. . . . When the puzzle is completed, read the caption to the students, 'You're One of the Bunch' and discuss what *belonging* means. . . ." The puzzle activity is followed up by discussion questions, such as:

1. "How did you *feel* while you were looking to fit your puzzle piece on the outline?"
2. "Did anyone help you find a match for your piece? How did that make you *feel*?"
3. "How do you think you would *feel* if yours was the only piece that didn't fit the puzzle?"
4. "How would you have felt if you had not received a puzzle piece?"[13]

The teacher is to "conclude by pointing out that it took everyone's efforts to complete the puzzle. Everyone is an important and needed class member." The teacher is also encouraged to reinforce the lesson by incorporating it into other subject areas, such as language arts: "Have a discussion using the yarn spider-web technique, where each student who speaks holds onto a piece of yarn ball. Encourage each child to contribute so they are *all part of the web*" (emphasis added).

The hidden assumption of this lesson is obvious: It is important to be one of the bunch! Or, as stated by a leading proponent of cooperative learning in the public school: "Students must feel that they need each other in order to complete the group's task, that 'they sink or swim together.'"[14] Unknown to trusting parents is that the process their children go through

35

to feel comfortable opening up with the group subtly trains the children to begin group thinking. Thus, group think, not independent thinking, is the value learned.

Group think is precisely the stated goal of atheist and socialist John Dewey, who is described as the most influential educational philosopher of the twentieth century. According to Dewey, who coauthored the *Humanist Manifesto I*, individualism has to be destroyed to elevate and promote the group. Dewey is quoted as saying, "Children who know how to think for themselves spoil the collective society . . . , where everyone is interdependent."[15]

It is alarming that developers of Christian youth curricula and such supplemental material are enthusiastically buying into and encouraging this same humanist-collectivist mindset. For instance, in his book espousing the philosophy of Group Publishing, Inc., Thom Schultz unequivocally admits that an individual should be assigned the job of making "sure that everyone understands and agrees with the answers *arrived at by the group*" (emphasis added).[16] In fact, by their own admission, Group discredits a traditional back-to-basics curricula, stating that it negatively programs us to believe "individualism and competitiveness are superior structures for learning."[17] Even more disturbing is their claim that in order for learners to "feel better about themselves," they must be taught in an environment of interdependence, not independence. Hence, the name of this publishing house, Group, and its overriding collectivist group philosophy go hand in hand.

National president of Young Life, Denny Rydberg, also asserts that "group building is important to the extent that it serves as a building block to growth: the growth of the group, and the group's ability to minister to one another. . . ."[18] This same national leader even admits that children will indeed lose their individuality to the group. In fact, after students have moved through what he describes as "the community building process," he boasts that "the kids are probably less a collection of individuals than they used to be. Your teenagers have begun to develop a meaningful sense of community."[19]

One of Rydberg's books on group building not only contains such foolish activities as the group hug, but also an activity that is strikingly similar to Your One of the Bunch, called "The Outsider":

> Pick one or two people to be the "outsiders." Have the remaining members of the group stand in a circle close together. The people forming the circle are supposed to try to keep the "outsiders" from getting inside the circle. Instruct the "outsiders" to try to get inside the circle. Let each person have the opportunity to be an "outsider." [20]

The discussion questions sound similar as well:

1. "How did you react to being an 'outsider'?"
2. "How did you feel trying to keep the 'outsiders' from gaining entry into the group?"
3. "What did you learn about yourself from this experience?"[21]

It is disturbing to discover that The Outsider is also found in Jeffrey Shrank's previously mentioned book, *Teaching Human Beings: 101 Subversive Activities for the Classroom.* Jeffrey Schrank claims in his 1972 book that the exercise is "a technique borrowed from the encounter groups" and "the ability of this game to generate feelings is amazing."[22] The goal of both humanist Schrank and the previously mentioned national leader for Christian youth, Denny Rydberg, are the same!

It is unthinkable that leaders in Christian education would adopt the same ideology, mindset, and terminology as the encounter-group crowd. As Christian authors, curricula developers, and youth leaders borrow ideas from each other, this philosophy spreads like wildfire and is unchallenged in the church. Conditioning Christian youth to think in terms of the group or the community is a deviation from teaching Christian youth to stand alone and *not* just go along. Group thinking is creating new thought processes in the church: from individual responsibility before God to group responsibility. Since when does the church need fads of the world to teach Christian youth to minister to one another and the world? On the contrary, the church of America needs strong Christian individuals who, like the biblical character Daniel, are willing to stand alone regardless of what those in the group—even church groups—may or may not think. The ultimate authority is not the group, but the Word of God.

The Intensive Group Experience

These group experiences, as already mentioned, have become known as group encounters. Other names, each with its own particular emphasis, include sensitivity training groups, T-groups (group dynamics), task-oriented groups, team building groups, and group psychotherapy. Often these terms are used interchangeably, since they all attempt to explore group interaction. According to the editors of *Sensitivity Training and Group Encounter*, group interaction is used "for dealing with various forms of interpersonal relationships, from ongoing social issues to the isolation, alienation, and distrust felt by the members of a group."[23] The editors acknowledge that the distinctions between the different names used to describe intensive group experiences are blurred due to the fact they all involve "complex human behavior and intense emotion."[24] Rogers himself confirms that the group experience is intense and powerful:

> [It] is a highly potent experience. . . . As a phenomenon it has been both praised and criticized, but few people who have participated would doubt that something significant happens in these groups. People do not react in a neutral fashion toward the intensive group experience. They regard it as either strikingly worthwhile or deeply questionable. All would agree, however, that it is potent.[25]

Even though there may be different emphases in individual encounter groups, there are several general characteristics that make group encounters identifiable. According to Rogers, a basic encounter group emphasizes "personal growth and the development and improvement of interpersonal communication and relationships through an experiential process."[26]

Differences between Discussion and Encountering

One must not confuse discussion or conversation among individuals in a group setting with group encounters. Discussions and group encounters may appear on the surface to be the same, but both have distinguishing characteristics. It is critical to be able to tell them apart, because if one thinks he is discussing but is actually encountering, then he has been duped into participating in a form of psychotherapy.

According to one definition, the act of discussing is an informal debate where one examines possible solutions for a given situation or problem. Conversations are simply informal verbal exchanges of thoughts and information between two or more individuals. On the other hand, a group encounter is a group of people who get together often under the direction of a leader/facilitator with the intention to increase self-awareness and encourage intimate personal relationships. Often unknown to the participants involved, however, is that their behavior and previously held beliefs may be changed through self-disclosure and/or strong emotional expression.

The Road of Error

The mixing of the Christian faith with humanistic philosophies and techniques is like the wolf in sheep's clothing. William Kirk Kilpatrick, an associate professor of educational psychology at Boston College, warns, "True Christianity does not mix well with psychology. When you try to mix them, you often end up with a watered-down Christianity instead of a Christianized psychology. But the process is subtle and is rarely noticed."[27]

Charles H. Spurgeon, the dynamic nineteenth-century preacher, reiterates, "There must be doctrine—solid, sound, gospel doctrine. . . . Getting children to meet in the morning and afternoon is a waste of their steps and yours if you do not set before them soul-saving, soul-sustaining truth."[28] Spurgeon admonishes all who teach children and youth,

> You are teaching children, so mind what you teach them. Take care what you are doing! . . . It is a child's soul you are tampering with. . . . It is a child's soul you are preparing for eternity. . . . If it is evil to mislead grey-headed age, it must be far more so to turn aside the feet of the young into the road of error, in which they may forever walk.[29]

Using psychology to replace the authority of Scripture is leading youth down the road of error. Employing gimmicks, fads, and mind games in an attempt to teach biblical truth not only takes valuable time away from the disciplined study of God's Word, but leads to false knowledge and faulty doctrine that may cause our youth to stray from their faith. As one pastor succinctly stated: "If you mix human wisdom, secular business, and psychology with biblical truth, you compromise the purity, the power, the clarity, and the effectiveness of the Word of God."[30]

Christians must be alert and trained to discern truth from error, right from wrong, and good from bad. Authentic biblical principles and practices must also be distinguished from ungodly theories and psychotherapeutic methods because ungodly theories and methods minister to the flesh rather than the spirit. Romans 1:22–23 gives the following warning to those who profess to be wise in their own eyes and vain about their own knowledge and abilities to reason: "Professing to be wise, they became fools, and exchanged the glory of the incorruptible God for an image in the form of corruptible man. . . ."

What will be the fruit of a church that tries to appeal to Christian youth by using the same gimmicks, fads, and mind games used to teach morality in the public school? Perhaps what is even more thought provoking is the following question: When a teacher in the public school plays amateur psychologist and invades the privacy of other people's children through the use of encounter-group activities, we call it "child abuse in the classroom," but what do we call it when it is takes place in the church?

(hapter 3

~~~~~~

It *Is* a Duck!

Be on your guard lest, being carried away by error of unprincipled men, you fall from your own steadfastness.

—2 Pet. 3:17

Working from the Rogers definition, which encompasses Maslow's theory of self-actualization, there are several key components to an encounter group. It is our intent to show that what Rogers called the "psychological climate" produced in an encounter group is the same psychological climate produced in numerous church curricula and programs for children and teens.

Perhaps the most glaring use of a psychological climate is found in certain youth ministries for middle and senior high students. Unknown to well-meaning youth leaders, Christian youth groups are frequently taking on the role of secular encounter groups only shrouded in religious terminology. Even though some say that Christian youth groups are not secular encounter groups, we say: If it walks like a duck, quacks like a duck, and looks like a duck—it is a duck!

According to Carl Rogers, the psychological climate produced in an encounter group is meant to encourage a reduction in one's defenses so that mutual trust can develop. This mutual trust allows one the freedom to express both negative and positive feelings as "each member moves toward greater acceptance

41

of his total being—emotional, intellectual, and physical."[1] The encounter group is also meant to foster a psychological climate in which an individual can receive feedback on how he appears to others while at the same time experiencing the various feelings and emotions "which have been hidden within."[2] The most important thing in group encounters (group psychotherapy) is to get people to talk openly.[3] Self-disclosure is critical to the encountering process.

Key words signifying the basic components of an encounter group include:

1. opening up
2. mutual trust
3. affirmation
4. feedback
5. experience

A Climate for Opening Up

Carl Rogers described how the group process encourages opening up and relating to one another.

> Only gradually does it become evident that the major aim of nearly every member is to find ways of relating to other members of the group and to himself. Then as they gradually, tentatively, and fearfully explore their feelings and attitudes toward one another and toward themselves, it becomes increasingly evident that what they first presented are facades, masks. Only cautiously do the real feelings and the real persons emerge.

When opening up, one becomes particularly vulnerable. As a result, an encounter experience may elicit extremely powerful emotions. Rogers added, "Participants feel a closeness and intimacy which they have not felt even with their spouses or members of their own family, because they have revealed themselves here more deeply and more fully than to those in their own family circle."[4]

The main focus of much of today's Christian youth curricula is also on bonding and opening up to one another in the group. Sometimes the objectives established by developers of Christian curricula are stated in slightly different terminology from the goals of the secular encounter group, but the meaning and intent are essentially the same. Such developers state their curricula is designed to "give teenagers a feeling of belonging" and to support teens by having "a family of peers."[5] The goal of much of it is to build a "close-knit community" where "individuals learn to trust the group enough to share their deepest feelings."[6] The emphasis is to create a climate where "individuals become more comfortable with each other . . . with the idea of sharing their ideas more openly."[7]

Often the words used by developers of curricula for Christian youth groups are almost the exact words used by secular psychologists describing the objectives of encounter groups. For example, the climate in today's youth group is to "help kids put down their armor and begin to trust within the group."[8] One curriculum series states that it is "highly relational" with a "personal growth emphasis."[9]

A Climate of Mutual Trust

The concept of "trust" is another key component to the secular encounter group. In order to freely share innermost thoughts and feelings, and to build bonds and a climate of sharing, one must have a certain level of trust of others in the group. Rogers wrote,

> It is a hunger for relationships which are close and real; in which feelings and emotions can be spontaneously expressed without first being carefully censored or bottled up; where deep experiences—disappointments and joys—can be shared; where new ways of behaving can be risked and tried out; where, in a word, he approaches the state where all is known and accepted.[10]

Is it coincidental that many of the Christian youth activities deal with trust? It appears that Christian curricula developers and

43

publishers are unaware that they are parroting humanistic philosophies. Denny Rydberg states in his book *Trust Builders: 71 Activities to Develop Community in Your Youth Group*, that a comfort level needs to be established so kids can trust each other. Once trust has been established, "they need to move to a new level—a level of discomfort." According to Rydberg, the exercises provide for the student "an opportunity to move beyond the comfort zone and achieve growth in relationships." He adds, "A youth group at this level offers an environment in which students can express their inner hurts, visions, and struggles without fear or ridicule."[11] It is important to note the similarities between Rydberg's goal for youth groups and what Rogers wrote about the group encounter.

Rydberg's statements that show the strong influence of Carl Rogers are also paralleled by Zondervan/Youth Specialties in *High School Talksheets*. "Creating a climate of acceptance" so students can "feel secure before they share their feelings and beliefs" is foundational to the *Talksheet* discussions. We contend, however, that *Talksheets* should more appropriately be called *Encountersheets*. The directions to the youth leader state: "Peer approval is paramount with teens. They are fearful of being ridiculed. . . . They need to know they can share what they are thinking, no matter how unpopular or 'wild' their ideas might be." To foster sharing and mutual trust, the teens are reminded, "What is said in this room stays in this room. Confidentiality is vitally important to a healthy discussion."[12]

Lyman Coleman, author of the Serendipity Youth Bible Study series, uses *team building* instead of using the word *trust*, but essentially he is talking about the same thing. A course description states that the Serendipity series is a "formula of group building, starting off light and moving deeper in sharing as the group is ready." Each lesson has a disclosure scale, which rates the level of personal disclosure in the lesson from "No Risk" to "High Risk." The disclosure level gradually increases throughout the series. The series boasts of teens becoming a "part of a caring, supportive group, where members help each other through the wear and tear of life."[13]

A Climate of Affirmation

Carl Rogers described affirmation as,

> . . . a warm regard for him as a person of unconditional self-worth—of value no matter what his condition, his behavior, or his feelings. It means a respect and liking for him as a separate person, a willingness for him to possess his own feelings in his own way. It means an acceptance of and regard for his attitudes of the moment, no matter how negative or positive, no matter how much they may contradict other attitudes. . . .[14]

Rogers also stated,

> Each person is an island unto himself, . . . and he can only build bridges to other islands if he is first of all willing to be himself and permitted to be himself. So I find that when I can accept another person, which means specifically *accepting the feelings and attitudes and beliefs* that he has as a real and vital part of him, then I am assisting him to become a person.[15] (empahsis added)

Interestingly, another key component of today's Christian youth groups that parallels secular humanistic reasoning is the act of affirming. One author states, "We also need to create a climate in which affirmations are the norm rather than the exception."[16] He adds, "Accept rather than confront. . . . Remember, the purposes of these activities [are] to help students begin to share in a safe environment. . . . When students share from their hearts, they need to experience acceptance first."[17] Still another curriculum developer says that one of his program's goals is to help "youth bring out the best in one another."[18] As noted previously, in one resource material by a leading publisher, the youth leaders are instructed to "let each person know their comments and contributions are appreciated and important. . . . Affirm even those comments that seem like 'heresy' to you."[19]

A Climate for Feedback

Feedback, according to Carl Rogers, is described as a process by which an individual, through freely expressive interaction, rapidly acquires a great deal of data as to how he appears to others. An example of one kind of feedback is for members in a group to describe each other as animate or inanimate objects. According to Rogers, powerful and highly constructive feedback can be the result of such an activity as long as the activity is done in the context of a caring group.[20]

Incredibly, in one activity book for youth groups there is an exercise called Zoo Keepers. This activity provides the same psychological climate for encouraging feedback. The youth are to form groups of no more than five, after which they form a cage by sitting in a circle. Each teen takes his turn in the cage. The teens forming the cage "take turns saying what kind of animal the caged person is most like and why."[21]

The goal, according to Rogers, of feedback is to accept each other once the facade and the mask have been let down. So it quickly becomes obvious that feedback will also be a significant component to many contemporary youth curricula and supplemental material. One publisher of activities for Christian teens writes: "It is important to bring some sort of closure to the session without negating the thoughts and opinions expressed by the group. A good 'wrap-up' should affirm the group." According to that publisher, the feedback from the youth leader to the teens also needs to reflect an attitude of mutual respect and acceptance regardless of the opinions and attitudes expressed—regardless if what the teens "say is opposed to the teachings of the Bible or the church or their leader."[22]

The Authority of Experience?

Rogers believed that an individual's experiences are even more authoritative than the Bible or a revelation of God.

> *Experience is, for me, the highest authority.* The touchstone of validity is my own experience. No other person's ideas, and none of my own ideas, are as authoritative as my experience.

It is to experience that I must return again and again, to discover a closer approximation to truth as it is in the process of becoming in me. Neither the Bible nor the prophets—neither Freud nor research—neither the revelations of God or man—can take precedence over my own direct experience.[23]

He also added:

I find I am at my best when I can let the flow of my experience carry me, in a direction which appears to be forward, toward goals of which I am but dimly aware. . . . When I am thus able to be in process, it is clear that there can be no closed system of beliefs, no unchanging set of principles which I hold. Life is guided by a changing understanding of and interpretation of my experience. It is always in process of becoming.[24]

The humanistic theory of experience is the same concept contemporary Christian curricula developers label "to learn by doing," or *active learning*. This is a key ingredient in youth group activities. As Group states,

Learning by doing is what active learning is all about. No more sitting quietly in chairs and listening to a speaker expound theories about God—that's passive learning. . . . With active learning, kids get to *do* what they're studying. They *feel* the effects of the principles you teach. They *learn* by experiencing truth firsthand.[25]

Also, according to Group, experiences evoke an emotional reaction, a statement to which Carl Rogers would have undoubtedly agreed. The publishers of Group go on to say that when using open-ended questions to probe feelings after an active learning experience, "Let your learners know that there are no wrong answers to these 'feeling' questions. Everyone's feelings are valid."[26]

Follow this philosophy to its natural conclusion: If the beliefs and feelings of an individual gained through his own personal learning experiences are all considered valid, the implication is that each individual is his own authority. It is then a small step away from thinking, albeit erroneously, that the authority of an individual takes precedent over even the authority of God and the Bible.

Copying the Counterfeit

In a section titled "A Word to the Youth Leaders," the author of the Serendipity Youth Bible Study series, Lyman Coleman, openly states, "If this sounds like something out of educational psychology, it is. The dynamics are the same."[27] By his own admission, Coleman is bringing psychology into the church.

In the *Encyclopedia of Education,* educational psychology is defined as "the scientific study of the behavior which occurs during the educational process"[28] The *Handbook of Educational Psychology* further explains that educational psychology deals with the fact that people are different, thus the focus on behaviors, thoughts, and individual interactions.[29] The study of man's behavior is gaining popularity in the church as evidenced by contemporary youth curricula. Church leaders and parents, therefore, must adamantly reject the youth leader's new role of becoming an educational psychologist to the unsuspecting teens who have been entrusted to his care.

The focus on opening up, the building of trust, affirmation of self and others, and the importance of experiences are not only key components of secular encounter groups, but they are also key components of numerous popular curricula for Christian youth. According to Rogers, the objective is to establish "a psychological climate of safety in which freedom of expression and reduction of defensiveness gradually occur."[30] Rogers words are paralleled by Coleman, "The purpose of this course is to become a Christian community in which you can talk about the real issues in your life with trust and respect for one another."[31] It quickly becomes obvious that the focus is on the individual, his behavior and thoughts, and his interaction with others, rather than on God. Coleman omits any mention of God—but shouldn't the purpose of a youth group be to get to know God and His Word better?

Theologian and biblical expositor Dr. Martyn Lloyd-Jones warns, "You must be careful in your observation of what a man does not say, as well as what he does."[32] Then he adds:

> I have discovered over the years that subtraction from the truth is something that members of churches are very, very slow to observe. I have almost come to the conclusion that the acid test to apply, to know whether a preacher [or youth curriculum] is evangelical or not, is this: Observe what he does not say![33]

If a curriculum developer emphasizes relationships with peers and neglects, or only superficially addresses, an intimate fellowship with the Lord, he is subtracting from the truth.

Authentic Christian Fellowship

We are *not* saying that Christian youth should not get together to get to know one another. Scripture tells us to fellowship with one another. We are not to give up meeting together, so that we may spur one another toward love and good deeds (see Heb. 10:24–25) and encourage one another to trust (see Prov. 3:5) and obey God (see Acts 5:29). However, authentic Christian fellowship cannot be prescribed. It is a natural outflow of worshipping God and studying God's Word together.

Fellowship with other believers is also not like other friendships in the world. As Christians get to know God better through worship, study, and prayer, they will also get to know one another better. Jesus Christ is the vine connecting each believer to Himself and, subsequently, to each other. Unlike many contemporary, trendy youth groups, self-disclosure is not a requirement. Genuine Christian fellowship is different from the contrived attempts to manipulate intimate relationships within an intensive encounter group experience.

In an article on group dynamics, W. R. Coulson argues that authentic Christian fellowship and trust "will simply not yield to gimmickry."[34] Coulson warns that "gimmicks being used on the unsuspecting . . . [is] contemptible." In other words, contrived gimmicks to foster fellowship just won't work. Authentic Christian fellowship acknowledges Jesus Christ at the center, "For where two or three have gathered together in My name, there I am in their midst" (Matt. 18:20). However, this biblical principle does not appear to be central to activities used in contemporary youth groups.

We have discovered that because of the emphasis placed on games and activities that often employ psychological gimmicks and techniques, time frequently runs out before teens get to the Bible study. As a result, the students do not have an opportunity to study God's Word together. It is through studying Scripture that our youth will grow in the knowledge of God. It is through Bible study and prayer that friendships will develop naturally and biblically.

Dr. M. Lloyd-Jones talks about the early church and the importance placed upon meeting together for the purpose of worshipping God and growing in knowledge about Him. He expounds,

> They meet together—for what reason? To worship God, to praise His blessed Name, to thank Him for the grace which has led to the forgiveness of sins, and for new life in Christ. They meet together also so that they may know Him better and come to understand His providence more perfectly. They hunger and thirst after righteousness. They also thirst for the sincere milk of the Word, and there is nothing they enjoy more than to study the Word, and to listen to it being proclaimed.[35]

The attitudes and lack of desire of today's Christians to study God's Word, compared with those of the New Testament church, show a real defection from a spiritual longing to have "knowledge of God, in a relationship in accord with His commandments." If Christians today are bored hearing God's Word proclaimed and instead want to dabble in current worldly trends, what does that say about their spiritual condition?

The Consequences of Ideas

Lyman Coleman is not the only author using psychotherapy on children; he is just the only one that we have found who openly admits it. Even though other authors and major publishers have not been so open about their use of psychotherapy in their youth curricula, they are using the methods and techniques just the same.

It is equally disturbing to realize how major authors and publishers have collaborated together in youth ministry resources and curricula. For example, Lyman Coleman and Denny Rydberg united efforts in the writing and production of the Serendipity Youth Bible Study series. Coleman wrote the foreword to Rydberg's book *Building Community in Youth Groups* while Group published Rydberg's book and its sequel. In his Serendipity series, Coleman reprinted by permission games taken from Group's *Quick Crowdbreakers and Games for Youth Groups.* The author of Group's Active Bible Curriculum *Psalms* recommends Rydberg's book *Trust Builders.* Zondervan/Youth Specialties recommends Rydberg's *Building Community in Youth Groups* in their *Talksheet* series.

The collaboration goes on. Interestingly, Rydberg, who for several years was the vice president of Youth Specialities, has built his five-step program for building community in youth groups upon the same five-level philosophy used by Reachout Expeditions, a division of Youth Dynamics. Reachout Expeditions, David C. Cook Publishers, Group, Zondervan's Youth Specialties, Gospel Light, Rydberg, and Coleman, all emphasize active and interactive learning and the importance of taking risks, while trust and relationships are also key themes.

It appears that the major contemporary authors and publishers are building upon each other's ideas, as evidenced by the same terminology being used and the stated philosophies articulated in the different curricula and resource material for youth. These prevailing ideas being repeatedly espoused reflect a mindset that, in far too many cases, is seeping into the church undetected, even if churches are not using the questionable material.

No Such Thing

Leaders of Christian youth groups, Christian curricula developers, and publishers may argue that they are not basing their work on secular psychology, but rather "Christian psychology." However, the Bobgans, who have followed and written about the infiltration of "psychoheresy" into the church for the past twenty years, argue that there is no such thing as Christian psychology. They state,

> "Christian psychology" involves the same confusion of contradictory theories and techniques as secular psychology. Professional psychologists who profess Christianity have simply borrowed the theories and techniques from secular psychology. They practice what they consider a perfect blend of psychology and Christianity. However, they use the same psychology as non-Christian psychologists and psychiatrists. They use theories and techniques contrived by such men as Freud, Jung, Adler, Fromm, Maslow, Rogers . . . none of whom embraced Christianity or developed a psychological system from the Word of God.[36]

Perhaps even more telling are the words spoken at the 1976 meeting of the Christian Association for Psychological Studies (CAPS), which is an organization of psychologists who are Christians. They admitted,

> We are Christians who are psychologists but at the present time there is no acceptable Christian psychology that is markedly different from non-Christian psychology. It is difficult to imply that we function in a manner that is fundamentally distinct from our non-Christian colleagues. . . . As yet there is not an acceptable theory, mode of research, or treatment methodology that is distinctly Christian.[37]

By their own admission, there is no distinction between the theories and methodology of secular and Christian psychologists. As a result, curricula developers and publishers who are employing "Christian psychology" are really engaging in secular psychology clothed in Christian vernacular. It can be concluded, therefore, that much of contemporary curricula is not being based upon the solid rock of Scripture, but rather upon the shifting sands of psychotherapy.

Moral Obligation

All Christians have a moral obligation to speak out against the use of humanistic philosophies and unbiblical methods with Christian youth. After all, what goes on in youth groups will affect countless numbers of Christian teens. One author boasts that his book has been used "by over 40,000 youth workers and by probably over a million students."[38]

In the beginning no one worried about group therapy interfering and taking time away from academic study; participants all welcomed group discussion. To use contemporary, faddish buzzwords taken from public school curricula and secular humanist authors, the participants were to become acquainted at a "deeper level" as they developed team spirit, a sense of community, and "respect for each other." However, just as academics suffered after the introduction of encounter group philosophy into the public school classroom, so will knowledge of the Bible decline in the church as youth group leaders strive to educate the emotions and senses rather than the intellect of our youth. Sadly, in the initial stages, one doesn't see the dangers that lurk on the horizon when participating in psychotherapy practiced on normal children by amateurs, but there are definitely dangers.

Warning! Encounter Groups Are Dangerous

In 1967, Carl Rogers wanted to test his hypothesis that good things would result if you took a major school system and got virtually everyone in it—administrators, teachers, students—to participate in a sustained, ongoing program of encounter groups. The school system run by the nuns of the Order of the Immaculate Heart of Mary volunteered for the experiment. They operated a Los Angeles college, eight high schools, and fifty elementary schools located up and down the West Coast. "Just one year after the educational experiment began, however, several dozen nuns left the convent, and within three and a half years, some 315 Immaculate Heart nuns had announced their desire to leave the religious order (an unprecedented defection in the history of the Catholic Church)."

Tragically, the religious school system was basically destroyed. Why? According to W. R. Coulson, "The groups destroyed learning. Teachers would come back from one of the encounters and they'd be fluttering around the ceiling. They wouldn't want to teach. They'd want to 'relate.'" After the failure of the Immaculate Heart experiment, Carl Rogers "went on to undertake similar experiments in five other major setting (including the Louisville, Kentucky, public school system), all of which ultimately failed."[39]

The following year, Coulson hinted of the dangers associated with group dynamics in an article he wrote, but said that he failed to state it strongly enough at the time, because long-term effects emerged only later. He states, "The problem of community will simply not be solved by group dynamics. . . ."[40]

Even Carl Rogers himself admitted—an admission that has been ignored by the education establishment—that what he called the person-centered, nondirective approach being used in group dynamics had proven to be "thoroughly insidious in religion."[41] By 1975, he questioned the direction of the encounter group movement and asked, ". . . did I start something that is in some fundamental way mistaken and that may lead us off into paths that we regret? . . ."[42] Coulson's answer to his friend and colleague's question was, "Yes, it's nothing to fool around with, even if one is a master psychologist."[43]

Law against Dabbling in Classroom Psychology

It is interesting to note that in 1984 regulations were put into US law in an attempt to protect students from the invasion of psychotherapy in the public school classroom. Under this federal law, commonly known as the Hatch Amendment, the following terms were defined:

1. Psychiatric or psychological examination or test means a method of obtaining information, including a group activity, that is *not* directly related to academic instruction and that is designed to elicit information about attitudes, habits, traits, opinions, beliefs, or feelings, and
2. Psychiatric or psychological treatment means an activity involving the planned, systematic use of methods or techniques that are *not* directly related to academic instruction and that is designed to affect behavioral, emotional, or attitudinal characteristics of an individual or group.

Using the above definition of psychiatric treatment or examination, it is clear that just as public schools are dabbling in classroom psychology, contemporary publishers of Christian youth activities are also using methods that are *not* directly related to the academics of biblical instruction. Moreover, it is perplexing why Christians would feel the necessity to combine psychological techniques with the absolute authority of the Word of God. Referring to how the laity often fails to recognize what is happening, especially in the early stages, Abraham Maslow comments on the welcome he received when he spoke before religious institutions: "They shouldn't applaud me—they should attack. If they were fully aware of what I was doing, they would."[44]

Spiritual Counterfeit

Today the emphasis has radically shifted from meeting together to worship God and to study God's Word, to meeting together to learn to relate to others. Missing in the early church were such terms as *opening up, mutual trust, affirmation, feed-*

back, and *experience.* A survey of contemporary youth curricula failed to consistently find the words *sin, forgiveness,* and *obedience.* How can our youth even begin to understand the righteousness of a holy God without confronting the sin in their own lives? It appears that a good psychological feeling about self and others is replacing the remorse and grief that comes with a personal confrontation with sin.

Are Christian youth being duped into believing they have had an authentic spiritual conversion, when in fact a psychological technique has only imitated and given the illusion of the real thing? In light of the psychological techniques that have found their way into the church, William Kirk Kilpatrick explains:

> It is not surprising that psychology would sooner or later also come up with its own version of the born-again experience. The best example of this is the encounter group, with its remarkable claim of exchanging old lives for new and the equally remarkable emotionalism that attends it. . . . In encounter groups people confess their sins, share fellowship, claim to feel the workings of the spirit, and come out anxious to convert others to their way.[45]

"For the truth is," expounds Kilpatrick, "psychology bears a surface resemblance to Christianity." He elaborates:

> Not doctrinal Christianity, of course. Most psychologists are hostile to that. And naturally enough, so are non-Christians. Nevertheless, there is a certain Christian tone to what psychology says and does: echoes of loving your neighbor as yourself, the promise of being made whole, avoidance of judging others. Those ideas are appealing to most people, no matter what their faith.[46]

Kilpatrick concludes with the following thought-provoking observation:

> Some Christians have been too quick to notice the similarities between Christianity and born-again psychology, and too

slow to notice the differences, with the result that many church activities have taken on a distinctively "encounter group" flavor. And group methods have begun to substitute for Christian practice.[47]

Unfortunately, the "encounter group flavor" has infiltrated church groups of all ages from Sunday school classes to adult Bible studies and everything in-between. It is not the scope of this book to critique small group ministries, but many adult Bible studies are embracing and incorporating the same psychological climate that is being fostered in youth groups for middle and senior high students. It appears that everyone wants to encounter! The word *encounter* is not as popular these days due to a negative connotation. Therefore, new buzzwords, such as *support* and *task groups* and even the familiar and positive word *fellowship* may be used in both the secular and church setting.

In addition, other Christian-sounding words and phrases found in contemporary youth curricula, such as *intimate relationships, building community, mutual trust,* and *affirming the unconditional self-worth of another* are yet more examples of the values being espoused that indicate the therapeutic culture has found its way into the church.

Missing the Mark

There is overwhelming evidence that the main objective of many contemporary youth group curricula is not about getting to know God, it is about getting to know yourself. The apparent objective is not about putting trust in God, it is about putting trust in others in your group. The inferred goal is not about seeking fellowship with God, it is about exploring your own thoughts, feelings, and experiences in an environment of relativism rather than absolutes.

It appears that Christian youth curricula have undermined a basic Christian principle: If our vertical relationship is right with God, then our horizontal relationship will be right with others. Christian youth curricula have it backward. They start on the horizontal plane, encouraging and developing relationships with others by learning about self, with the hope that the lessons learned will transfer to a loving, intimate fellowship with God. Wrong premise! We must first start by learning about God as we spend time in fellowship with Him, then out of obedience and love for our God, a natural and biblical relationship will develop with others.

Michael Horton, author and biblical expositor, makes a rather disturbing observation concerning a Christian's over emphasis on relationships with others.

> To whom are we introducing people? To Christ or to ourselves? Is the "Good News" no longer Christ's doing and dying, but one's own "Spirit-filled" life? More sobering still, this implies that instead of the Word as a means of grace, "victorious Christians" are themselves mediating divine grace through the example of their own holiness. That makes us sacramental, rather than the Word. This is not good news. . . .[48]

What is taking place under the guise of Christian youth group activities makes what parents across America have been fighting in the public schools look mild in comparison. Tragically, youth leaders using material from contemporary Christian curricula developers and publishers may unintentionally be turning their youth groups into a group encounter in which the youth will be unknowingly receiving psychotherapy. Godly men and women are falling for modern gimmicks and fads that incorporate psychotherapeutic theories and techniques. In other words, many are being duped by a spiritual counterfeit.

~~

Chapter 4

More Child Abuse in the Classroom

If anyone advocates a different doctrine, and does not agree with sound words, those of our Lord Jesus Christ, and with the doctrine conforming to godliness, he is conceited and understands nothing.

—1 Tim. 6:3–4

The following youth group activities found in contemporary curricula and supplemental material for middle and senior high students prove without a doubt the depth of spiritual despair that exists. Instead of Christian youth learning Bible facts and the basics of their faith, they are wasting time with nonsense and psychobabble. The spiritual development of teens is being dumbed down with silly games and activities at a time in their life when the Word of God needs to become their solid foundation. The extent of this travesty is no small matter.

Besides being silly and dumb, many of the following activities employ philosophies and methods that may undermine the spiritual well-being of youth. The harmful philosophies being taught include relativism, death and sex education, tolerance, self-esteem, and rebellion against authority. Some of the destructive teaching methods involve moral dilemmas, sensitivity/diversity training, situational ethics, values clarification, decision making, critical thinking, privacy-invading questions, and active learning. Developed and marketed by those who are respected in the field of Christian youth ministry, the activities described in this chapter will not bring the minds of our youth into the captivity of Jesus Christ. To the contrary, these activities will lead students away from truth found only in God's Word, to a dependency on what each individual thinks and feels.

There is no rational reason for the activities and games that follow. W. R. Coulson emphatically states, "One has to be wary of leading young people to do things they can give no rational reason for doing. It makes them impulsive. It also turns out to give them emotional handicaps."[1]

Best Praiser: Affirmation

Does it make sense for Christian teens in a senior high youth group to be learning how to praise God by discovering which one in the group is the "best praiser"? They do this by taking turns telling the person next to them "why he (or she) is the most wonderful person in the world" and then voting to see who did the best job praising.[2] This activity is far removed from the authentic praise of God.

At a time when teens need to learn to resist peer pressure, it does not make sense to encourage vulnerability to another's flattery that may result in the possible submission to another's controlling influence. In the Book of Jude, we are told that the Lord will "execute judgment upon all, and convict all the ungodly of all their ungodly deeds which they have done in an ungodly way" (Jude 1:15). Included in that list of ungodly deeds is "flattering people for the sake of gaining an advantage" (v. 16). It is impossible to comprehend how giving phony praises to one another will transfer to an understanding on how one should praise God.

The respected preacher and author A. W. Tozer had a different attitude toward the world's praise than what is being promoted in contemporary youth curricula. He expressed the desire to "be among those who are unknown, unsung, and unheralded doing something through the Spirit of God . . . than to be involved in some highly recognized expression of religious activity."[3]

Butterfly Experiences: Self-Esteem

In an attempt to deter students in the public school from experimenting with drugs and sex, an increased emphasis has been placed on building a student's self-esteem. However, in its cover article of February 17, 1992, *Newsweek* discussed "the tremendous influence of self-esteem in the nation and the problems it caused." The article concluded that much of the self-esteem industry in the country was simply dealing in nonsense and suggested that "teachers, parents, and children who believe that emphasis on self-esteem will improve their performance are fooling themselves. . . ."[4] In addition, according to *US News & World Report*, there is "almost no research evidence that these [self-esteem] programs work."[5] It is hard to believe that in spite of the research, developers of Christian youth curricula have brought into the church so much of the world's preoccupation with self. As you can see from the following activity, even though it has been designed for Christian youth, it is indistinguishable from the nonsense that goes on in our nation's public schools.

In this activity titled Butterfly, the youth leader tells the participants after they have formed a circle, "Some of us may feel like we're in the caterpillar stage of life. Or we may feel as if we're still wrapped in a cocoon. But wherever we are in life today, someday we're going to have 'butterfly' experiences. Let's think about what those experiences might be for each other." The youth leader then instructs the students:

Say something you appreciate about the person on your left, followed by a description of a possible "butterfly" experience that person might have in the future. For example, you might say, "Heather, I appreciate your enthusiasm. Someday I believe you'll be an outstanding teacher and coach as you inspire others with your joy." Have kids continue around the circle, using the same "I appreciate . . . , Someday you will . . ." format.[6]

Self-esteem exercises are particularly dangerous and insidious for Christian students to participate in. William Kirk Kilpatrick warns,

> The self-cultivator doesn't necessarily stop believing in God, but his concept of God will likely change. . . . We will begin to adjust our idea of God to correspond with our ideas about human potential. The more self-reliant we feel ourselves becoming, the less we will feel a need to rely on Him. . . . From here it is just a small step to the belief that the self is a kind of god.[7]

The Butterfly exercise omits God's sovereign role in directing and shaping an individual's life. Sadly, teens are turning to one another to get direction for their lives rather than to God. After giving words of flattery, teens are making lofty predictions about another teen's future career or possible exalted experience. Encouraging teens to consult God through prayer about their future is strangely missing.

Emotional Grab Bag: Sensitivity Training
There is absolutely no rational reason for Christian youth to sit around in circles doing bond-building exercises so that they will somehow discover they can trust the group enough to share their deepest feelings. For instance, in one exercise students are to make a list of different feelings—such as depressed, bitter, angry, afraid, etc.—write them on a slip of paper to be placed in a box, and then have everyone choose one at random. Students are instructed to silently think of a time in their life when they experienced the chosen emotion, and then go around the circle, one person at a time, and answer questions like: "What's one time in

your life when you experienced this particular feeling? How long did the feeling last? Was it easy or difficult to think of a time you experienced these emotions?"[8] Interestingly, the exercise is called Emotional Grab Bag. However, a more appropriate title would be Emotional Basket Case.

It is not difficult to see the potential for emotional problems to arise when the emotional pot is stirred by adults playing amateur psychologists. Dr. Thomas P. Miller, a child psychologist, states that sensitivity training (of which the Emotional Grab Bag is an example), is inappropriate in schools. Why? "Its purpose is not instructional, it is therapeutic, and as such beyond both the mandate and competence of education. For a teacher to involve a child in such an activity is a gross invasion of parental prerogative."[9] We would add, that for a Christian youth group leader to involve teens in a sensitivity training activity is also a gross invasion of prerogative of parents in the church. Therapy is particularly inappropriate when done by a Christian leader playing amateur psychologist on unsuspecting Christian youth in the church.

Suitcase Relay: Diversity Training

The Suitcase Relay is sensitivity training in action. Sensitivity training is a technique designed to change through desensitization the standards, attitudes, and behaviors of individuals. To become desensitized is to become tolerant of a behavior or attitude that was once objectionable. Sensitivity training—also called "diversity training," particularly in the public school and the work place—is a technique that is frequently used to "train" (mentally manipulate) students and employees to be accepting and nonjudgmental of current "socially acceptable" attitudes and values.

In this crowd-breaker activity, the youth are divided into two equal teams: as many boys as girls. Each team is given a suitcase that contains a lady's dress and man's suit—complete with shirt and tie. "On the word *go*, a first couple (boy and girl) from each team must run with their suitcase to the opposite end of the room, open the suitcase, and put on everything in the suitcase—the boy putting on the lady's dress and the girl putting on the man's suit. Then they carry their suitcase back to the starting line. Undress. Put the clothes back into the suitcase and hand the suitcase to the next couple."[11]

We would expect this type of game/activity to surface in the public school in a class on diversity training, to teach tolerance and acceptance of different lifestyles, but not in Christian youth groups. With all the gender confusion going on in our culture, we do not need any more blurring of the lines between acceptable and unacceptable dress traditionally associated with one's gender.

With the emergence of the homosexual and feminist movement, parents of public school students discovered that assignments and activities often served a political purpose in the school: the undermining of traditional roles of men and women. It is apparent that if the church is going to adapt the games and fads of the public school, the very same checklist used to help parents evaluate school programs and public school material needs to be shown to parents in the church.

Duck, Duck, Goose: Dumbing Down

In the introduction to an elective Bible study for senior high students, youth leaders are told that "though some kids may at first think certain activities are 'silly,' they'll enjoy them." Youth leaders are then instructed to "Have fun with the activities you lead. Remember, it is Jesus who encourages us to become 'like little children.'"[12]

Incredibly, Scripture has been totally taken out of context and misapplied. Jesus teaches, "Truly I say to you, unless you are converted and become like children, you shall not enter the kingdom of heaven" (Matt. 18:3). Jesus was not teaching people to act childish, but rather to be childlike as they came to God. Jesus wants us to come to Him as a child, with a humble, trusting heart. Jesus is *not* teaching that adults or teens should revert back to childhood and play silly, childish games. It appears that developers of this curriculum are advocating that immaturity should be embraced by our teens, while at the same time misapplying the words of Jesus to justify their objective.

After playing games such as Duck, Duck, Goose; Red Rover; Dodge Ball; etc., snacks in memory of childhood, such as Twinkies, fruit pies, and cookies and milk are served.[13] This is certainly not an activity that will help teens press on to maturity. It is a silly, frivolous activity, an activity that encourages youth to act out behavior contrary to Scripture. The Bible states believers are to be dignified (see Titus 2:2), sensible (see 1:8), and sober (see 1 Pet. 1:13).

Unknown to most youth leaders, the technique "to go back in time to rediscover the little child we once were" is one of the many values-clarification strategies developed by secular humanist educator Sidney Simon. According to Simon, "By 'playing' these 'games,' people strip away the layers that hide their inner selves. . . ."[14] Therefore, the preceding activity would not be complete without its privacy-invading questions. "What is something you did as a child that got you in trouble? If you could be a child again, what is something you'd do differently? Why?"[15] For a teen to answer the questions candidly, he opens himself up to possible ridicule that may be detrimental in a social context of young people who are vulnerable to the influence of their peers. This activity is just another example of child abuse in the classroom, but this time the classroom is inside our churches.

There is another hidden problem associated with this teaching method of asking for personal information. It has been documented that, after hearing others confess their wrongdoings in a safe environment of acceptance, a student is apt to feel his own wrongdoings are not so bad after all, thus running the risk of causing one to accept lower moral standards. But that is not all. After discovering that one's own family standards are far different from those of the group, there is a real tendency on the part of a teen to doubt whose standards are correct. Teens may also receive the impression that one's own Christian teachings are out of step with current times—once again, according to the group.[16]

User Friendly: More Dumbing Down

This dumbed-down lesson is based upon the passages in Exodus that describe how "Bezalel helped build the tabernacle using the special gifts God gave him." In a "Leader Tip" the youth leader is instructed: "If the kids have trouble saying that name [Bezalel], have them give him a nickname, as if he were one of their friends."[17] Tragically, the teens have now become the standard, not the Bible. One can only imagine the confusion that will result from everyone calling a given character in the Bible by a different name. No one will know who anyone is talking about! Developers and publishers of youth curricula must not cultivate a lower standard by encouraging the simplification of words in an attempt to make Scripture more "user friendly" for teens.

One worldly trend responsible in part for the dumbing down of public school students is minimizing the importance of memorizing facts. This destructive fad has also found its way into the church. Evidence of the dumbing down of Christian youth is made obvious by an author of youth curricula who states: "There is [sic] no right or wrong answers, because the purpose is not to test your knowledge of the Bible."[18] A contemporary publisher of youth curricula also states that their curricula series is "about people. Not memory verses."[19] Incredibly, these curricula go against Scripture's directive to hide God's words in ones heart to prevent sinning against God (see Ps. 119:11).

An Average-Looking Raw Egg: Still More Dumbing Down

Another activity using a worldly technique that will contribute to the spiritual dumbing down of Christian youth is one in which the importance of a person's inner traits versus a person's outer appearance is compared to an average-looking raw egg. The teens are instructed to decorate the egg with brightly colored markers. Then to show that the useful part of the egg is on the inside, the raw egg is cracked into a glass and a volunteer drinks the yoke.[20]

Once again, it is difficult to imagine the apostles using such a gimmick to capture the interest of their audience. The implication is that God's Word alone is insufficient to capture the attention and hearts of those gathered together. Instead, the false assumption is that entertainment and faddish gimmicks are needed to nab the audience's attention. Appealing to sensationalism, this activity defies common sense and has little if any biblical relevance.

Shipwreck: Moral Dilemma

The Life Boat activity used in the public schools is a moral dilemma exercise that parents have vehemently opposed. In a similar church activity, Shipwreck, teens are told to role-play that their ship has been damaged beyond repair and is sinking. After each teen has been assigned an identity, they must decide as a group who will live and who will die. Since the lifeboat can only take two-thirds of the people in the room, that means that the one-third left will go down with the sinking ship.

This is appalling! Why is this controversial values-clarification exercise being presented in the church with Christian youth? A Christian's response should be an attempt to save everyone on the sinking ship, rather than judge those in society who are more important and deserving of life and sentence to death those who are deemed less important or less worthy. The Shipwreck exercise is a psychological technique to subtlely coerce students to disclose and then reevaluate their attitudes, values, and beliefs.

William Kirk Kilpatrick argues that concentrating on moral dilemmas, also called "situational ethics," puts the cart before the horse.

> Before students begin to think about the qualifications, exceptions, and fine points that surround difficult cases they will seldom or never face, they need to build the kind of character that will allow them to act well in the very clear-cut situations they face daily. . . . The great danger of the open-ended method of moral education is that students will come away with the impression that morality is not a solid and ob-

vious thing but a series of quandaries subject to innumerable interpretations and qualifications. From here, of course, it is only a short step to finding the appropriate provisos and saving clauses necessary to make one's own conscience comfortable in all situations.[21]

In other words, if a teen is subjected to moral dilemmas, he may become tolerant of behaviors or ideas he would have been intolerant of before. Situational ethics desensitizes individuals to absolutes, since right and wrong, good and bad are made to appear relative to the changing situation or circumstance.

A sick enticement to this so-called Christian version of a simulated shipwreck is that the participating teens are told by their youth leader that at the end of the activity "those on the lifeboat will get ice cream sundaes and those who are left on the sinking ship will not. This will add incentive to want to get on the lifeboat."[22] This psychological mind game has absolutely no business in a Christian youth group—or a public school classroom, for that matter. The unspoken lesson learned from this exercise is that greed and/or selfishness will be rewarded. It appears that narcissistic self-gratification is being encouraged rather than a sense of duty and self-sacrifice.

Let's Get Physical: Sex Education, Planned Parenthood Style

It is hard to imagine how so many ill-considered curricula have infiltrated the church. Consider a lesson called "Let's Get Physical," another objectionable values-clarification strategy, where teens go through a list of physical sensations, such as "oral sex, full body massage, mutual fondling to the point of arousal, playing post office, spin the bottle, etc.," and place it on a scale from "clearly wrong" to "perfectly acceptable."[23]

Kilpatrick describes how to identify an activity in which values clarification is used. "In values clarification the usual strategy is to ask a student to rank in order from a list of values those that he most likes or dislikes. Although there are variations . . . , in the end it is the student's own personal preference that determines right and wrong."[24] In the Let's Get Physical exercise, instead of listing values from those the teen likes most or dislikes, he lists physical sexual sensations that are clearly wrong to perfectly acceptable. A personal value judgment is made in an atmosphere of tolerance for other points of views.

Values clarification, even "Christian values clarification," destroys biblical absolutes and promotes relativism. A noted researcher specializing in the history of ideas, Thomas Sowell, argues: "The very phrase 'values clarification' is fundamentally dishonest. . . . Clarification is merely a word used to camouflage this process of undermining the child's existing values."[25]

Questions to supplement this exercise include, "Why do we think some people are sexy and others aren't? If sex is a personal, private thing, why do many people try so hard to look sexy? How do you think God feels about the question of what's sexy and what isn't?"[26] This exercise sounds more like something out of a Planned Parenthood manual—not something out of a curriculum for Christian youth.

Blushing over Sex: Touch Therapy

It should come as no surprise that sexuality is also the subject of this youth session. This activity, which incredibly is listed under "Fellowship and Worship," is to help "kids get to know each other." The teens are directed to form pairs, one boy matched up with one girl. One person in each pair then brushes "a little blusher on his or her partner's cheeks while the one receiving the blush describes an 'embarrassing moment' he or she has experienced."[27]

This is just one example of many in Christian youth curricula of how kids are encouraged to touch in order to get to know someone. W. R. Coulson warns that personal touching to get to know someone is backward from the norm.[28] Intimate touching on the face, which gives teens permission to act in a manner outside of normal and acceptable behavior, puts into question the qualifications of the writer of this curriculum and the capability and maturity of a youth leader who may decide to use this activity with his youth group. A teen should never be put in the position to be touched with familiarity by someone he or she does not know while at the same time having to share an embarrassing moment he or she has experienced. This is outrageous!

It is also incomprehensible that curriculum developers think that they are sex-education experts and that they have the authority to decide that our kids should *feel* comfortable talking about sex. The youth leader is instructed to "Challenge each person to learn to enjoy the physical sensations that are appropriate for him or her at this time. . . ."[29] This is dangerous ground! It appears that the lesson's objective is to have teens feel comfortable talking about sex with each other rather than to make a commitment to remain sexually pure until marriage.

Charting Independence: Questioning Parental Authority

Incredibly, not only do curricula developers think that they are sex experts, they also think they are qualified to counsel in parent-teen relationships using psychotherapy techniques. In one elective study, the first statement in the first lesson assumes tension and conflict. "When parents and teenagers get together, there's often conflict. While teenagers fight to build their own identity, parents continue to try to shape it. Both end up frustrated and angry—all because they failed to communicate."[30]

In one lesson, "Charting Your Own Independence," teens are told "parents and teenagers often have different perceptions of what kind of independence is appropriate at certain ages."[31] The teens are encouraged to decide at which age they should be allowed to have their girlfriend or boyfriend in their room, when they should begin dating, and when they should be able to see R-rated movies or videos, etc. This activity pits child against parents.

Throughout the rest of the lessons, the teens are encouraged to "talk about the good and bad qualities of parents," "how they feel when communication breaks down with their parents," and what it is "like trying to keep up with [their] parents' expectations?"[32] In one activity, the teens are to draw pictures of animals that best represent their family members.[33] These activities and discussions are disrespectful in nature toward parents and will only drive a wedge between a healthy, normal parent-child relationship.

It is not until the very last lesson that to love and honor parents is discussed as a biblical command, but after all that has been said and done, the discussion to love and honor parents would be nothing more than lip service. As one pastor articulates, "Parents are given a God-ordained right to act as the authority of the lives of their children. It is unbiblical for that authority to be attacked or even questioned."[34] In the previous lessons found in this contemporary youth curriculum, however, family privacy has been flagrantly invaded while the biblical model for parents to raise their children up in the discipline and instruction of the Lord has been violated (see Eph. 6:4, Prov. 1:8).

Once again, Christian youth group leaders using certain youth curricula will be placed in the role of playing amateur psychologists with other people's children. William Kilpatrick talks about the weakening of loyalties brought on by a psychological society:

> The business of the psychological society seems also to be the business of weakening loyalties. It's done in the name of personal independence, to be sure. . . . The fact is that the breakdown of natural groupings usually heralds less freedom, not more. One thing you notice about totalitarian states is that they have little use for the family or parish or the local government. They like nothing better than to liberate the individual from his local bonds.[35]

Activities in which young people are put in the position to question parental authority weakens family ties by fostering a disrespectful attitude toward parents rather than promoting an attitude of love and respect. Kilpatrick has yet more to say on this important topic:

> The worst indecency of the totalitarian mind is that it wants to wipe out all special ties of emotion or allegiance such as

might exist between husband and wife or parent and child. These kinds of loyalties threaten the only allegiance considered important, the one owed to Big Brother. It is in this atmosphere, of course, that children willingly denounce their parents to the secret police.[36]

Obviously, Christian curricula developers are not intentionally encouraging weakening family ties in order to promote an allegiance to Big Brother; but whether curricula developers realize it or not, questioning parental authority and the integrity of the family is always the groundwork for the acceptance of a totalitarian mind.

Weekend Curfew: Decision Making

This particular activity centers around a family debate over a weekend curfew. Teens are given roles to play. In this case, one teen is given the role of a teen who argues that it is unfair to set a specific curfew time on weekends, while another teen is given the role of a parent whose goal is to convince the teenager that a 12:30 A.M. weekend curfew is reasonable.[37] It appears that whoever has the best argument or debate skills wins. Whatever happened to teaching obedience?

When a teen is encouraged to debate his own point of view, W. R. Coulson warns that the teen "becomes the subjective center of his own decision-making world, no longer an obedient subject of his family's." Coulson uses the issue of drug education in the public school to make his point:

> What happens is that the student's identity is recast. . . . He learns that among the options of his life are drugs. . . . He might not have realized it before, but with enough interaction with peers of questionable character . . . and enough 'clarification' of previously unrealized 'values,' he has come to believe that he can become whatever he wants or 'needs.'[38]

In this activity, the teen is given the mistaken notion that challenging a parent's time for a curfew is valid. Unknown to parents, permission is being granted to challenge a parent's authority concerning the standards they have set for their children. Teens would not necessarily have any experience with the rules established in other families, which may be more lenient or perhaps more strict than their own. Coulson observes,

> Having been energized and then parked in a circle for heart-to-heart discussion; having exchanged feelings and found that deep down, his classmates were persons with feelings, too, the inexperienced student will have been said to have 'grown.' In the process, he's lost his fear of offending against the prohibitions of his home and the commandments of his church. The outcome (confirmed in the research) is that he's become more likely to give into what before he would have seen as temptation to be resisted.[39]

Tragically, the teen is being enticed to disrespect the guidelines for a curfew set down by his parents. Once again, there is a weakening of a teen's loyalty to his parents. A teen is being tempted not to honor his parents by obediently submitting to their rules—and he has learned it all within the walls of the church!

Society for More Decent Bibles: Questioning God's Authority

At a time when the authority and sufficiency of Scripture are waning, it is disturbing to find an activity that sets youth up to question Scripture. In this activity, teens debate whether the members of the Society for More Decent Bibles, who believe all references to sex should be removed from Scripture, should censor all or part of Genesis 38.[40]

It is beyond comprehension why curricula developers would incorporate an activity that not only encourages youth to question the authority of Scripture, but that also sets them up to be an authority on Scripture interpretation. Christian apologist, and respected lecturer on the existence of God, Ravi Zacharias, points out, "The big question Adam and Eve were asked by the serpent in the garden was, 'Has God really said? . . .'" Zacharias explains, "When [Adam and Eve] questioned the reality of His voice and supplanted it with their own authority, they made themselves the measure of all things."[41] Opinions espoused during a youth group discussion should not be confused with extensive study and research to seek out the truth contained in a given passage of Scripture. Opinions must never be confused with the inerrant authority of God's Word.

Outspoken leader of the Protest Reformation, Martin Luther, is quoted as saying, "As for the right of private interpretation, that would mean that each man would go to hell in his own way."[42] Michael Horton, pastor and vice chairman of the Alliance of Confessing Evangelicals, explains why private interpretation is condemning. "No one has a 'right' to interpret Scripture in isolation from the communion of saints." He adds, "There is a 'cloud of witnesses,' from the patriarchs and apostles to the early fathers, doctors, and reformers, and the individual believer is responsible to this catholic community."[43]

W. R. Coulson seconds Abraham Maslow, who grieved for the academic decline of his students and who later advocated that one cannot learn to be a professional under the discussion method, but rather one learns under authority.[44] The discussion method is nondirective, while the authoritative method of teaching is directive. In drug- and sex-education curricula used in the public schools, program developers—frequently from the pharmaceutical and tobacco industries—knew that if they could get children to make their own decisions without direction from their parents, then children would become vulnerable and available to exploitation.

According to Coulson, if teachers do not teach and instead let the children have their own discussion, "the good children become subject to the influences of the bad children, not the other way around."[45] As children turn their chairs inward to form a circle and openly share feelings and attitudes, it is the child who is the experimenter and risktaker who will win the admiration of his classmates, not the obedient, "good" child. The risktaker's life sounds full and exciting, while the disciplined, obedient child's life appears dull and boring.

The Bible clearly teaches to avoid bad company. "Do not enter the path of the wicked, and do not proceed in the way of evil men. Avoid it, do not pass by it; turn away from it and pass on" (Prov. 4:14–15). As Coulson points out, children are not allowed to decide whether or not to slash the principal's tires, or whether or not to attend school, so why should they be encouraged to decide about moral issues, such as sex outside marriage, taking illegal drugs, or in this case, deciding on the inerrancy of Scripture.

Scripture teaches in the authoritative, imperative voice. "All Scripture is inspired by God and profitable for teaching, for reproof, for correction, for training in righteousness" (2 Tim. 3:16). Awe and reverence for the authority of God and His Word is taught in 2 Peter 1:20–21, "But know this first of all, that no prophecy of Scripture is a matter of one's own interpretation, for no prophecy was ever made by an act of human will, but men moved by the Holy Spirit spoke from God." These statements are fact and not intended for discussion and subjective interpretation.

Pleasure Police: Critical Thinking

In this exercise, the youth are divided into two groups: the pleasure seekers and the pleasure police. A member of the pleasure seekers tries to make it across the room to pick up a cookie while a member of the pleasure police tries to keep him from accomplishing his goal. The contest continues until the time limit is up.[46]

The game is followed by a discussion on whether or not God is like the pleasure police, trying to keep people from enjoying their natural sexuality. Instructors are to accept all responses as equal, since according to the teacher's manual, there are no right and wrong answers. Teens, therefore, may come away from this activity believing God to be unfair! After all, the pleasure police got all the cookies at the end of the game! There is no guarantee that because teens played this game, they will realize that God gives limits to protect His children, not to deny them what is good. In crucial matters, such as the character of God, a conscientious teacher would want to teach the true character of God and not leave a teen's conception or misconception of God up to chance.

Critical thinking sounds desirable as a skill that should be taught to students. However, critical thinking is just another name for values clarification. Critical thinking is not the process to seek out absolute truth, as one might assume, but rather it is a means to justify relativism. Again, everyone's viewpoint is equally valid if they have critically thought through their problem or situation. However, discovering God's truth does not depend on one's intelligence or one's ability to critically think. If anyone sincerely desires to know God, God will reveal Himself to him. Scripture teaches: "You will seek Me and find Me, when you search for Me with all your heart" (Jer. 29:13). It is the condition of the heart that God honors and rewards, not the ability to critically think or to reason using man's worldly wisdom.

Icebreakers

As we have already seen, questions are often used following a game or activity in order to elicit personal information from teens. Sometimes such icebreakers are used at the beginning of a Christian youth group function to get the teens interacting with one another. It was surprising to discover that there are entire books that deal exclusively with questions. As documented earlier, the use of questions is a key technique in an encounter group to get young people to open up and relate to one another. It is also through questions that a value may be taught. In fact, one humanistic author admits, "Many questions are really statements of belief, feeling, or opinion masquerading as a question."[47]

Parents keep their children out of the public school to avoid the previously mentioned kinds of activities, yet these senseless and sometimes sick exercises and questions for Christian youth groups go on and on, in book after book. It is absurd for Christian curricula to suggest that in some way these preposterous activities will lead Christians to a deeper relationship with Christ.

Good Intentions? Not Good Enough

Youth leaders may mean well and have good intentions, but through ignorance they end up playing amateur psychologists with the potential of emotionally harming children. Pastor Gil Rugh states in his book *Psychology: The Trojan Horse,* "Good intentions, however, are not the issue. Nowhere in the Bible do we find God accepting of people with good intentions who put aside the clear teaching of the Word. Much damage can be done with good intentions."[48]

A. W. Tozer articulates stronger and more sobering words for anyone who acts out of ignorance:

> The words *through ignorance* should not cause you to picture in your mind a starry-eyed, honest-hearted person who just happens to sin accidentally. Realistically we must face up to the fact that here is a careless person, one who perhaps has neglected the Scriptures and their warnings. He or she has followed the intent of his or her own deceptive heart and had sinned against the commandments of the Lord.[49]

Anyone dealing with Christian youth has a grave responsibility to know biblically sound teaching techniques and methods so that they do not find themselves carelessly playing the dangerous role of an amateur psychologist with other people's children. We must heed the serious warning in 2 Timothy 4:3–4, "For the time will come when they will not endure sound doctrine; but wanting to have their ears tickled, they will accumulate for themselves teachers in accordance to their own desires and they will turn away their eyes from the truth, and will turn aside to myths." We are told in Scripture to "take every thought captive to the obedience of Christ" (2 Cor. 10:5). We must be continually on guard against the secular masquerading as the sacred.

The Subtle Serpent

Giving youth conflicting messages in a "psychological climate" of openness causes absolute truth to be compromised as teens are encouraged to find their own truth from within themselves. Subtle deceptions have slithered into the church through philosophies that have distorted the truth, and through teaching methods that appear Christian because of the Christian terminology used. This infiltration of the secular into the sacred can be likened to a frog placed in a pan of cool water on the stove: If the heat is slowly turned up, the frog is unable to detect the increase of water temperature, eventually resulting in its own demise. Like the frog, Christians are not aware of what is happening to them. A gradual change in theology and teaching methods influenced by worldly philosophies is much less likely to be noticed than an obvious or drastic shift. If Christians are not trained to detect subtle compromises to God's truth, Christians will experience the same fate as the complacent, undiscerning frog.

We must be on the alert and must be trained to detect error. The apostle Paul also gave a solemn warning to the church at Corinth almost two thousand years ago, a warning that is just as pertinent for Christians today, "But I am afraid, lest as the serpent deceived Eve by his craftiness, your minds should be led astray from the simplicity and purity of *devotion* to Christ" (2 Cor. 11:3).

Chapter 5

Judge Not! Tolerating Tolerance

Do not believe every spirit, but test the spirits to see whether they are from God; because many false prophets have gone out into the world.

—1 John 4:1

A dominant cultural value today is tolerance and open-mindedness. Once the pursuit of absolute truth is shoved aside and even rejected, tolerance and the acceptance of any belief, opinion, and lifestyle will be the natural consequence. According to one pastor, discernment is perhaps the greatest need facing the church today, for discernment dares to make the judgment between good and bad, truth and error, and right and wrong.[1] The distinguished biblical expositor D. M. Lloyd-Jones makes the following thought-provoking observation:

> There have been periods in history when the preservation of the very life of the church depended upon the capacity and readiness of certain great leaders to differentiate truth from error and boldly to hold fast to the good and to reject the false; but our generation does not like anything of the kind. It is against any clear and precise demarcation of truth and error.[2]

Is it any wonder that even our churches have fallen victim to the world's war on standards when activities in youth curricula no longer engage in an earnest pursuit of truth but instead engage in the pursuit of tolerance? Contemporary youth activities, patterned after techniques of psychotherapy, are now focusing on helping youth feel accepted and understood—regardless of behavior. There does not appear to be a sincere search for truth with a desire to act upon that truth in obedience to God.

Accept Rather Than Confront?

Denny Rydberg coined the phrase "Accept rather than confront." He instructs youth leaders to do the following:

> Don't use opening-up exercises as teachable moments to instruct or correct. Remember the purpose of these activities: to help students *begin* to share in a safe environment. . . . Instruction and correction will come later. When students share from their hearts, they need to experience acceptance first.[3]

Other writers and publishers agree with the philosophy espoused by Rydberg in his material designed for Christian youth. Tragically, the philosophy reflects a humanistic mindset. The perceived need to protect a teen's fragile self-concept however is not more important than earnestly and diligently seeking truth. To allow a teen's incorrect answer is unprincipled advice. God's Word clearly warns against anyone adding to or deleting from Scripture (see Deut. 2:4).

Youth leaders are also instructed: ". . . do not jump in at opportune moments to teach the participants a lesson. Simply listen, affirm, and accept them."[4] This so-called acceptance, or tolerance, indicates an indifference to God's truth.

It should not come as any surprise that *acceptance* and *absence of judgment* are found in a promotional package sent out by Quest, a popular drug-education curriculum used in the public schools across this nation. The program "emphasizes creating the right kind of classroom climate—primarily, one of acceptance, trust, and an absence of judgment . . ."[5] The climate created by Quest in the public school classroom sounds almost identical to the climate described by Rydberg and others for the contemporary Christian youth group.

Researcher and scientist W. R. Coulson articulates his objections to Quest and other similar drug programs: "It's precisely the *necessity* of judgment, not its absence, that must be promoted with the young today, given the magnitude of the drug problem."[6] The same argument should be used with our youth in a church setting. It is precisely the necessity of judgment, not its absence, that must be promoted with Christian youth today if they are to contend for the faith. Our teens must learn to examine everything carefully in order to hold fast to that which is good (see 1 Thess. 5:21).

It is important to note that there is a huge difference between being taught to appreciate a person for his own unique individuality, and being taught to accept all of their values, opinions, and beliefs are equally valid. We can be respectful of another's point of view without agreeing with it. There is a difference between being "judgmental" and exercising good judgment about what is right and wrong. In fact, as Christians, if we sincerely desire the best for someone, we show we truly care by being willing to judge sinful behavior and then confront a fellow Christian if he is in error. Of course, confrontation should be done out of love, with a humble spirit, and for the purpose of restoring the individual back to Christ.

Christian Values Clarification—an Oxymoron

One teaching method used in Quest and other public school curricula that we have also seen used in curricula for Christian youth is values clarification. Lyman Coleman openly promotes the use of so-called Christian values clarification, which on the surface sounds noble and worthy of pursuit.[7] After all, don't we want our children to clarify their Christian values? However, Christian values clarification is an oxymoron. There is no such thing.

Values clarification is a misleading phrase because values clarification is not based on absolutes.

Clarifying one's values sounds like an important and even necessary thing to do, but one needs to understand that values clarification, even so-called Christian values clarification, is a process that destroys biblical absolutes and promotes relativism. A significant clue that Coleman's Serendipity Bible Study series does not deal in absolutes can be found in the introduction to the mini-course *Hassles*. The introduction explains, "The Bible study is designed around a two-part questionnaire. . . . The questionnaire has multiple-choice options—and there is [sic] no right or wrong answers. . . ."[10]

When there are no right and wrong answers, then each view or opinion is equally satisfactory. A youth's belief becomes only one of many supposedly equally authoritative views. By accepting all views as equally valid, then the implication is that there are no absolutes. Paul C. Vitz, professor of psychology at New York University and noted author, elaborates in his book *Psychology as a Religion* that if there are no right or wrong answers, then one's beliefs are relative and will continue to change throughout one's life.[11]

Dave Hunt and T. A. McMahon, in their book *The Seduction of Christianity*, elaborate:

> Obviously, if everyone comes up with his own standard of good and evil, utter chaos would be the result. The idea that man can know what is right and wrong by consulting himself is a lie that caters to our pride. Man had rejected God as the personal Creator who sets all standards, and in so doing had set himself up as his own god. Moral absolutes were out; doing one's own thing was in.[12]

W. R. Coulson emphatically concludes, "Values clarification is the philosophy that everybody has within them, and ought to express, their own values. . . . Values clarification, then, is an evil approach to moral development. It leaves behind many victims, young and old, stranding them without an authoritative conscience."[13]

Unfortunately, the author of the Serendipity Youth Bible series and other Christian publishers and writers who rely on values clarification strategies do not appear to understand the power of the psychological technique they are using in their curriculum. It will not accomplish their learning objective: to have Christian youth clarify their Christian values.

What Do You think?

On the assumption that feelings have everything to do with education, Group has aggressively moved from the traditional educational position of the objective realm (the acquisition of knowledge) to the subjective realm (the exploration and expression of thoughts and feelings). Group justifies its use of open-ended questions to probe feelings in their instructions to youth leaders: "Avoid questions that can be answered with a 'yes' or 'no.' Let your learners know that there are no wrong answers to these 'feeling' questions. Everyone's feelings are valid."[14]

Yet another publisher of Christian curricula, Zondervan, states, "When asking a question . . . phrase it to evoke *opinions*, not *answers*." The instructions continue:

> In other words, if a question reads "What should Bill have done in that situation?" change it to "What *do you think* Bill should have done?" The addition of the three words "do you think" makes the question a matter of opinion rather than a matter of knowing the right answer.[15]

These instructions, which disregard the proverbial warning that "a fool does not delight in understanding but only in revealing his own mind" (Prov. 18:2), read like a page out of one of the many books on values clarification written by Sidney Simon, a noted secular author and a leading professor of humanistic education. Simon states: "THERE ARE NO 'RIGHT' OR 'WRONG'

ANSWERS, ATTITUDES, OR RESPONSES. Whatever way a person feels is valid for that individual." Simon goes on to say:

> You might act differently in a similar situation, but that does not deny the reality of the other person's feelings. But we cannot and don't want to control the ways people of any age think and feel.[16]

Because Sidney Simon is a secular humanist and does not believe in God, he does not understand that the way one *thinks* and *feels* often dictates the behavior. That is why we are told in Scripture to take every thought captive to Christ (see 2 Cor. 10:5). Jesus said:

> You have heard that the ancients were told, "You shall not commit murder." . . . But I say to you that everyone who is angry with his brother shall be guilty before the court. . . . You have heard that it was said, "You shall not commit adultery"; but I say to you, that everyone who looks on a woman to lust for her has committed adultery with her already in his heart. (Matt. 5:20–21, 27–28)

Simon's teaching is contrary to Scripture. Wrong thoughts and feelings are not valid; they are sinful. Sinful thoughts, feelings, and attitudes may lead to sinful behavior. Thoughts, attitudes, and responses must be held up to the yardstick of Scripture so that a judgment between good and bad, truth and error, and right and wrong can be made.

It should come as no surprise that Simon believes that one's values constantly change. He writes, "The intelligent person is likely to change attitudes and opinions many times in the course of a lifetime."[17] Individuals who determine their own moral standards set themselves up as their own god, rather than acknowledging and submitting to God and His standard. This is a tragic repeat of history as told in the Book of Judges, "In those days there was no king in Israel; everyone did what was right in his own eyes" (Judg. 21:25). The attitude in the 1990s appears to be: Today we are as gods; everyone does what is right in his own eyes.

Values Clarification: A Challenge to Authority

Sidney Simon developed his teaching method known as values clarification in the early 1970s based on the approach formulated by Louis Raths, who in turn built upon the thinking of John Dewey. Values clarification was promoted as "an ideal way to deal with values without taking sides or indoctrinating students in one particular value position."[18] However, in the book *Values Clarification: A Handbook of Practical Strategies for Teachers and Students,* Simon states the real intent behind values clarification:

> . . . the young person is ultimately left to make his own choice about whose advice or values to follow. But young people brought up by moralizing adults *are not prepared* to make their own responsible choices. They have not learned a process for selecting the best and rejecting the worst elements. . . . Thus, too often the important choices . . . are made on the basis of peer pressure, *unthinking submission to authority*, or the power of propaganda.[19] (emphasis added)

It quickly becomes evident that Simon has disdain for Christian parents who want to pass their values and beliefs onto their own children. The obvious intent of values clarification in the public school is for youth to challenge authority and also for Christian youth to challenge their faith. One of the important steps in values clarification is to choose one's beliefs and actions freely from alternatives. Youth, therefore, are encouraged to "consult themselves" for the best choice after looking at all possible options. In other words, they are to consider alternative modes of thinking and acting. For a teen to choose the values or beliefs of his Christian parents indicates that he had not freely chosen his values or beliefs, but rather that he had blindly submitted to authority. W. R. Coulson laments, "The sad fact is that children can indeed be converted to believe that what's most important is not to do the right thing but to make their own decisions."[20]

Even though Zondervan does not use the words *values clarification* in their material for youth, teens are encouraged to clarify their own values just the same. Youth leaders are informed, "While discussing the questions . . . your students will be encouraged to think carefully about issues, to compare their beliefs and values with others, and will learn to make the right choices." The questions and activities "will challenge your group to evaluate, defend, explain and rework their ideas. . . ."[21]

Many of these calculated strategies include: asking the student to complete unfinished sentences; ranking ideas and values in the order of importance; stating whether or not they are undecided, strongly agree or disagree with a specific idea or value; or identifying on a graph where they believe they rank personally on an issue. Tragically, as the teens are encouraged "to consider what the Bible has to say," the Bible is relegated to just one of many options. The statement that a teen will learn to make "right choices" implies that human nature is basically good and that an individual has the innate ability to come to the right conclusion. Once again, this is a position in sharp contrast to the truth of Scripture.

An Insideous Attack

Simon's various strategies for values clarification have also been expounded upon in a book for parents, *Helping Your Child Learn Right from Wrong: A Guide to Values Clarification*. It is important to note that the introduction to this book was written by Dr. Thomas Gordon, author and founder of Parent Effectiveness Training (PET). Gordon promotes the psychological technique of active listening, a nondirective, nonjudgmental approach to teaching. Many parents who have taken this course in a secular or Christian setting were unaware that they were being indoctrinated into accepting a form of relativism.

Once again, parents must be on guard. Christian parents must not embrace a philosophy that espouses "changing one's mind is a sign of growth." Simon goes on to emphasize: "Instead of ridiculing each other for inconsistency when someone says something at odds with a previous statement or action, we learn to rejoice in each other's growth."[22]

In the chapter "Religion Strategies," Simon suggests that parents use the following values clarification strategies with their children. He writes: "We often perform the same religious rituals that our parents did before us, without really thinking about what our religion means to us." He then suggests listing "thirteen rituals connected with your religion. If you were limited in your practice of religion, which three would you give up first? Which three would you defy authority to continue?" In yet another strategy, Simon writes: "These commandments [the Ten Commandments] are the basis for much of Judeo-Christian morality. As a religious person, do you feel it is important to obey all the commandments totally? If not, under what conditions would you or would you not obey each one?"[23]

William Kilpatrick points out that the use of a psychological technique to present a Christian theme will only serve to undo it. Kilpatrick expounds,

> The idea of presenting doctrines of the faith as a matter of choice clearly shows the influence of humanistic psychology. Since humanistic psychologists believe that truth is a personal construct, they are forced to utilize that kind of technique over and over. They have no other alternative but to encourage students to choose their own truths or values. But that is not the Christian position on truth. These techniques when used in Christian education will subtly condition youngsters to believe that faith is a matter of personal opinion.[24]

Obviously, faith is not a matter of personal opinion if one believes in the authority of Scripture; so this teaching technique is nothing less than an insidious attack on the Christian faith.

We recall a conversation we had twelve years ago with a pastor and a Christian high school principal who ardently defended placing Sidney Simon's *Values Clarification* on the desk of every teacher in the principal's school. Unfortunately, they were unwilling to even consider the negative outcome of values clarification methods being used on Christian youth. Besides their indifference to the concerns that we raised, we left stunned that they were not even open to thinking about the possibility of a negative impact being left on a church and a Christian school willing to flirt with humanistic philosophies.

Bernie says, "Judge Not!"

In a curriculum for young children, *The Gospel According to Saint Bernard,* one of the lessons is entitled "Judge Not!" The stated biblical truth for this lesson is that "we should not judge other people." Information presented as background for the lesson states that "children can more easily put aside differences if they learn early to not judge people and to accept them as they are."[25]

This potentially dangerous lesson confuses Scripture by equating a girl who is quiet and unattractive with a boy who shows a marijuana joint around school. Obviously, children should not be critical of other children based upon their physical characteristics, such as weight, skin color, or attractiveness. On the other hand, children must be taught to judge illegal and immoral behavior as wrong. One has to question why the author of this curriculum would put together two very different scenarios. This lesson is not only confusing, but it is an example of distorted and twisted reasoning.

Much of what is taught through youth group curricula is not as blatant as what was taught in this curriculum for younger children, but the message to "judge not" is promoted just the same. When youth curricula and ministry resources state that there are no right and wrong answers, then it is implied that there is nothing to judge. Youth, therefore, are not being trained to discern, but rather to unconditionally accept a variety of opinions and attitudes. Being tolerant of all points of view appears to be the new Christian role for youth.

When situational ethics and moral dilemmas are used with Christian youth, they are subtly, and sometimes not so subtly, taught a tolerance for moral relativism. The underlying precept in situational ethics is that values are flexible and that they change as situations change. An exercise presenting a moral dilemma infers that a value or belief is not absolute and needs to change to fit different circumstances.

In fact, Carl Rogers wrote, ". . . this increasing ability to be open to experience makes him far more realistic with new people, new situations, new problems. It means that his beliefs are not rigid, that he can tolerate ambiguity. He can receive much conflicting evidence without forcing closure upon the situation."[26] This is dangerous territory for a Christian. Christians must not put themselves in situations or experiences where a relativistic mindset is being promoted. One also cannot help but wonder if this toleration for ambiguity is at least in part responsible for the apathy toward biblical truth that we see in the church today.

Finding Common Ground?

In a mini elective study dealing with church unity, teens are asked to play a game that is basically an exercise in values clarification. The teens all start in one spot but move in different directions depending upon their responses to given statements. This activity corresponds to strategy 6, "Values Spectrum," developed by Sidney Simon. According to Simon, "The Values Spectrum is a good strategy for 'compulsive moderates'—people who try to avoid conflict and commitment by straddling every fence they come to. . . . This strategy helps [individuals] to realize how many different shadings there are on every issue and to share [their] thinking."[27]

The purpose of the activity on church unity is to show that regardless of differing opinions and responses, the teens participating are all Christians. The conclusion: "God's people aren't perfect. But that doesn't mean we can't grow in unity. . . ."[28] A sampling of the questions the teens were asked to respond to include:

1. "If you believe it's unchristian to smoke or chew tobacco, move left one space. If you believe it's OK, move back one space."
2. "If you believe Christians shouldn't wear jewelry, move . . ."
3. "If you prefer a different color of carpet in the sanctuary, move . . ."
4. "If you believe women can be ordained as ministers and pastors, move . . ."[29]

Implied in this lesson is the necessity to find common ground and promote unity. However, there was no discussion that authentic unity centers around the person of Jesus Christ. There was also no discussion on the importance of encouraging and even challenging one another to check attitudes and behavior against Scripture. This lesson implies that just because the teens are all Christians, they should accept differing points of view in the name of unity. The attitude appears to be: You can believe whatever you want, and I will believe whatever I want. However, the conviction to uphold Scripture is essential if a church truly believes in the authority of Scripture.

We must *not* pursue unity at all cost! Instead, we must defend Scripture *regardless* of the cost. It is ludicrous to compare ordaining women as ministers and pastors in the church with the preference of carpet color in the sanctuary. Once again, two confusing scenarios have been put together. The ordaining of women as pastors is directly addressed in the Bible, while the preference for carpet color in the sanctuary is not.

A Taboo

In the lesson "For His Eyes Only: Leaving the Judgment to God," the main point is: "Only God has the right to judge people's hearts."[30] That is true. Not only does God have the right to judge people's hearts, God is the only one who *can* judge people's hearts. However, as Christians, we are to judge right from wrong, and good from evil. As Christians we are not able to judge a person's heart to determine his eternal destination, but we are able to judge another's behavior to determine whether it is in accordance with Scripture. This distinction about judging was not made in the lesson. Teens are most likely to come away with the thought that they must not judge. Period.

"The church in our age," according to John MacArthur, "has abandoned the confrontive stance. . . . Christians today are obsessed with finding areas of agreement." The disturbing question that MacArthur asks following his astute observation should cause all Christians to evaluate the importance of upholding the truth of the gospel: "What will happen to the church if everyone proceeds down the slippery path of public opinion?"[31]

Affirmation and acceptance, which are key components in Christian youth curricula, appear to have taken precedent over discernment and judgment. MacArthur makes the insigtful observation that in many churches today it is taboo to be intolerant of tolerance. He elaborates:

> In the world of modern evangelicalism, it is allowable to advocate the most unconventional, unbiblical doctrines—as long as you afford everyone else the same privilege. About the only thing that is taboo nowadays is the intolerance of those who dare to point out others' errors. Anyone today who is bold enough to suggest that someone else's ideas or doctrines are unsound or unbiblical is dismissed at once as contentious, divisive, unloving, or unchristian. It is all right to *espouse* any view you wish, but it is not all right to *criticize* another person's views—no matter how patently unbiblical those views may be. When tolerance is valued over truth, the cause of truth always suffers.[32]

Religion of Civility

Os Guinness, Christian thinker and author, has some poignant comments concerning tolerance, which he calls the

91

religion of civility. He believes tolerance to be a corrupt form of civility: "This pseudocivility, or intolerant tolerance, begins with a bland exterior of permissive ecumenism—everybody is welcomed—but ends with a deep-rooted relativism hostile to all serious differences and distinctions."[33]

"Tolerance," G. K. Chesterton writes, "is the virtue of those who don't believe anything."[34]

Today, to be intolerant and judgmental are synonymous with being narrowminded. To be accused of being narrowminded has become a flagrant insult, rather than a desired compliment. D. M. Lloyd-Jones said, "We must not mind being thought 'narrow.' . . . This charge of intolerance is a compliment. For, surely, if our position is that in which God has ordained His elect should stand, we must necessarily be intolerant of all that would divert us from it."[35]

Scripture teaches, "Enter by the narrow gate; for the gate is wide, and the way is broad that leads to destruction, and many are those who enter by it. For the gate is small, and the way is narrow that leads to life, and few are those who find it" (Matt. 7:13–14). As one pastor succinctly stated, "Truth by its very nature is narrow and exclusive."[36]

The opposite of tolerance is conviction. Conviction, not tolerance, is essential to the Christian faith. A contributing author to the book *The Coming Evangelical Crisis*, Gary L. Johnson, stated, "Convictions are the root on which the tree of vital Christianity grows. No convictions, no Christianity. Scanty convictions, hunger-bitten Christianity. . . . An anemic Christianity that is not virile enough to strive for the truth can never possess the nerve to die for it. A truth not worth defending very soon comes to be seen as truth not worth professing."[37]

As one Puritan stated, "Indifference in religion, is the first step to apostasy from religion."[38] Since the church is not impacting the culture, could it be that we do not think the truth needs defending? We are told in Scripture to always be ready "to make a defense to everyone who asks you to give an account for the hope that is in you" (1 Pet. 3:15).

Subtleties That Deceive

It is true that we did not go through each activity in every curricula for Christian youth, but in all that we reviewed, we did not find one activity that dealt with judging truth from error, right from wrong, and good from bad. We found no lesson that taught how to practice discernment. The difference between a babe in Christ and a mature Christian is his ability to discern (see Heb. 5:12–14), but no where did we find developers of Christian youth curricula encouraging teens "to press on to maturity" (Heb. 6:1).

Obviously, curricula developers are not blatantly saying "Believe in relativism, not absolutes" and "Be tolerant of all points of view; do not judge." If such statements were found in youth curricula, hopefully there would be a cry of outrage arising from the Christian community. However, even though such statements do not appear to exist, the educational philosophies and teaching methods used in numerous contemporary youth curricula are subtly reinforcing the secular humanist concept to "judge not."

Youth leaders, must critically judge the material they use with their youth group. They must not assume that just because a given curriculum has gained popularity that it is scripturally sound. John MacArthur argues, "Our only defense against false doctrine is to be discerning, to distrust our own emotions, to hold our own senses suspect, to examine all things, to test every truth-claim with the yardstick of Scripture, and to handle the Word of God with great care."[39] A Christian must carefully scrutinize philosophies and diligently analyze methods in order "to present [himself] approved to God as a workman who does not need to be ashamed, handling accurately the word of truth" (2 Tim. 2:15).

Christians must also be willing to judge. MacArthur admonishes that a "truly biblical ministry *must* hold forth truths that are absolute. . . . We must take an unmovable stance on all issues where the Bible speaks plainly. . . . Sound doctrine divides, it confronts, it separates, it judges, it convicts, it reproves, it rebukes, it exhorts, it refutes error. None of those things is very highly esteemed in modern thought. But the health of the church depends on our holding firmly to the truth."[40]

~~

Chapter 6

A Pseudo and Reckless Faith

Trust in the Lord with all your heart, and do not lean on your own understanding. In all your ways acknowledge Him, and He will make your paths straight.

—Prov. 3:5

An activity used to teach the concept of trust and faith that appears frequently in youth group curricula is the trust walk, sometimes called the "blind walk."[1] The trust walk, however, is also found quoted in humanistic books, such as *Carl Rogers on Encounter Groups* and *Teaching Human Beings: 101 Subversive Activities for the Classroom* by Jeffrey Schrank. In the introduction to the latter book, Schrank admits that "running through this cook book of ideas is the theme of 'unlearning . . . By the time a child becomes a teenager and enters high school he is filled with myths, misconceptions, fears, and doubts which schooling and parents have forced upon him. One role of the activities in this book is to help the student see the possible dangers in what he already has learned and now takes for granted."[2]

A Christian parent or youth group leader should become immediately suspect of any activity found in Christian curricula that is also found in a book dealing with subversive activities to help children see the possible dangers in what they have learned from parents. Children who have been taught to put their confidence in God (see Ps. 78:7) by parents who have followed God's command to train and teach their children in the ways of the Lord (see Eph. 6:4) are in danger of having their faith undermined. What knowledge is Schrank saying teens need to unlearn? "Some knowledge which a vast number of teens have learned and which desperately needs to be unlearned is: I am not important; my feelings cannot be trusted and should be controlled; I need permission to do things; adults usually know better."[3]

It quickly becomes obvious that Schrank believes children should be autonomous from their parents. Throughout Schrank's book, parental authority, as well as all authority, is undermined, which sets Christian children up to question God and the authority of the Bible. Children are encouraged by Schrank to trust and act upon their own feelings, while at the same time they are encouraged to distrust the knowledge, values, and morals taught by their parents and other Christian adults. Children are being taught to trust, but it is a trust in themselves and their own feelings and not a trust in God.

Ten years ago we asked public school administrators why they were using techniques developed and used by secular humanists who openly admitted that they want children to unlearn traditions and values of parents. Now we are asking church leaders the same question. Why are these humanistic activities and techniques being used on our Christian youth? Francis Schaeffer said before his death, "Show me what the world is saying today and I will show you what the church will be teaching in five years." Something is terribly wrong when the church becomes a copycat of the world.

A Subversive Activity

In Schrank's book, the stated purpose of the trust walk is to help "a group explore its need and ability to trust each other."[4] Carl Rogers's daughter, Natalie Fuchs, says in her father's book

Carl Rogers on Encounter Groups that the trust walk should be used at the right time so feelings can be explored in order to build trust. [5] The concept of trust is central to Schrank and Fuchs, but it is a trust in each other and not a trust in God.

In a popular secular variation of the trust-walk exercise, one partner is blindfolded. The other partner communicates verbally, telling the blindfolded partner where to walk. After both partners have had their turn at being blindfolded, the participants come together for a group discussion led by a facilitator. The participants are asked to answer each question posed by the facilitator, who may or may not tell the participants that it is permissible not to answer the questions. More than likely the participants will be encouraged to take an active part in the discussion.

Some questions include:

- "When you were blindfolded, what were you thinking?"
- "What kind of emotions did you experience?"
- "Did your level of trust change between the first minute and the last minute?"
- "Did you ever feel that your partner may not completely communicate something?"
- "When you were the partner doing the leading, what were you feeling?"[6]

In a secular encounter group, the trust walk followed by "feeling" questions is a technique used to break down a child's natural inhibitions by getting him to reveal his innermost thoughts, feelings, or reactions to a situation. "Feeling" questions encourage youth to reveal personal information about themselves so others can supposedly see them as real. In theory, and according to Carl Rogers, all "masks and facades" are torn down.[7] So why are the trust walk and related questions such bad things for Christian youth?

A Christian Trust Walk?

We have been told by a Christian youth group leader that, since her *objective* is different from that used in a secular setting, there is nothing inherently wrong with the activity. "If our objective is right in God's eyes," she argued, "if we are not trying to mislead or manipulate anyone, if our hearts as leaders are in the right place as we try to honor God, and if we are not violating anyone's privacy with pressure to participate, then little if any harm will result in the method used."[8]

According to W. R. Coulson this type of exercise is dangerous, even if it is used in a Christian setting. Coulson makes it clear that this type of exercise is still simulated therapy, and anyone who thinks they can make anything good out of it is arrogant.[9]

There are numerous variations of the trust walk found in different Christian curricula, and the purposes stated by the curricula developers for using that exercise are just as varied. However, it is invariably followed by questions that require a teen's personal response to "What do you think?" and "How do you feel?" The blindfolded teens share why they were able or unable to trust their sighted partners as the group explores their need and ability to trust one another.

According to the Christian youth leader previously mentioned, the purposes for using this exercise are for getting to know one another better and for building trust in others and, ultimately, in God. Her lesson plan stated that Christian brothers and sisters will develop trust as they share themselves—their feelings.[10] Once again, Coulson identifies this activity as simulated therapy, but this time with the implication of an eleventh commandment: "Thou shalt be open."[11] The youth leader continues to justify the use of the trust walk by arguing, "If we cannot trust others, whom we can see and know, how can we completely trust God, when we can't even see Him?"[12] Unfortunately, this comment is an all-too-common example of man's attempt to explain God through his own pitiful experiences.

Since getting to know one another and building trust in others are the same objectives promoted by secular humanists in their publications, it does not make sense that this activity should naturally transfer to a trust in God, as assumed by this Christian youth leader. Why would secular humanists, who are anti-God, promote an activity that could also be used to strengthen trust in God?

A Lesson in Confusion

This lesson on trust will more than likely end up as a lesson on confusion. What kind of trust will develop if one youth gave directions for his blindfolded partner to walk into a stationary object, such as a table or a wall? This individual may be clowning around, or he may simply have his left mixed up with his right. What would that experience teach about trust? There is a good possibility that the person blindfolded may quickly learn that he cannot trust his partner and that he must peek in order to be safe and not get injured. In other words, there is no control over what is learned. The experience may be either positive or negative.

Since the game may not be taken seriously by the participants, it is doubtful that the lesson's goal on trust would be achieved. Even if the game were taken seriously, it is questionable that a feeling of trust in each other would transfer to a trust in God. In fact, according to Coulson, the experience is so overgeneralized that it may not be applicable in the real world, only to a world of abstract theory and ideology.[13] It appears that Schrank's objective to have kids unlearn what Christian parents have taught—in this case, to trust in God—will more than likely be the outcome of the lesson. Schrank will have accomplished his goal.

A Grave Error

The majority of youth leaders have a sincere love for the Lord and are orthodox in their faith, but they have the mistaken notion that, because they believe the right things, the application of what they believe will take care of itself. The late Dr. Martyn Lloyd-Jones believed that this kind of thinking is in grave error. He argued,

> Anyone who is tempted to speak in that way ignores not only his own weakness, but, still more, the adversary of our souls, who is always attempting to frustrate the work of God. . . . I am concerned to show you how you cannot take it for granted that a man who believes the right thing is of necessity one who can present that right thing in the right way.[14]

Lloyd-Jones reiterated, "It is not enough that you believe the truth; you must be careful to apply what you believe in the right way."[15] Trusting in God is fundamental to the Christian faith. No Christian youth leader would deny the importance of teaching this basic concept, but upon reviewing the types of activities being used to teach trust in God, there is obviously a severe breakdown in the truth and teaching of that truth.

Unscriptural Teaching

The critical question that needs to be asked is if it is even scriptural to trust others as promoted by both the secular humanists and developers of Christian curricula. The answer is an adamant no. One must wonder why so much emphasis is placed upon trusting others in youth curricula, for nowhere in Scripture are we told to trust others, only God. We are told to *love* others (see John 13:34), even our enemies (see Luke 6:27), and we are admonished to *forgive* those who wrong us (see Eph. 4:32).

We are commanded to *honor* and *obey* our parents (see Exod. 20:12). We are also told to *pray* for those who persecute us (see Matt. 5:44) and to show *compassion, kindness, humility, gentleness,* and *patience* toward others (see Col. 3:12). But nowhere in Scripture are we ever instructed to *trust* others. The Bible clearly teaches that man's basic nature is sinful, which is contrary to the belief of secular humanists and humanistic psychologists that man is basically good. Scripture admonishes believers to "... put your trust in the Lord your God ..." (2 Chron. 20:20). The prophet Isaiah proclaimed, "Trust in the Lord forever, for in God the Lord, we have an everlasting Rock" (Isa. 26:4). And Isaiah warned, "Stop regarding man, whose breath of life is in his nostrils; for why should he be esteemed?" (Isa. 2:22). Scripture also instructs, "It is better to take refuge in the Lord than to trust in man" (Ps. 118:8), and, "We should not trust in ourselves, but in God" (2 Cor. 1:9).

Proverbs 28:26 admonishes, "He who trusts in his own heart is a fool." The strongest admonition, however, comes from the Lord, Himself, "Thus says the Lord, 'Cursed is the man who trusts in mankind'" (Jer. 17:5).

The concept to trust in God is essential to the Christian faith, but the concept of trusting in self and in one another is *not* scriptural. The object of one's faith becomes *self* and *others* rather than God. Yet no one seems to be questioning this heresy. Lloyd-Jones warned,

> There is a constant danger of error and of heresy, even among the most sincere, and also the danger of a false zeal and the employment of unscriptural methods. There is nothing to which we are exhorted more frequently in the New Testament than the need for a constant self-examination and a return to the Scriptures themselves.[16]

Another Subversive Activity

The trust fall, which is also listed in *Teaching Human Beings,* has been recently highlighted in a Christian publication as a worthwhile activity to be used with Christian youth. The caption under a picture of youth participating in the trust fall at a Christian camp reads: "... teens ... illustrating their need to trust others and to trust God."[17] In a misguided attempt to justify the use of the trust fall with Christian youth, Denny Rydberg, in his book *Building Community in Youth Groups,* wrote: "When a high school girl successfully falls backward into the outstretched arms of her peers, she can begin to visualize what it means to trust God and trust *the group*" (emphasis added).[18] Implied in that statement is the heretical belief that it is just as important to trust the group as it is to trust God.

This activity, which is yet another secular exercise designed to build an unbiblical trust in others, has several variations. One variation of the trust fall requires a young person to stand on a chair or a table. The other children form two lines side by side, interlinking but not joining their arms. The person on the table turns his back to those who are going to catch him and then free-falls backward into the line.

You may have done one or more variations of the trust fall as a child yourself, so you might be asking, "What is the problem? Is this not nitpicking?" According to W. R. Coulson, it is not. These types of activities are experimental and problematic, for they are not like everyday life. *Touching* often is a key component. The subtle message is that in order to trust, you must touch and be touched by others.[19] In the publication *The Active Listening Hoax,* Coulson quotes Carl Rogers:

> Whether we recognize it or not, we're experimenting with helping people develop in ways that have never been a main part of the cultural stream: that is, to be more open and nondefensive and expressive of feelings. So that we really are engaged in a new cultural enterprise which places value on behaving differently in social groups than individuals have customarily behaved.[20]

Touch to Trust

There are many intimacy games/activities suggested for use in youth groups that involve touch. At the close of one activity, teens are instructed to "close with a warm group hug."[21] In another "touching" activity, the teens form pairs. One person in each pair is to be the message giver, and the other the message receiver. Partners stand face to face and place a hand on each other's shoulder. The message giver then gives the message receiver an encouraging message.[22]

Yet another example of an activity employing intimate touching has the teens stand single file, facing the same direction, before sitting down. The teen at the end of the line uses his or her finger to draw a picture on the back of the person in front, and so on up the line.[23]

Close physical contact also takes place in the Lap Sit. In this exercise, the teens stand in a tight circle. On command "everyone sits down on the lap of the person behind him or her." If unsuccessful the first time, the teens are instructed "to get closer together and try again."[24]

One final example is called Circle of Love. In this activity, the teens are to express their feelings for each other nonverbally. The teen in the middle of the circle goes to each person in the circle, looks them in the eyes for a few seconds, then takes their hand and tries to express the care he has for each person by doing something to their hand—such as gripping it firmly, stroking it, shaking it, etc.[25]

In his book *Groups, Gimmicks and Instant Gurus,* W. R. Coulson, tells of the CBS-TV documentary on encounter groups called *Circle of Love,* which was made at the Western Behavioral Sciences Institute. Even though the title of the documentary is the same as the title in the preceding activity in a Christian curriculum, it could have been coincidental—that is, until one reads that the participants in the encounter group presented in the documentary were asked "to express their feelings to one another, but not in words."[26]

Parents: Beware! Under the guise of teaching children trust, Christian curriculum developers are exposing children to touch stimulation, a controversial technique used in secular encounter groups.

Indiscriminate Touching

According to W. R. Coulson, when youth are exposed to encounter group or sensitivity training activities that consistently involve touching, they are at an increased risk for sexual seduction by the instructor or peers.[27] Encounter games that involve touch are very powerful, particularly when used with teens. Coulson states, "Sometimes participation in one can cause a person's body to get so far beyond his head that he can't take responsibility for what happens."[28] A sobering observation is given by Coulson:

> For personal growth to be solid, the body and the head have to grow in tandem. A game can give permission for one to do what he might have longed to do but could not take responsibility for. . . . It can rush his body beyond his head, his behavior beyond his person. If the game thus provides too powerful a stimulus, the participant may later find himself needing to disown abruptly what he made happen under the special rules of the game.[29]

Touching in order to get to know someone is backward from the norm. Coulson elaborates,

> Ordinarily, in daily life, if one wants to touch someone, it is to express a closeness that he feels already. First you get to know somebody, then you feel close to him, then you even might want to express it physically. But according to what the students had learned earlier, . . . the everyday process could be reversed and lack of acquaintanceship bypassed. First you could touch a total stranger, *then*, because of the touch, feel close to him, then maybe even want to talk.[30]

Be Still and Know

These touching activities not only have the potential to be psychologically harmful, they also take away time that can be spent with God and studying God's Word. The message to "be still and know that I am God" (Ps. 46:10 KJV), and to "rest in the LORD and wait patiently for Him;" (Ps. 37:7), is missing from most contemporary youth curriculum. It is through silence before God and reading and meditating on His Word, that God will reveal Himself to us. According to Lloyd-Jones, "Being busy subdues the mind, the heart, and the conscience."[31]

Great Christian leaders of our past stressed the importance of spending time alone with God and warned against being busy in what may even appear to be worthwhile Christian activities. Andrew Murray, a pastor and evangelist during the 1800s, in one of his writings expounded:

> . . . let us day by day set ourselves at His feet, and meditate on this word of His, with an eye fixed on Him alone. Let us set ourselves in quiet trust before Him, waiting to hear His holy voice—the still small voice that is mightier than the storm that rends the rocks—breathing its quickening spirit within us, as He speaks: "Abide in me."[32]

Trust Is Not a Feeling

Unlike secular humanist author Jeffrey Schrank, who believes that feelings *can* be trusted and that feelings need *not* be controlled, Christians have traditionally believed that feelings are subjective and unreliable and, therefore, are not to be trusted. Feelings and emotions are powerful, causing one *not* to think clearly when ruled by them.

On the other hand, God and His Word are unchangeable, dependable, and true for every person, for every circumstance, and for all time. Not only can feelings not be trusted, trust is *not* a feeling. William Kilpatrick counsels, "We are not to believe in God only so long as we can feel His presence. Indeed, the real test of our faith is when we cannot feel it at all."[33]

The Old Testament book Habbakuk teaches that to trust in God is to keep your eyes on God and not on your problem. To look at your problem and then to God will only cause confusion and despair. To look to God and then your problem is to put life's unfair, perplexing, and sometimes tragic circumstances in the proper perspective. Even though our feelings are telling us differently, we must trust that God is working out His purposes even if we do not understand. The world's response is to act on the impulses of our feelings, but the supernatural response is to wait patiently upon the Lord.[34]

It appears, however, that much of the contemporary youth curricula and resource material available violate this important biblical principle. In one popular ministry resource, young people are encouraged to "express their inner hurts, visions, and struggles" within their youth group of peers.[35] The focus is on the individual's problem and the group's interaction with one another rather than on God. In fact, God is strangely omitted. One needs to ask: Are we subtly conditioning our youth to have trust and faith in *the group* instead of God? Is this encounter-type group interaction giving the impression that God is only a figurehead and real help for life's trials comes from the group?

Blind Faith?

Even though trusting in self and others is a doctrinal divergence that must be guarded against, Christians should continually strive to be trustworthy and to become more Christlike. There is a big difference between unreservedly trusting someone and striving to become more trustworthy oneself.

Words and ideas are important because their applications have consequences. We must not only be very careful how we use words and ideas, but we must be careful to critique how others use them as well. Christians must hold words and ideas up to the yardstick of Scripture.

For example, it is alarming enough that a small-town newspaper in Washington state featured a large picture of students from their local Christian school leading blindfolded partners around the parking lot and into buildings on campus. However, the travesty of Christian students playing this sensitivity game was exacerbated by the newspaper's heading that read: "Blind Faith." The heading suggested to the reader that a Christian's faith is blind and is nothing more than a walk in the dark. John MacArthur, in his book *Reckless Faith*, states:

> Authentic faith can never bypass the mind. It can never be irrational. Faith, after all, deals with truth. Truth is objective data to be known, studied, contemplated, and understood . . . elevating feelings or blind trust cannot legitimately be called faith, even if it masquerades as Christianity. It is actually an irrational form of unbelief.[36]

Christian author Paul Little adds, "Christianity goes beyond reason but not against it."[37] In other words, an authentic Christian's faith is *not* blind.

The printed word has an aura of authority, so the heading was read and more than likely not even questioned. Christians always need to critique what they read and check it against Scripture. If an idea is expressed often enough, it is likely to be accepted as true. William James, a philosopher who is considered by many to be the father of modern psychology, is credited with the saying, "There is nothing so absurd but if you repeat it often enough, people will believe it."[38] Yes, words and ideas have consequences.

There are hidden dangers when Christian youth leaders use secular activities clothed in religious terminology. To do so is to promote modern thought through the smoke screen of religious words. Youth, as well as leaders, will eventually be unable to distinguish between the secular and the sacred. Also, if an activity or teaching method is used in the church or Christian school, it is likely that Christian youth will think it is OK to participate in such activities outside of a Christian setting—without realizing that the activity may be led by those whose motives are hostile to the Christian faith. Christian youth would not necessarily think to question a game used in a secular setting if it had been used at church, since they would naturally assume that church leaders would not endorse or use anything contrary to Scripture.

Presumptuous Assumptions

Christian youth are continually being bombarded with "innovative" and "relevant" methods to teach trust. In a promotional brochure for a Christian wilderness adventure program, the following description for whitewater rafting is found:

> It's a foaming MONSTER! It's gonna eat us alive! WHAAM!
> We hit so hard it knocks our breath out and shoots us straight
> into the sky! . . . Water's flying everywhere! And just as we

open our eyes to see how much worse it's gonna get, we break over the top, swallow our stomachs, and slide down the backside. We're still together, soaked and screaming like a bunch of crazies, but who cares . . . that was too cool.[39]

Following this dramatic description are these questions: "So, how do we set up for the whitewater in our lives? Do we slide into the rapids sideways and get flipped over, or do we take them head on? Do we let them eat us alive, or do we trust God to guide us over the top?"[40] In an attempt to make an experience in whitewater rafting relevant to problems or crises in a teen's life, the analogy between whitewater rapids and whitewater problems breaks down. There is something wrong with the entire idea of looking at life's problems like a screaming crazy with the attitude of "Who cares?" because a problem or crisis is "too cool." What is really being taught here? Are problems adventures in which we "trust" God to come to the rescue?

Christians must be careful that they do not intentionally put themselves in a potentially hazardous or challenging situation and expect (trust?) God to bail them out. Participating in this type of man-devised experience, expecting God to answer or respond in a preconceived way, is not only unscriptural, but it is presumptuous. It also trivializes God to the position of a benevolent grandfather who simply grants our selfish and childish requests.

In yet another example, Christian teens participating in an internship for youth ministry are also exposed to an unbiblical method for teaching trust. In the middle of the night, a group of six or seven Christian teens are awakened and blindfolded by their leaders and taken out to a field one hundred miles away. The kidnapped group has only a day and a half to make it back to campus. There is a list of dos and don'ts. For example, the teens may only ride in a vehicle for twenty miles at a time, and they must stay together at all times, etc. The teens are also instructed that they can only witness to and answer questions that may be posed by individuals outside their group, but they may not ask any questions (such as, where are they?).

The purpose of this exercise is for the teens to turn to God to meet their needs for food and shelter and guide them safely back to campus.[41]

Teens may come away from that experience and *think* and *feel* themselves quite spiritual, since they "called upon" and "trusted" the Lord to meet their needs while getting them safely back to campus. However, those teens will have been deluded into a pseudotrust. Hypothetical situations do not teach faith or trust. One learns authentic faith by learning biblical principles and practicing them in real-life situations.[42]

Temptation to Trust Self

The apostle Paul also warned that we must not put confidence in our own intellect. "And my speech and my preaching was not with enticing words of man's wisdom, but in demonstration of the Spirit and of power: that your faith should not stand in the wisdom of men, but in the power of God" (1 Cor. 2:4–5).

Tozer elaborated, "There is no truth apart from the Spirit. . . . For a man to understand revealed truth requires an act of God equal to the original act which inspired [the Bible]."[43]

This relatively new trend of relying on philosophy and man's ability to comprehend the deep things of God without the aid of the Holy Spirit is partly responsible for many of the games, gimmicks, and contrived experiences that are finding their way into church curriculum. Subtly, the message has become that the Bible is not all-sufficient: We need the Bible *and* philosophy, or the Bible *and* psychology, or the Bible *and* whatever.

The idea is being promoted that one can participate in simulated activities in order to grow in one's faith and trust in the Lord. Granted, God is able to use any activity or circumstance to draw individuals to Himself, but knowledge of God is given by divine initiative and not attained through an individual's feeble attempts to discover his own path to God through unscriptural methods. We must be challenging the false premise that games and gimmicks devised by humanists and borrowed by Christians will cause one to grow in Christ.

Nothing but Foolishness

Walking blindfolded and falling backward from tables will not teach teens to trust in God. Why would one even need to trust God if he can trust others to catch him when falling, or to listen to him nonjudgmentally as he expresses himself? Teens may question their need for God and wonder what it is they are supposed to be trusting in God for?

After reading a large number of youth curricula, one gets the distinct impression that Christian curricula developers believe individuals have within themselves the power and ability to trust God by participating in games patterned after those developed by secular humanists. Activities based upon this unbiblical concept will only deceive teens into a pseudotrust, encouraging a reckless and shallow faith in God. Authentic faith cannot be attained through participation in contrived, psychologically based games, but rather "faith comes from hearing, and hearing by the word of Christ" (Rom. 10:17).

The root problem with those games is that they are actually statements of disbelief in the all-powerful, all-knowing, ever-present living God. The temptation to trust in self is dangerous, because when self is elevated, God is "abridged, reduced, modified, edited, changed, and amended until He is no longer the God" of the Bible.[44] Tozer admonished, "It is vitally important that we think soundly about God. Since He is the foundation of all our religious beliefs, it follows that if we err in our ideas of God, we will go astray on everything else."[45]

Chapter 7

The Idolatry of Self-Worship

But realize this, that in the last days difficult times will come.
For men will be lovers of self, . . . rather than lovers of God; . . .
—2 Tim. 3:1–2, 4

In reviewing Christian youth curriculum, one is made aware of the overwhelming focus on self. Youth are continually encouraged to explore their innermost thoughts and feelings while unconditionally accepting themselves and others. Not surprisingly, unwarranted claims to authority, dignity, and self-worth are made in the absence of humility. This worldly emphasis on self is contrary to Scripture and is nothing less than a form of idolatry.

The widespread self-esteem movement has its roots in secular psychology. A biblical counselor and noted author, Jay E. Adams, is quick to point out that "the self-love, self-worth movement did not originate out of new exegetical and theological study; it was accommodated and incorporated into the teaching of the church."[1] Should Christians be embracing the self-esteem movement that has its roots outside the church? Does this movement undermine a biblical foundation that could hinder or even damage a child's relationship with the Lord? It is important to discover just how extensive this movement of self-love is in the church and what dangers it may pose for Christian youth.

A Worldly Response

Upon investigation, the number of activities in popular Christian curricula that attempt to bolster a child's self-esteem is astonishing. There are also numerous mini-courses, often called elective studies, lining the shelves in Christian bookstores that deal solely with improving a child's self-concept. An example of such a mini-course is titled *Just Look at You!* This five-lesson course for junior high school students has deviated from biblical truth. As a result, the course will undoubtedly contribute to a teen's worldly and unhealthy obsession with self.

Many of the activities in this study deal with a teen's perception of a poor image of their body. According to Darrell Pearson, one of the authors of *Just Look at You*, junior high kids struggle with the way "God put them together," and the question "Why did God make me look like this?" poses a big dilemma. Pearson even contends that such responses as "You really are beautiful because God made you that way, . . . [and] God looks on the heart . . . often trivialize a very important issue, even if the statements are true"[2] Sadly, Pearson's response to a teen's poor self-image is a worldly one rather than one based upon godly principles.

The following are some activities from this elective study. Even though many of these activities that encourage teens to focus on their negative characteristics appear to be contrary to bolstering a positive self-image, the teens are still focusing on self rather than focusing on God.

Your Secret Identity

In the lesson "Your Secret Identity," the middle-schoolers are given a "chance to create a superhero alter ego" for themselves.[3] First, they are to describe themselves as they think they appear to the rest of the world most of the time. Then they are to create the secret identity for themselves, complete with strengths, special abilities, and at least one weakness that makes them vulnerable.

If the late A. W. Tozer, who is often referred to as a twentieth-century prophet, were to read this activity, he would be grieved. This godly man wrote a stinging indictment about the human ego. He asserted, "Every man with moral intelligence must be aware of the curse that afflicts him inwardly; he must be conscious of the thing we call *ego*, by the Bible called *flesh* or *self*, but by whatever name called, a cruel master and a deadly foe."[4]

Paul Vitz, associate professor of psychology at New York University, also talks about how the glorification of self is contrary to what Scripture teaches.

> It should be obvious . . . that the relentless and single-minded search for and glorification of the self is at direct cross-purposes with the Christian injunction to *lose* the self. Certainly Jesus Christ neither lived nor advocated a life that would qualify by today's standards as "self-actualized." For the Christian the self is the problem, not the potential paradise. Understanding this problem involves an awareness of sin, especially of the sin of pride; correcting this condition requires the practice of such un–self-actualized states as contrition and penitence, humility, obedience, and trust in God.[5]

Some Body to Admire

In this exercise, which tends to stir up envy and arouse a Barbie mentality, the teens are to list the ten people (five men and five women) that have the best bodies. Some of the questions following the activity include: "Do you think people with good bodies are generally better liked than those who are skinny or overweight? If so, how do you think it makes the skinny and overweight people feel? To what extent does another person's body influence how you feel about the person?"[6]

For the session in which this activity is listed, the stated goal is to "help kids recognize that self-image involves a lot more than just body image" and "to help kids begin to shift their thinking from caring only about outer appearance to include an emphasis on inner character as well."[7] This activity, however, does not address the stated goals. In fact, this activity appears to be in direct opposition to the goals. As a result of participating in this exercise, teens would have a difficult time not comparing themselves to the "best bodies" they listed, and more than likely would find themselves coming up lacking. This will only further encourage teens to have a fixation on their own bodies and the bodies of others.

The Magical Genie

In "The Magical Genie," teens are told that they are to imagine that they found an "awesome-looking lava lamp at a garage sale." As they start to rub off some of the dust, a genie "wearing a tie-dyed T-shirt and wide-flared bell-bottom jeans, and humming a Grateful Dead tune" appears. The genie tells them they can make all the wishes they want, but since he is only an apprentice genie, he only knows how to change them in physical ways: their bodies or their personalities. The children are then instructed to list everything about themselves that they would like to change, "both outer characteristics and inner traits."[8]

This will result in the preoccupation of teens with their own bodies. This self-absorption is unbiblical and will more than likely be detrimental to a teen's spiritual growth. It is unscrupulous for authors and publishers of youth curricula to foster a self-centered approach to teenhood. Pearson justifies this approach, because he believes "most junior high students struggle with their appearance more than any other single area." He also believes that teens "can't help feeling awful about the way they're made, questioning the validity of a God who seems so cruel."[9] What Pearson has failed to acknowledge is that to list perceived flaws shows a disrespectful attitude toward God, who fashioned each of us in His image and by His own hand.

One cannot help but wonder why teens would be encouraged to put their confidence in a magical genie who hums tunes from a counterculture rock group. If this activity is not already bad enough, it also validates the era in our nation's history that ushered in rebellion and disrespect for authority. This era, which coined the slogan, "If it feels good, do it," also became known as the Me generation.

Self-Love in Disguise

Public schoolteachers and school officials frequently argue that children do poorly in academics and exhibit negative behavior because they have low self-esteem. Children are, therefore, taught to accept and love themselves. Since children must be taught to love themselves, implied is the faulty concept of dissatisfaction with self or even self-hate, a concept that is tragically being embraced in churches, as demonstrated in the preceding examples of curriculum activities. However, one pastor sagaciously reminds us: "Teaching one to love oneself has no biblical foundation. The Bible already assumes we have a self-love, which because of sin is often twisted and confused."[10]

One would think that the person who is always putting himself down hates himself or at least has a poor self-image. But, in essence, he is making it known that he has not measured up to the standards that he has set for himself. According to the research done by David Hunt and T. A. McMahon, this is not a symptom of a low self-concept but rather one of pride. They give the following example:

> The person who says, "I'm so ugly, I hate myself!" doesn't hate himself at all, or he would be *glad* that he was ugly. It is because he loves himself that he is upset with his appearance and the way people respond to him. The person who grovels in depression and says he hates himself for having wasted his life would actually be glad that he had wasted his life if he really hated himself. In fact, he is unhappy about having wasted his life because he loves himself. The apparently remorseful criminal, who says he hates himself because of the crimes he has committed, should then be glad to see himself suffer in prison. Yet he hopes to escape that fate, which proves he loves himself in spite of his protestations of self-loathing.[11]

David Powlison, author and lecturer in practical theology at Westminster Theological Seminary in Philadelphia, concurs with

Hunt and McMahon. Powlison states that low self-esteem is actually "a form of pride and the compulsive drive toward self-righteousness that operates in everyone."[12] He elaborates, "People generate their own faulty expectations and idealized images of what or who they ought to be. Sometimes they fail to meet them. Their own lie-distorted conscience accuses them. Hence, they suffer symptomatic 'low self-esteem.'"[13]

Low self-esteem is actually a disguised form of pride. The Bible condemns self-righteous pride and arrogance and considers them evil (see Prov. 8:13). If the self-esteem movement encourages self-righteous pride and arrogance, why is it being taught in the church? The self-esteem movement belies common sense and sound biblical teaching.

Best Body Parts

This activity also from *Just Look at You* is a take-off from the Some Body to Admire activity already mentioned. This contest judges body parts among members in the group. For example: best big toe, best elbow, best ear, and best lips. It is suggested that these body parts be projected through a hole cut in a piece of paper to help the judges focus and so that the judges will not be influenced by who the people are.

Our teens should not be encouraged to compare themselves with others. Students voted as having the best ear or the best lips may become vain about a particular body part. Vanity is yet another example of unhealthy self-absorption and has always been considered an undesirable character trait. It rapidly becomes apparent that vanity is encouraged, and all under the auspices of developing one's self-esteem, a secular humanistic concept to elevate self.

There are negative effects that may result from activities that encourage an elevated self-concept, whether it is vanity over a particular body part or an inflated ego about perceived intelligence or abilities. This movement of self-love poses hidden dangers for Christian youth. A. W. Tozer makes the observation that "young Christians often hinder their own usefulness by their attitude toward themselves."[14] He expounds:

> They begin with the innocent notion that they are at least above the average in intelligence and ability. . . . They want to begin at the top and work upward! What happens is that they usually fail to secure the high place they feel qualified to fill and end up developing a chronic feeling of resentment toward everyone who stands in their way or fails to appreciate them. And as they grow older that comes to include almost everybody. At last comes a deep permanent grudge against the world.[15]

Affirmation As a Mighty Warrior

Affirmation is a technique frequently used to help teens build up another's self-esteem. One activity in this mini-course encourages "spending time on each individual, bestowing affirmation on him or her as a mighty warrior." It is suggested to "raise each warrior on the shoulders of others in the group" while the group offers "cheers and applause as well as relevant positive comments."[16]

Insincerely bestowing affirmation or positive comments on another is called *flattery* in the Bible. It is wrong to instruct a teen to flatter someone he may hardly know. Psalm 5:9 has harsh words concerning those who flatter: "There is nothing reliable in what they say;/ Their inward part is destruction itself;/ Their throat is an open grave;/ They flatter with their tongue."

To flatter calls into question the motive of the flatterer and the gullibility and the ego of the one being flattered. How sincere are comments of praise when the affirmation is given because of a required assignment? In other words, "If someone will say things to your face they would never say behind your back, it is insincere praise."[17] Contrary to what is being practiced during these affirmation-type activities, the Bible teaches, "He who rebukes a man will afterward find more favor, than he who flatters with the tongue" (Prov. 28:23).

There are additional dangers in affirmation-type activities. First, if teens become dependent on worldly praise, their motivation to do good deeds may become skewed. Good deeds with wrong motives will be burned as dead branches on Judgment Day (see John 15:6). Second, the Bible instructs Christians to seek God's praise, not man's praise, and asks the question, "How can you believe, when you receive glory from one another, and you do not seek the glory that is from the one and only God?" (John 5:44). Third, and perhaps the most important reason not to seek self-praise, "Jesus sets forth self-denial rather than self-affirmation as the way to enter into a proper relationship with God."[18] Jay E. Adams adds, "It should grieve us to think of children . . . being encouraged to think they deserve 'a pat on the back' and being told to 'feel good' about themselves, thereby being led in the very pathway to selfishness that God condemns. . . . The proper thing to encourage, according to the Word of God, is self-denial."[19]

It is disturbing that individuals who should know better are leading youth astray. Affirmation and self-esteem activities are hindering our youth's proper relationship with God. Kilpatrick reminds us that "Our Lord's greatest wrath wasn't directed at obvious sinners, like Mary Magdalene, but at those who were convinced of their own self-worth."[20] Therefore, it can be concluded that affirmation and self-esteem activities are nothing more than spiritual junk food, which will produce only feeble, anemic Christians.

Delusions and Self-Deception

But there is still another secular method promoting self that is so subtle, many are unaware of its presence. This is found in the seemingly harmless questions "How do *you* feel?" or "What do you *think*?" As a result, what a child thinks or feels is validated as being the authority for him, and delusions of self-importance overshadow how small and sinful he really is.

Such questions become solely a means of self-expression and an avenue for narcissism, because what one thinks and feels has nothing to do with seeking truth. Truth is, regardless of what one thinks and feels. Solomon, known as the wisest man who ever lived, wrote, "A fool does not delight in understanding, but only in revealing his own mind" (Prov. 18:2).

Instead of validating different opinions based upon limited Bible knowledge or on feelings, youth should be encouraged to use the Bible, reliable supplemental resources, biblical scholars, creeds, and great teachers of the past to seek real understanding of God's Word. But unfortunately, according to pastor and author Michael Horton, "Everyone believes that his or her own personal feelings are more valuable than the collective intellectual wisdom of the ages."[21] The question should not be "What do you think?" but rather "What does God say?"

If children minimize the authority of God and instead rely on their own perceived authority, they become easy prey for false doctrine. If God is trivialized, it is easier to elevate self and embrace the heretical doctrine of self-worship. An awe and reverence for God should permeate all curricula. A. W. Tozer is quoted as saying, "What we believe about God is the most important thing about us."[22]

The late Paul E. Little, in his book *Know What You Believe*, added, "Our belief or lack of it inevitably translates itself into our actions and attitudes."[23]

Self-deception is the work of our own sinful nature. Instead of encouraging our own delusions of self-importance, we should be developing an attitude of humility. John MacArthur wrote "It is humility that acknowledges our own potential for self-deception (The heart is more deceitful than all else and is desperately sick; who can understand it?—Jer. 17:9). It is a humility that distrusts personal feelings and casts scorn on self-sufficiency."[24]

To be self-sufficient is to deny our need of God. If we can look within ourselves and base our decisions and actions on what we think and how we feel, we are subtly removing God from His throne. We may go to church regularly, openly profess our faith to others, and be a part of a community outreach to the homeless, but unless we acknowledge God as all sufficient, relying solely upon Him and not ourselves, then we are victims of the subtle serpent of deception.

Experiencing Emotion

Another secular method of focusing on self is that of experiencing emotion. When a person experiences emotions, according to Carl Rogers, ". . . he has experienced *himself,* in all the richness that exists within himself." Rogers argues that experiencing emotions and feelings is "really the discovery of unknown elements of self."[25]

A client of Carl Rogers relates the excitement she felt while exploring and experiencing her feelings: "I have all the symptoms of fright. . . . It really seems like I'm cut loose and very vulnerable. . . . Still, I have a feeling of strength. . . . I'm feeling it internally now, a sort of surging up, or force . . . something really big and strong."

Rogers critiques his client's response. He explains, "This is an example of what I mean by experiencing a feeling fully and acceptantly. . . . It represents, in my judgment, a moment of change—probably physiological, irreversible change . . . the changed self that emerged would be based on her organismic reactions, her inner experiencing, and not on the values and expectations of others."[26] After reading this woman's personal description of the excitement of experiencing herself through emotions, it becomes easier to understand how a Christian can confuse and attribute the exhilaration of such an experience with an authentic spiritual conversion by the Holy Spirit. Perhaps that is why in the past, experiences that stimulate the emotions have been rejected by the Christian church.

In one resource book for Christian youth groups, youth leaders are instructed to: "Focus on the students' personal experiences and feelings. Once personal feelings are discussed, the philosophical and theological implications of the exercise can come alive." Incredibly, the youth leader is also instructed, "If the group seems reluctant to share . . . , go around the circle and ask each person to respond with his or her feelings."[27]

Discovering self by experiencing emotions rather than discovering God by studying His Word is a radical shift in church practice. How many church leaders are even aware that this shift in philosophy is taking place in youth curricula?

Spiritual Deception

Christians who love the Lord do not wake up one morning and say "Today, I am going to start worshipping myself" any more than the Israelites consciously decided to start worshipping idols. The Israelites let down their guard. They were not watching, nor were they discerning. They were not diligently guarding their faith in God and passionately protecting His holy character. Instead, the Israelites let down their defenses as they did business and socially intermingled with their heathen neighbors. As a result, the Israelites became involved in worldly practices. They even intermarried with those who worshipped pagan gods. The Israelites, however, did not totally reject God; they worshipped both God *and* other gods.

When God is worshipped along with other gods, God no longer is perceived as all-knowing, all-powerful and ever-present. William Kilpatrick points out that even "the secular mind does not always find it necessary to deny God, but it must always reduce Him to a comfortable size. Above all else He must be a manageable God who does not watch or judge."[28] Many activities in contemporary youth curricula set students up for this mindset. For example, in the directions for an affirmation exercise from a resource book for youth, the students are told to "include God as one of the group."[29] These instructions demean God to be just one of the guys—a peer who is instructed to unconditionally love and not judge.

The Israelites did not intentionally decide to compromise God, but compromise they did. Many Christians today are doing the same thing. Christians say they love the Lord and desire to follow Him, but because of the subtle practices of the world, they are being encouraged to worship God and self. If the worship of self was to replace the worship of God, our idolatry would be easier to identify; but the world has encouraged us to worship self *in addition* to God, making our idolatry more difficult to recognize.

God tells us in His revealed Word, "I, the LORD your God, am a jealous God" (Exod. 20:5), and commands, ". . . you shall not worship any other god, for the LORD, whose name is Jealous, is a jealous God. . . ." (Ex. 34:14).

Moses instructed God's people, "For the Lord your God is a consuming fire, a jealous God" (Deut. 4:24), and Joshua also warned the Israelites, "He is a jealous God. . . . If you forsake the Lord and serve foreign gods, then He will turn and do you harm and consume you. . . ." (Josh. 24:19–20). These are sobering words that should cause every Christian to sincerely search his heart to determine where self-worship is being idolized in his own life.

We Are to Decrease

The message proclaimed by John the Baptist "He must increase and I must decrease" (John 3:30) should be the message taught and reinforced in Sunday school classes and youth groups. We should be continually asking ourselves, Does this Sunday school or youth group activity honor God, or does it cause the child to focus on self? What would Jesus say about this activity? Would Jesus approve of this activity to teach about Himself and our relationship to Him?

Martin and Deidre Bobgan, in their book *Psychoheresy*, state, ". . . the Bible teaches one to be Christ-centered and other-oriented. Loving God above all else and with one's entire being, and loving neighbor as much as one *already* loves oneself, are the primary injunctions of the Bible. The admonition to love oneself or to esteem oneself is missing."[30] Teens should not be encouraged to draw attention to, or boast in, their own abilities and accomplishments. Instead, teens should be continually reminded, "He who boasts, let him boast in the Lord. For not he who commends himself is approved, but whom the Lord commends" (2 Cor. 10:17–18).

The Doctrine of Natural Goodness

Certain Christian curricula continually reinforce the focus on self, a self which proponents of humanistic psychology believe to be intrinsically good. The concept that man is basically good is contrary to Scripture. Scripture says that man is fallen and has a sinful nature:

- "For all have sinned and fall short of the glory of God" (Rom. 3:23)
- "There is none righteous, not even one" (3:10)
- "There is none who does good, there is not even one" (3:12)

We must acknowledge our sinful nature and recognize that there is nothing we can do to save ourselves. Salvation is initiated by God. No one can come to our Lord Jesus Christ unless the act has been granted by the Father (see John 6:65). Christian leaders must scrutinize church curriculum to ensure that material and methods are not fostering a reliance on self. Pride and self-righteous attitudes promoted in church curriculum will hinder the spiritual growth and the maturity of our youth. A. W. Tozer warned, "Self-righteousness is an effective bar to God's favor because it throws the sinner back upon his own merits and shuts him out from the imputed righteousness of Christ. And to be a sinner confessed and consciously lost is necessary to the act of receiving salvation through our Lord Jesus Christ."[31]

It is by addressing one's sin, not one's self-worth, that will lead to an authentic trust in God as one begins to comprehend the depths of God's love and forgiveness. When one sincerely addresses his own sin, confidence and sufficiency in self are destroyed. It appears, however, that the majority of youth curricula avoid the topic of sin altogether. Kilpatrick warns that the church is in danger of embracing the doctrine of natural goodness implied in most theories of self-esteem. He argues that Christians must be careful not to reduce

> the good news of the gospel to the status of "nice news"—
> "nice" because there was never any bad news in the first place.
> If psychology's great optimism about raw human nature is
> correct, then Christianity is not necessary: Christ's redemp-
> tive action on the cross becomes superfluous. After all, why
> should He have suffered and died to redeem us if there is
> nothing wrong with us? If all we need do to find wholeness is
> just be ourselves, then His death sums up to a meaningless
> gesture, a noble but unneeded self-sacrifice.[32]

The Sense of Nothingness

The opposite of positive self-esteem is humility. If there are lessons on humility in youth curriculum, they are not very easy to find. Most of the lessons are much more concerned with developing a child's positive self-image. Andrew Murray stated that humility is "simply the sense of entire nothingness, which comes when we see how truly God is all, and in which we make way for God to be all."[33] Murray elaborates, "Where God is all, self is nothing."[34] Murray encourages one to think about humility in relationship to faith.

> Is [faith] not the confession of nothingness and helplessness,
> the surrender and the waiting to let God work? Is it not in
> itself the most humbling thing there can be—the acceptance
> of our place as dependents, who can claim or get or do noth-
> ing but what grace bestows? Humility is simply the disposi-
> tion which prepares the soul for living on trust. And every,
> even the most secret breathing of pride—in self-seeking, self-
> will, self-confidence, or self-exaltation—is just the strength-
> ening of that self which cannot enter into the Kingdom,
> because it refuses to allow God to be what He is and must
> be—the all in all.[35]

As the great Charles H. Spurgeon expounded, "It is the Holy Spirit's work to turn our eyes away from self to Jesus: but Satan . . . is constantly trying to make us regard ourselves instead of Christ."[36] Could it be that youth leaders are working at counter purposes to the Holy Spirit every time they do an activity that elevates self rather than Christ? According to what Spurgeon said, could it also be argued that anyone who encourages a focus on self is in fact assisting Satan? This is a sobering thought!

While an Enemy of God
The Bible tells us that God loves all mankind so much that He sent His Son, Jesus, to die on the cross for our sins. "For God so loved the world that He gave His only begotten Son, that whoever believes in Him should not perish, but have eternal life" (John 3:16).

David Powlison makes an important distinction about God's love that Christians would do well not to forget. Powlison reminds us that God loves us "*despite* who we are and *because* of who *He* is."[37] Adams elaborates on this truth:

> The Scriptures teach that "while we were helpless," "while we were sinners," and "while we were enemies," Christ died for us (Rom. 5:6, 8, 10). . . . We were unlovely, unloving, and unlovable. Of what worth is a weak, sinful enemy of God to Him? Yet in spite of all that there was in us that might repel Him, God out of His great mercy alone determined to set His love on us. This cannot help but turn our eyes away from ourselves and any supposed self-worth and instead toward God, who is truly worthy of *all* of our love and praise for redeeming us![38]

There is nothing we can do to make ourselves holy and acceptable to God. It is only through what Jesus did on the cross that God's righteousness is imputed to us. Rather than focusing on self, Christians should focus on God and His great mercy and grace. Adams reiterates,

> It is not because of man's great value to God that He cares for him, but in spite of his lowliness. This care shows something of *God's* greatness—not man's. In His amazing grace and un-

deserved love, God cares for man. The great fact is that the Scriptures everywhere point us to the grace of God and not to the worth of man.[39]

Adams solemnly warns that Christians should not tamper "with the precious doctrine of grace in order to support a non-Christian humanistic theory."[40] The "non-Christian theory" is the unbiblical theory of self-esteem.

In His Steps

Jesus was obedient to His Heavenly Father, even unto death, but His death did not exemplify self-worship or affirmation by others. On the contrary, Jesus was rejected, mocked by His enemies, and betrayed and abandoned by His friends. Jesus demonstrated humility as He humbly and obediently submitted Himself to God's will. Submission to God's will in order to glorify God is what Christians should strive for. "Christ suffered for you, leaving an example for you to follow in His steps" (1 Pet. 1:21).

Andrew Murray argues the importance of seeking humility: "We must seek a humility which will rest in nothing less than the end and death of self; which gives up all the honor of men as Jesus did, to seek the honor that comes from God alone; which absolutely makes and counts itself nothing so that God may be all, that the Lord alone may be exalted."[41]

Contrary to the humanistic philosophy of self-esteem, a Christian's meaning and security in life are found by looking to God. Activities in contemporary curricula that focus on praises from peers and public applause so that "self" can feel good, is pointing our youth in the wrong direction. Our own importance reflected in the unbiblical self-esteem movement is made irrelevant and self-serving when compared to Jesus' model of humility.

Missing: Reverence and Holy Fear

The attributes of God's holiness and righteousness are missing from contemporary youth curricula. Even though it is right and good that we spend time in fellowship with God, we must be careful that we do not assume a familiarity that does not exist. In fact, in his book dealing with the dangers and delights of spiritual intimacy, Michael Horton adamantly warns against a feel-good faith that encourages a chummy relationship with God.[42] There are countless passages from Scripture that should cause us to seek fellowship with God in awe and reverence and not casual familiarity.

It is not popular today to talk about fearing God, and youth curricula appear to avoid the topic altogether. Still, the response of those in the Bible who had a personal encounter with the living Lord is one of fear as their own sinfulness was exposed before the righteous, holy God. Their response was not one of feeling good about self. When the prophet Isaiah came face to face with the living God, he cried: "Woe is me, for I am ruined! Because I am a man of unclean lips" (Isa. 6:5). Job had a similar response when his sin was exposed during his encounter with God. He said, "I repent in dust and ashes" (Job 42:6). After witnessing a miracle by Jesus, Peter, who was also convicted of his own sinfulness, fell down at Jesus' feet, saying, "Depart from me, for I am a sinful man, O Lord!" (Luke 5:8). Fear should be a natural response from us when our depravity is exposed before God; we deserve death. But God through His infinite mercy and unconditional grace sacrificed His own Son as propitiation for our sin. To comprehend such a sacrificial act is difficult for finite human minds.

It is disturbing to think that youth leaders using contemporary youth curricula are, in essence, encouraging our teens to have an unholy relationship with the righteous God of the universe. Before a rightful relationship with the Lord can be established, our teens must acknowledge their own depravity and sinfulness. However, it is difficult for a teen to confront his sins when others are telling him how great he is and he is being encouraged to focus on his own special strengths and abilities.

Worship, honor, and praise must be directed to God the Creator and not to man—the created. God is for eternity. He has always been and always will be. Unlike man, whose flesh is like grass and will wither, God's Word stands forever (see Isa. 40:7–8). Man's talents and accomplishments are dwarfed when compared to the greatness of the living God. In awe and reverence for our God, Isaac Newton wrote, "We are therefore to acknowledge one God, infinite, eternal, omnipresent, omniscient, omnipotent, the Creator of all things, most wise, most just, most good, most holy. We must love Him, fear Him, honor Him, trust in Him, pray to Him, give Him thanks, praise Him, and hallow His name. . . ."[44]

Religious Fraud

In view of the greatness of our God, Christian youth curricula that dwell on self are teaching a false doctrine. Activities in contemporary curricula that focus on praise from peers and public applause so that "self" can feel good are pointing our youth in the wrong direction. Our youth must be taught and encouraged to diligently seek God and His righteousness while at the same time giving no thought to themselves. God is God, and it is His praise our youth should seek, and not the praise of peers. Games that affirm them as a mighty warrior or activities that encourage delusions of self-importance are spiritually fraudulent. Instead of self-adoration and self-worship, our teens should be taught to humbly pray, "Lord, I renounce my desire for human praise, for the approval of my peers, [and] the need for public recognition. I deliberately put them aside today, content to hear You whisper, 'Well done, thou good and faithful servant.'"[45]

Even though curricula found on shelves in Christian bookstores may have Christian-sounding titles with Scripture verses scattered throughout, they are not teaching a humility before God or an awe and reverence for Him. In fact, Paul Vitz suggests that God has been reduced "to a useful servant of the individual in his quest for personal goals."[46] Christian curricula are elevating self, the created, rather than praising, fearing, trusting, and loving God the Creator. A. W. Tozer concluded,

> No matter how attractive the movement may appear, if it is not founded in righteousness and nurtured in humility, it is not of God. If it exploits the flesh, it is a religious fraud and should not have the support of any God-fearing Christian. Only that is of God which honors the Spirit and prospers at the expense of the human ego. "That, according as it is written, He that glorieth, let him glory in the Lord."[47]

Chapter 8

Encounter in the Trees

For the time will come when they will not endure sound doctrine; but wanting to have their ears tickled, they will accumulate for themselves teachers in accordance to their own
desires.

—2 Tim. 4:3–4

Respected evangelical leaders have foretold of a coming evangelical crisis if we continue on the course we have followed for
the past twenty-five years. Pastors, elders, and deacons, Sunday
school teachers, and Christian men and women—all of whom
faithfully serve Jesus Christ need to understand that the sufficiency and authority of Scripture are under attack. We see this
assault taking place not only in Christian youth curricula, but
in outreach and wilderness adventure programs for both
churched and unchurched youth.

Since Christianity has been built upon the principle that
Scripture is to be our sole guide for message and method, one
cannot help but wonder what the church of tomorrow will look
like if the Christian youth of today play loose with their faith
and expect an experience to move them closer to God. What
will be the consequences of participating for years in Christian
youth activities that educate the emotions rather than the mind?
Will the Christian youth of tomorrow know what it means to be

led by the Spirit when their minds have been captive to man-made experiences that stimulate and manipulate the emotions? Will our young people develop into spiritually mature Christian men and women when the disciplined study of Scripture is replaced with a constant diet of touchy-feely activities? Are the Christian youth of today being deceived into accepting a faith not grounded on a solid scriptural foundation?

Manipulating Emotions

Can you imagine youth leaders intentionally creating fear in teens in order to teach them that they can trust in God? Well, a prominent national Christian youth organization, Young Life, is using a popular and trendy rope course to do exactly that. In an article featuring this organization, the caption under a picture read: "A 40-foot ropes course at Lake Champion challenged participants' fears as they grow to trust Christ."[1] Another Christian organization, Reachout Expeditions, a division of Youth Dynamics, Inc., uses a rope course they describe as a "curious collection of ropes, logs, and cables . . . dangling from the trees of a quiet forest."[2]

An informational brochure about Reachout Expeditions entices its readers: "Imagine standing on platforms and hanging from cables strung between treetops forty feet high. Its crazy. We'll spend the day pushing through our *fears* and finding out about ourselves along the way"[3] (emphasis added). Once again, it is apparent from their own material that the intent of this artificially simulated activity is to create fear. Along with learning more about themselves, the purpose of creating fear is so that the participants will reach out to help each other. Those at Reachout Expeditions also have expressed a hope that, by participating in their wilderness adventures, participants will reach out and "embrace the challenge of knowing God in a new way."[4]

We find it difficult, however, to picture the apostle Paul swinging from ropes in trees in order to learn to trust Christ, nor can we see the apostles Matthew, Mark, Luke, or John using this method. It is incomprehensible that the apostles would attempt to manipulate the emotions and senses of individuals in order to draw them closer to Jesus. Using experiences to manipulate the emotions in an attempt to teach a biblical concept is unscriptural. To overcome fear, one simply trusts in God; one does not need to participate in a ropes course or any other contrived, fear-producing activity.

Experience Fear, Frustration, and Hopelessness

A concerned mother, whose teenage son attends a Christian school, brought to our attention yet another example of an experience used to manipulate children's emotions. This overnight experience in which her son was expected to participate is called the 18-Hour Encounter, sponsored by WAKE UP AMERICA!— a movement launched by World Concern. The biblical concept supposedly being taught during this "Encounter with the Real World" is that of compassion for those who are suffering. According to the national chairperson, Tony Campolo, one goal is to "enable [children] to experience some of the frustrations and fears felt by those in poverty." [5]

The ministry philosophy of the 18-Hour Encounter states:

> The students will also be educated about what's really happening in our world—the true conditions that millions of desperate people endure. Through the various games and exercises, students will discover not just facts about poverty. They will feel and experience for themselves some of what hopeless people face every day. [6]

To *feel* and to *experience* are key words that indicate that the objective of this activity is to educate the emotions and senses and not the intellect. The psychological nature of the 18-Hour Encounter becomes even more evident after reading the promotional material: "Students will be integrated together through the activities and the small, caring groups. They will begin by getting to know more about each other on a deeper level than before. The bonds of community will develop and barriers will go down. By the end of the encounter, students will be sharing their hearts. . . ."[7] Once again, the secular psychotherapeutic techniques of the encounter group are being applied to youth. The importance placed upon "sharing on a deeper level as barriers go down" shows the strong secular influence of Carl Rogers and Abraham Maslow in this Christian organization. In their own words, the 18-Hour Encounter is not only learning about those in poverty, but also learning about themselves and each other.

This 18-hour Encounter, a sensitivity training exercise, serves to manipulate a man-made experience with the hope of developing compassion and empathy in youth. Christians must realize that playing mind games with youth is a questionable method to help them grasp biblical truth. Throughout early and modern-day history, men and women have proven and acted upon their empathy for the homeless and those in poverty without attempting to experience their plight through a simulated activity. In fact, it is impossible to imagine the apostles Peter and Paul manufacturing an experience as a means to impart to the early Christians compassion for those who are suffering.

It is not difficult to imagine, however, the anxiety that could be generated in youth as they experience strong emotions in a situation over which they have no control. To intentionally induce frustration and anxiety in a child by overloading him with problems beyond his control is unprincipled. The potential to harm the emotional health of children by thrusting the problems of the adult world on their young shoulders is undeniable.

Psychological Conditioning

The 18-Hour Encounter has many of the same political and social overtones, and uses the same psychological conditioning, as the secular *World Game* developed by socialist and atheist Buckminster Fuller. The *World Game*, which is being used in the public schools across the country, is promoted as a means to "allow people to experience global issues such as economics, diversity, environmental problems, hunger, literacy, population. . . ."[8]

Interestingly, it is the Humanist Manifesto, not the Bible, that states, "We affirm that moral values derive their source from *human experience.*" Again we ask the question, Why is a worldly technique developed by those who are anti-God being used on Christian youth? It has been suggested by a respected researcher, Thomas Sowell, that these psychological conditioning methods, which change fundamental attitudes, values, and beliefs, are actually brainwashing techniques.[9]

Isolation, one of the brainwashing techniques described by Sowell, is used in the previously mentioned 18-Hour Encounter.

> The success of brainwashing depends not only on the stress brought to bear on the targeted individuals but also on the extent to which their resistance can be undermined. Isolation—disconnecting them from the psychological support of those who share their values, or who are tied to them personally—is one way of undermining their resistance.[10]

The objective for the 18-Hour Encounter is to have youth experience what it is like to go hungry and to be cold, so that they will be guided "into a decision and lifestyle that will change the world for many hurting people."[11] To put a child in unfamiliar surroundings where he is forced to experience hunger and cold while being isolated from the physical and emotional support of his parents is a psychological technique that may cause a child to experience an unusual amount of stress and anxiety.

In psychological experiences, according to Sowell, stage-managing can be important.[12] In the letter sent home telling about the 18-Hour Encounter, the stage for the psychological experience was described, but the majority of the parents were unaware of the social experiment about to take place—an experience that had the potential to reshape their child's emotions, attitudes, and behaviors. The letter informed parents that "the lodge and bunkhouses are in the woods and rustic, without heat. There's a big stone fireplace to heat the lodge room. The caretaker on the property has a phone." The parents were also told that "a World Concern representative will assist in leading the activities, which will include games, videos, and problems simulating the experiences of refugee people." The letter concludes with, "This retreat is considered part of our fall curriculum, so it's *expected* that every student will attend."[13] The stage had been set.

Mental Molestation

Immediately upon arrival at the designated location for the encounter, the teens have all their belongings taken from them and locked in a room. The teens are then given beads and told, if they want any of the items they brought, they must pay for them with the beads they just received and/or with any additional beads they may gain as the encounter proceeds. "Students can gain beads for positive actions or be given beads for no reason at all. Everything costs something—going to the rest room, food, water, or even the use of their toothbrush."[14] The teens are also instructed:

DO WHAT YOU ARE TOLD. Assume everything is real. If someone says, "I've got a gun!" THEY DO! Don't try to be a hero—follow all directions so you can experience the world that many refugees and oppressed people live in. Those who violate the rules usually end up getting injured or sick and have to spend time flat on their back in the medical tent in isolation.[15]

During the second hour, everyone is instructed to line up for pizza. The following are instructions to the leaders:

Exaggerate how delicious [the pizza] will be. It will cost [the students] 3 beads. Collect all the beads. (Have no sympathy on those who don't have enough—don't suggest sharing.) After the first two people get their pizza, have two pizza hijackers burst in with Nerf guns shouting, "GET DOWN!" at the top of their lungs. Make sure everyone lies flat and follows the orders.[16]

The hijackers take all the pizza and steal all the beads they can get a hold of. After the hijackers leave, the remaining students get crackers and some watered juice. During the seventh hour, it is time for the teens to go to sleep. There is one problem, however, "all the sleeping bags and pillows were stolen by the villainous hijackers. But for the price of a couple of beads, blankets are available." At "Hour Nine" (2:00 A.M.) teens are startled out of their sleep by a loud obnoxious alarm. The instruction manual instructs the leaders to "round up all the sleepy participants and quickly organize them into a huddle. Speak sternly and seriously:

> We've got to move out of here. Lookouts have spotted some rebel forces in the area. We think they know where our camp is. We're going to have to change locations until they pass through the area. Keep track of each other and stay together.

As the group moves to another location, the teens are instructed to remain quiet in order to escape the hijacker's notice. "If somebody makes a noise and draws attention" the hijackers have been directed to "harass the group, take any beads [and] a couple of blankets or whatever they can find."

"Hour Fourteen" is breakfast. Leaders are to "line everyone up [and] get 2 beads from each student for breakfast. . . . Choose two students at random to go to the front of the line. Give those two students hot breakfasts from a local fast-food place." When the third teen comes up, he is told there are no more hot breakfasts. He and everyone else are served simulated Unimix (a highly nutritious porridge commonly served to starving people in Africa). The teens are told, "Never mind the black stuff that looks like bugs or burned stuff. This is just a simulation!" A snack break is planned for "Hour Seventeen." The teens are told that there's food available if they can find it. They are then taken to a room where someone has hidden "little plastic bags (one per participant) with a piece of bread and a little piece of candy in each one."[17]

Regardless of the desired outcome by Christians who use humanistic exercises and techniques, there is inherent danger in allowing anyone to intentionally manipulate a child's mind and emotions—no matter how good their intentions might be. There is the unmistakable risk of setting up children for future emotional manipulations, but by those with motives and political agendas that are less than honest. Could this be a practical, contemporary example of the apostle Peter's warning: "Be on your guard lest, being carried away by error of unprincipled men, you fall from your own steadfastness" (2 Pet. 3:17)?

Disturbingly but not surprisingly, the ideas and methods presented in the 18-Hour Encounter are not isolated. A variation of this extended exercise has surfaced in other material developed by a major Christian author, showing how far-reaching ideas can be.[18] The 18-Hour Encounter espouses Christian-sounding goals punctuated with Christian terminology but is based upon the psychological manipulation of emotions through experiences—a method that has no scriptural basis. This method, however, goes beyond being unscriptural. This psychological conditioning exercise is the mental molestation of other people's children.

The Blind Retreat

Man-made activities designed to create emotional experiences in youth for the sole purpose of affecting their behavior and attitudes have the potential of backfiring. Dr. William Coulson warned that "whether the experience was totally positive, totally negative, or mixed, there were always risks in participation, and the risks were personal."[19] Even Carl Rogers eventually realized that some people "might be deeply hurt or greatly helped but [he] could not predict which."[20]

For instance, one young man personally told us about a bizarre experience called the Blind Retreat held overnight and the following day at his church. Teens were blindfolded for the entire day to experience what it felt like to be handicapped. While blindfolded, there were discussions and activities focusing on the need to trust each other, and of course, the infamous trust walk was on the list of activities to do. The youth described this simulated experience as torture and told how at the end of the day one boy "ripped off his blindfold in tears." The teen said everyone understood his outburst of emotion because many of the other youth were feeling the very same way.

More than likely, the well-meaning leaders had no idea how negative this potent, emotional experience would be for some of the youth. Yes, some of the youth may have enjoyed participating in the overnight encounter, but others did not. To some of the teens, this simulated exercise subtly planted seeds of distrust and a sense of betrayal as the teens questioned the wisdom of adults who would intentionally put them through this traumatic experience. Also, as a result of his own personal experience, the young man told us that he avoided attending the youth group's next overnight encounter—spending the night in cardboard boxes to experience what it felt like to be homeless, an idea that doesn't even come close to describing the plight of those without dependable food and shelter.

Hyped-Up Hype

There is a growing national ministry for teenagers called Teen Mania. The organization's name grabbed our attention because the word *mania* is not a word customarily referred to as a positive character trait. One definition equates *mania* with *madness* and also a type of mental disorder. Another definition refers to "excessive excitement, enthusiasm, or craze." This definition can also be extended to mean enthusiasm of an extreme and transient nature. One would hope that a teen's commitment to the Lord would be a lifelong commitment, not a transient one.

In Teen Mania's promotional brochure telling about the Acquire the Fire Convention (ATF), readers are told: "ATF bombards teenagers with the *reality of God* through relevant teachings by Ron Luce, a live band, intense worship, drama, video, lighting, and special effects. It's a nonstop, no-hype, 100%

authentic challenge to teenagers that is revolutionizing young people across North America" (emphasis added). Regardless of what the brochure says, this convention sounds like a lot of hype! The hype continues:

> One of the most powerful forces in the known world today is Teenagers. One problem: They don't know it. There are literally thousands of young people on this planet wanting to give their lives to a cause but don't even know how to begin to find one. . . . Imagine a massive army of young people from all denominations gathering in major cities *for an event that will change their very existence.* . . . One purpose: To set on fire the most powerful force in the world (maybe even the universe). . . .[21] (emphasis added)

The attitude of Teen Mania appears to be the same as that expressed by David C. Cook Publishing, who believes youth leaders "face a stiff challenge trying to bring biblical truth to MTV kids."[22] Based upon the previously mentioned excerpts from the Acquire the Fire publication, president and CEO of Teen Mania has apparently resorted to MTV hype in an attempt to draw youth to Christ.

We ask you to consider: Have we lost a sense of the sacred and reverence for an all-powerful, holy God when we think we need worldly drawing cards—live bands, videos, lighting, and special effects—to impact teenagers with the reality of God? Is it not presumptuous for anyone to emphatically claim that he has what it takes to create an event that will change a teen's very existence? Are we creating an atmosphere for youth that, instead of elevating them with a sense of the sacred, reduces them to the level of the world around them?

Hyped-Up Claims

More bold claims were made in Teen Mania's hyped-up letter: "What you have in your hand is your ticket to grab hold of the destiny God has for your life. He wants to use you to change the world! . . . God's raising up a new generation of young people just like you who are tired of doing the same old thing with their Christian life." This letter, a pitch for their summer mission trips, claims that these mission experiences "could cause you to be a successful man or woman of God for the rest of your life."

This letter sounds more like fundraising than the Spirit's call, but it goes on:

> Don't you dare put this down until you've read all the way through it, until you've prayed sincerely.... Even if you've never thought you could win anyone to the Lord, even if you've thought that you could never go on a mission trip, even if you don't have any idea how you'd get the money, don't you dare let any of those reasons stop you.... Don't wait a moment longer. Fill out this application. Get it in the mail. It's time to stand up with thousands of others.... [23]

This attitude of possessing the way to God, as expressed by Teen Mania and many other parachurch organizations, is one of arrogance. Why do they think their conference, their mission, their experience will transform a life when even the miracles performed by Jesus did not necessarily cause someone to believe (see John 12:37)? As one pastor lamented, "The weak, feeble picture of God all this hype presents is disturbing."

More Junk Food

Reachout Expeditions is yet another example of a Christian organization attempting to use emotions generated from an experience to teach their stated objectives. Their wilderness adventure programs centering around outdoor experiences, such as whitewater rafting, mountaineering, rock climbing, and mountain biking, claim to offer excitement and both mental and physical challenges. According to promotional material, participants will also "encounter life changing 'edge moments.' These 'edge moments' will encourage new attitudes that will transfer into new ways of coping with life's daily challenges."[24]

Reachout's mission "is basically a tweaked version of Matthew 28:19, 'Go therefore and make disciples of the next generation.'"[25] It must be acknowledged, however, that even when attempting to be clever or relevant, "tweaking" Scripture is not acceptable. Scripture reads, "Go therefore and make disciples of all the nations." In addition, Reachout makes the assertive declaration: "Wilderness-based ministry is effective—just ask the experts—Noah, Abraham, Moses, John the Baptist. . . ."[26] This arrogant and bold claim is yet another tweaking of Scripture. These men of God were *not* experts in wilderness-based ministries! In fact, for Reachout to make such a claim borders on disrespect for biblical accuracy.

Unfortunately, Reachout also uses elements borrowed from secular psychology in their adventures and expeditions. Bells should be buzzing and red flags going up when we read in promotional brochures such things as: "It takes several days in the wilderness for the masks we wear to fall and our REAL lives begin to shine forth," or when we read that another goal is to "help participants improve or establish relationships with trusted others."[27] These statements sound like they are right out of a manual on the Rogerian method of psychotherapy. Remember, according to Carl Rogers the solution to man's problems lies in man himself; thus, man has no need for God. One cannot help but wonder why a Christian organization would embrace these philosophies.

One promotional brochure for this wilderness program tells the perceived importance of one-day wilderness trips, which are termed "Adventure Intensives."

> Adventures provide a unique and effective setting for building trust and teamwork in relationships with others. *Faith in the safety systems, self,* and *others* is nurtured through the encouragement and sensitive support of the staff. Overcoming various physical, mental, and emotional challenges provides tremendous opportunity for improving one's self-esteem as well as for gaining personal spiritual insight.[28] (emphasis added)

Faith in safety systems, faith in self, and faith in others are not biblical concepts. Those sound like something promoted by secular humanists and psychologists, not something pursued by those professing to be Christians.

Faith can be a disarming word for those who do not have discernment. Faith is usually associated with the Christian faith—a faith in God, not a faith in safety systems, self, and others. It becomes apparent that the biblical concept of faith as presented in the "Adventure Intensives" is nothing more than the same old junk food!

It should also come as no surprise when we read or hear about secular enterprises that also provide adventure-based learning and rope challenge courses. These secular adventure-based enterprises are being promoted as a learning process based upon experiences. In these hands-on type approaches to experience "the issues of trust, support, communication, responsibility, commitment, problem solving, and facing fears" are addressed.[29] Not only are the secular enterprises dealing with the same subject matter as parachurch organizations, there appears to be little difference between the secular and the sacred in the vocabulary used and the objectives articulated.

Emotional Highs

John MacArthur observes, "More and more people are . . . encouraged to seek God through emotional experiences practically divorced from truth. They eventually get caught in an endless cycle where in order to maintain the emotional high, each experience must be more spectacular than the previous one."[30] Could this be what is happening with our young people today? According to pollster George Barna, Americans are biblically illiterate, with teenagers knowing even less about the Bible than adults.[31] Spiritual leaders need to be cautious that sound doctrine through disciplined study of the Bible is not replaced with experiences and emotions.

MacArthur, however, makes the important distinction that doctrine should not be divorced from experience. He quotes

James 2:26: "Just as the body without the spirit is dead, so also faith without works is dead." Even so, MacArthur argues, "Christianity must be doctrine before it can be legitimate experience." He elaborates: "Truth genuinely believed is truth acted upon. Real faith *always* results in lively experience, and this frequently involves deep emotion. . . . But genuine experience and legitimate emotions always come *in response to truth;* truth must never become the slave of sheer emotion or unintelligible experiences."

MacArthur then asks some thought-provoking questions: "Shall we now exalt experience at the expense of sound doctrine? Will we allow emotion to run roughshod over truth? Will evangelicalism be swept away with unbridled passion?"[32] We hope the answer will be no, no, and no! We must return to the basics of Scripture and not succumb to the temptation of relying on psychological experiences that make faith a subjective phenomenon.

William Kilpatrick explains why some Christians elevate experience over Scripture.

> For some Christians [experience] has a higher standing than Scripture. The reason . . . is that in our society one's personal experience is beyond criticism or judgment. If I say I've experienced true enlightenment, who are you to say I haven't? It seems somehow undemocratic to question the validity of another person's inner feelings. Yet, when we rely on this criterion alone, we run the danger of making our faith a purely subjective phenomenon. . . . There are persons who will swear by encounter groups or meditation or drugs because of the powerful experience these things have provided them. And there is, of course, no way to gainsay them. They will simply fall back on their experience. They know it's true, and that's that.[33]

Ravi Zacharias articulates the dangers of relying on one's personal subjective experience as the final authority. He argues: "If the critic can reduce all of Christianity to a 'religious experience' unverifiable by any other means, then we are confined to a privatized belief with no objective authority left to defend."[34]

Lack of Faith

There are many different ways in which Christians can be led astray by the world's beguiling philosophies and intriguing but deceptive techniques. Since Satan masquerades as an angel of light (see 2 Cor. 11:14), Christians need to be continually on guard. When teaching truth and godly principles to youth, Christian leaders must be careful not to succumb to the alluring appeal of substituting biblical methods for faddish worldly ones, remembering that God's ways are not man's ways (see Isa. 55:8). The preceding examples of swinging in trees, the 18-Hour Encounter, and the wilderness adventures each embrace secular methods in an attempt to teach biblical principles.

According to the late D. M. Lloyd-Jones, unscriptural methods discredit the gospel and bring it into disrepute. He implores us to examine ourselves, since the use of unscriptural techniques implies a lack of faith. He states, "Over-attention to techniques and methods . . . , is indicative always of a lack of faith in the work of the Holy Spirit." He poses the questions that many in our churches ask, "Why should not the Holy Spirit make use of these modern teaching techniques? Why set the Holy Spirit and modern teaching techniques in opposition to one another?"

He responds to his own questions: "The apostle Paul would never have argued like that, but deliberately avoided all that can be subsumed [included] under the heading 'man's wisdom.' He *could* have argued in that manner about the use of philosophy and rhetoric, but deliberately did not do so."

Lloyd-Jones goes on to say, "We are to present the truth, trusting to the Holy Spirit to apply it. I would urge, therefore, that on scriptural grounds we must not of set purpose decide to employ techniques. That is to go over on to the side of, and to the use of, psychology."[35] He concludes by reminding us "Not by might, nor by power, but by my Spirit, saith the Lord of hosts" (Zech. 4:6).

Chapter 9

Tweaking Scripture

You shall not add to the word which I am commanding you,
nor take away from it, that you may keep the commandments
of the Lord your God which I command you.

—Deut. 4:2

Risktaking is a theme that is emerging in youth activities, but it
too is an idea that originated with secular humanists.
Remember that Carl Rogers emphasized that new ways of be-
having should be risked and tried out. One takes risks in letting
down his mask so others can see him as he really is.[1] Sidney
Simon and others, in their book *Values Clarification*, also promoted the attitude-changing strategy of "learning to build trust
so that we can risk being open."[2] The concepts of trust and risk
are often presented together. However, the author of *Inside American Education*, Thomas Sowell, warns against risktaking experiences, which can desensitize normal inhibitions. He calls it a
technique of psychological conditioning.

> Much of what is done in trust-building exercises—having
> classmates lead a blindfolded student, for example—may seem
> to be innocuous, and perhaps pointless, when viewed in iso-
> lation. It is, however, one of a number of aptly named "strat-
> egies" designed to induce a certain state of mind, including a
> relaxation of inhibitions against the unknown and reliance

on peers. In short, youngsters are encouraged to extrapolate from these exercises in a highly controlled environment to the unpredictable dangers of real life.[3]

Sowell summarizes, "In attitude-changing programs, trust and risk are repeatedly depicted in a positive light, as if there were no dangers." He continues:

> More generally, such sweeping trust and corresponding willingness to risk are prerequisites for abandoning the values and inhibitions which have been distilled from the experience of previous generations. Unfortunately, the greatest risks are not taken by teachers or promoters of attitude-changing programs, but by vulnerable children and the parents who will be left to deal with the consequences.[4]

Unfortunately, this secular concept of risktaking in relationships has now been adopted by major developers and publishers of Christian curricula. Denny Rydberg stresses the importance of this in his five-step plan for youth groups, "Each step can help kids put down their armor and begin to build *trust* within the group," so that the kids "feel comfortable enough to *risk* sharing their deepest joys and most intense struggles" (emphasis added).[5] Rydberg also explains that "vulnerability can be defined as openness—the willingness to risk, to share even to the point of being misunderstood."[6]

Rydberg continually portrays risktaking as a positive and desired characteristic to be pursued by teens. In one activity entitled Risk, the teens are to discuss the handout *Risking Much,* which concludes with, "But risk we must, because the greatest hazard in life is to risk nothing. The man, the woman who risks nothing does nothing, has nothing, is nothing." Of course, the poem is discussed through the use of encounter-group questions that require a teen to reveal personal information about himself. The questions include: "What is one risk you've taken in the past? What was the result? What is one risk you need to take but have been avoiding? How can this group help you in taking that risk?"[7]

Lyman Coleman, also builds on the concept of risktaking. In his Serendipity Youth Bible Study series, Coleman has a self-disclosure scale for each lesson that measures the risk to participants. Evidently, he believes that in order for spiritual experiences and group building to take place, there must be risk involved. He, too, presents risk in the form of self-disclosure in a positive light.

Risktaking Adventures

Risky experiences that engage a wide range of emotions are also being presented as the ultimate or extreme thrill in some youth curricula and programs. The Cook Ministry even goes so far as to say that "Faith and risk are practically synonyms."[8] In the series, *Extreme: A Real Live Look at the Forerunners*, the concept of risktaking is explored by having the teens divide into pairs or small groups to do the following assignment:

> Design the Extreme Weekend. Money's not an object. Practicality's not an issue. You can fly anywhere and buy whatever you need. Your job is to find the Ultimate Thrill. Your mission is to squeeze the most adventure and excitement into one weekend possible. If you're a group of risktakers, will you bungee jump off the Eiffel tower? Will you rappel into a volcano in Maui? If you're a more romantic group, will you arrange to fall asleep under the stars on a beach somewhere on the Pacific coast?

An optional follow-up to the activity includes the following questions: "Are you a risktaker? A thrillseeker? Or is that not your scene? How do you feel about 'extreme' activities? If you consider yourself a thrillseeker, what do you get out of taking risks and challenging limits? If you're not into risktaking, why not?" This lesson, according to the author, Rick Wesselhoff, "will work particularly well with a group that thinks 'extreme risks lead to extreme life.'"

Just as in the brochure by Reachout Expeditions, Scripture is tweaked when Wesselhoff writes, "Jesus Himself promised us life to the Extreme."[9] Wesselhoff admits that "life to the Extreme" is his paraphrase of John 10:10b, "I came that they might have life, and might have it abundantly." It rapidly becomes obvious that the author believes "life to the Extreme" equates with "life abundantly." "Life to the Extreme" apparently refers to a life in which an individual is willing to take risks. Once again, it sounds like Carl Rogers, who said,

> Increasingly I discover that being alive involves taking a chance, acting on less than certainty, engaging with life. All of this brings change and for me the process of change is life. I realize that if I were stable and steady and static, I would be living death. So I accept confusion and uncertainty and fear and emotional highs and lows because they are the price I willingly pay for a flowing, perplexing, exciting life.[10]

What happens when risk-taking becomes a style of living? More particularly, what will be the outcome to teens participating in a therapeutic youth group focusing on risktaking? According to W. R. Coulson, Carl Rogers recognized that the very outcome of a successful encounter experience "was a 'risktaking style of living,' and he knew that, for the young, such a result, at the least, would interfere with academic learning and productivity. He knew this from research and more intimately in his own life."[11]

A Biblical Warning

Christian parents and youth leaders should be alarmed at the current emphasis on risktaking. In a letter from the apostle Paul to Timothy, Paul warns, "But realize this, that in the last days difficult times will come. For men will be lovers of self . . . without self-control, . . . *reckless*, . . . and lovers of pleasure rather than lovers of God" (2 Tim. 3:1–4, emphasis added). To be a risktaker is to expose oneself to the chance of physical and emotional injury or loss. Implied in risktaking activities is an attitude of recklessness.

Someone who is reckless tends to act too hastily, without due consideration about the consequences. Synonyms include *rash, negligent, imprudent.* Instead of the word *reckless*, the King James Version of the Bible uses the word *heady*, meaning "rashly impetuous." It is a sobering realization that the very thing the Bible warns as a sign of difficult times to come is being promoted in curricula for Christian youth.

This current trend toward recklessness is also captured in the title of a devotional book for youth, *Dangerous Devotions.* The back cover reads: "Do not read this book unless you are prepared for an adventure! *Dangerous Devotions* will take you where you've never gone before. Proceed, if you dare. The trip may get dangerous!"[12]

Costly, but No Risk

Jesus cautioned His followers to carefully consider the cost of a commitment to Him. In the parable of the tower, Jesus instructed:

> For which one of you, when he wants to build a tower, does not first sit down and calculate the cost, to see if he has enough to complete it? Otherwise, when he has laid a foundation, and is not able to finish, all who observe it begin to ridicule him, saying, "This man began to build and was not able to finish." (Luke 14:28–30)

It is costly to follow Christ, and according to Jesus, one must count the cost. Following Christ does not mean that one's life will be free of all troubles. On the contrary, being a disciple of Jesus Christ may mean the loss of wealth, popularity, and social status. Yes, to follow Jesus Christ may be costly. In fact, you may lose everything you hold dear, but there is no risk involved. Once you have committed yourself to Christ, you can count on God's strength to guide and support you even during difficult times and trials.

One biblical commentary elaborates on the parable of the tower:

> This parable represents the absurdity of those who undertook to be disciples of Christ, without considering what dif-

ficulties they were to meet, and *what strength they had* to enable them to go through with the undertaking. He that will be a true disciple of Jesus Christ, shall require no less than the *mighty power of God* to support him. . . .[13] (emphasis added)

Jesus Christ will give the strength and courage to stand for Him. "He Himself has said, 'I will never desert you, nor will I ever forsake you'" (Heb. 13:5). The apostle Paul reminds us that we can confidently say, "The Lord is my helper, I will not be afraid" (Heb. 13:6).

Crimes of Logic

Words have meanings, and meanings have consequences. As a result, one has to be careful with the words one uses. Ravi Zacharias argues the importance of logic and sound reasoning in defending truth. He states, "Playing word games when dealing with the most monumental issues of life—can be one of the most insidious and destructive forces in the life of a nation. History has shown that crimes of logic can be more catastrophic for humanity than crimes of passion."[14] Likewise, the church must diligently guard against using false and illogical reasoning.

In previous examples, it was shown that subtle changes in scriptures have occured. They may seem inconsequential, but the subtle play on words is a very serious matter. Another example of a play on words is found in a contemporary Bible study produced by one of the leading publishers of youth curricula. This study encourages teens to "compare their own tendencies toward teenage rebellion with Jesus' holy rebellion against religious leaders of his day."[15] The teens are told that "Jesus is a 'holy rebel' they can follow."[16] This is shocking! They are associating sinful behavior with the One who is sinless.

The words *rebel* and *rebellion* have negative connotations. Synonyms for rebel include *insurrectionist* (someone who rises in revolt), *mutineer*, and *traitor*, while *disobedience* and *insubordination* are synonyms for *rebellion*. More importantly, God's Word states, "For rebellion is as the sin of divination"

(1 Sam. 15:23). Plainly stated, rebellion is sin. Scripture also says that divination is "detestable to the LORD" (Deut. 18:12). Therefore, if rebellion is as the sin of divination, rebellion is also detestable to the Lord.

Nowhere in the Bible is Jesus ever referred to as a rebel leading a rebellion, but He is frequently referred to as a servant obediently doing the will of His Father in heaven. Other names for Jesus include Wonderful Counselor, Mighty God, Eternal Father, and Prince of Peace (Isaiah 9:6). In the Book of John, Jesus is called Son of Man (6:27); bread of life (6:35); light of the world (8:12); good shepherd (10:11); the way, the truth, and the life (14:6); and the true vine (15:1). This list of names is not exhaustive. Calling Jesus a rebel, even a holy rebel, is misconstruing the message and character of Jesus, thus presenting a different gospel.

The Adventures of Jesus?

Along with risktaking, adventures are also being introduced. *Risktaking* and *adventure* mean almost the same thing. It should come as no surprise that the word *adventure* means a bold, usually risky undertaking of uncertain outcome. What should come as a surprise, however, is that the word *adventure* is used with Jesus in a suggested Bible study series, "The Adventures of Jesus Christ."[17] Sounding more like a marketing device, it is appalling to think of Christ's birth as "the adventure in the stables" or Jesus' temptation by the devil as "the adventure in the desert." Perhaps the most distressing of all, however, is the "adventure of Jesus on the cross."

Once again these so-called Bible studies are followed up with inappropriate questions for discussion. Two of the questions are "What did you learn about the adventure of following Jesus Christ?" and "How can you keep your zest for adventure as you get older?"[18]

Unknown to many, the use of inaccurate words and phrases are planting ideas that undermine and change the gospel message. In the material we critiqued, we expected to see an emphasis on traditional words of the Christian faith, such as *humility, sacrifice, obedience, purity, sin, repentance, grace,* and *forgiveness.* Instead, we were shocked to find such unlikely words as *rebel, change agent, extreme, rebellion, risk, adventure, attack, revolution.* We question the introduction of these words into the church vocabulary, for these allegedly more relevant words have the potential of misrepresenting Scripture.

Active Learning

Not only is the gospel message being tweaked, but so are the methods. In the past, emphasis on emotion and experience were carefully avoided in the Christian church, but there has been a shift in thought that now embraces experience as a method to teach biblical concepts, especially in parachurch organizations and curricula for Christian youth. Other names for experiential learning (learning which engages the emotions) commonly used in contemporary Christian curricula include *active learning* and *learning by doing.*

Most parents and Christian educators would be surprised to learn that an outspoken guru for the current controversial reform in education, Ted Sizer, is a strong advocate of active learning. Sizer admits to following in the footsteps of Dewey (1859–1952), who is known as the father of progressive education and a strong proponent of the philosophy that a child learns best from experience.[19] It quickly becomes apparent that the contemporary concept of active learning was not established on biblical principles, but rather, active learning is a concept that originated with humanists and secular theories.

Group defends this latest fad. They state that the active leaning recommended in their material is designed to "evoke specific feelings in the students."[20] "Each active-learning experience is followed by questions that encourage kids to share their feelings about what just happened. Further discussion questions help kids interpret their feelings and decide how this truth affects their lives."[21] Group calls this process of discussion *debriefing,* but more appropriately it should be called *encountering.*

Some may argue that active learning, or learning by doing, has a place in motor-skill development. But why the emphasis on feelings? Can you imagine a class of apprentice plumbers, after learning how to solder a copper fitting, sitting around in a circle discussing how it felt to solder? It is even more ridiculous to think of them discussing how the experience will affect their lives.

Denny Rydberg defines active learning as a "learning environment where everyone is forced to participate and thereby forced to learn."[22] He directs youth leaders to: "Place people in situations [experiences] that require communication and cooperation to overcome physical and emotional barriers. . . ."[23] It is apparent that Group agrees. Group makes the following comment concerning the trust walk, an active-learning exercise promoted in their curricula: "Everyone needs to participate to learn the inherent lessons of trust, faith, doubt, fear, confidence, and servanthood."[24]

The use of active learning in order to accomplish Group's stated goals is nothing less than practicing psychotherapy on Christian youth. Christian leaders must seriously question the use of active learning. Obviously, the Holy Spirit is not being relied upon to direct and guide. Instead, a reliance on one's own subjective emotions and experiences become the focus. The shift is drastic, but is anyone paying attention?

William Kilpatrick warns against the subverting of the sacred through psychological techniques:

Psychology's inroads into Christian life are due primarily to psychology's ability to offer *emotional experiences* sufficiently close to the *experience* of faith to be mistaken for faith itself. Because evangelical and charismatic Christians place such a great emphasis on the experience of faith, they are particularly susceptible to these imitations. The part of the world the Christian finds most attractive will often seem like Christianity itself. There will be much talk in it of brotherhood and love and the spirit. It will sound right. It will feel right.[25] (emphasis added)

Servant Attack

In a Bible study by Group entitled *Why Jesus Christ Matters*, an active-learning exercise titled Servant Attack has the teens form trios. With large bowls filled with warm water and several towels, the teens are instructed to disperse throughout the congregation during the worship service and randomly select four people's feet to wash. This experience is prefaced by the reading of John 13:1–9, the story of Jesus washing his disciples' feet.

Group acknowledges that "active learning intrigues people."[26] Concerning the Servant Attack lesson in particular, Group adds, "Whether [teens] find a foot-washing experience captivating or maybe a bit uncomfortable, they learn. And they learn on a deeper level than any work sheet or teacher's lecture could ever reach."[27] The publishers of Group openly admit that there really is no control over what is learned; the experience may either be a positive or negative one. They acknowledge that the experience of washing the feet of another may either be captivating or uncomfortable. We ask, Why teach a lesson in which the learning is haphazard or that the outcome is extremely variable? If learning is haphazard or unpredictable, then a lesson could just as easily be undermined as reinforced.

The author, whether he knows it or not, is embracing the philosophy of risktaking as promoted by humanist Sidney Simon and others.

> All new experiences are risktaking experiences, because we never know how they might turn out. Generally, the more the student has to do, the newer the experience for him, the greater the risk he has to take, the deeper will be the sensitivity which results from it.[28]

Because all the aspects of even a planned experience cannot be totally controlled, an individual's resulting impressions are subjective rather than objective. The same experience may have totally different effects on different individuals due to the individual's background, personality, previous experiences, etc. Do adults and leaders in the church who are responsible for teaching the precious truths of God's Word want to jeopardize teaching God's truths through the use of experiences when the lessons to be learned from those experiences are left up to chance?

Denny Rydberg assumes, albeit falsely, that well-planned experiences will provide students with worthwhile positive experiences. Concerning the experiences he has listed in his book, he boasts: "Many of these experiences will be vividly etched in your kids' memories for years."29 One cannot help but ask the question: What happens if an experience proves to be a negative one?

Learning God's Word by doing or experiencing puts us in control. Is that biblical? Granted, an apprentice carpenter learns carpentry by doing carpentry. Learning by doing is applicable in that situation, but is learning by doing applicable in learning God's Word? Do we learn God's Word the same way we learn carpentry? If we do, then what is the role of the Holy Spirit? If we believe that we are in control, are we guilty of having the illusion that we are capable of ascending to God? Are we attempting to plug into the divine by using a particular method or technique? Are we arrogantly trying to understand God through our own contrived experiences? A disturbing trend appears to be that we are attempting to create God in our own image through our own experiences.

Kilpatrick adds the following thoughts:

> If you find yourself trying to manufacture these experiences or if you come to the point where you think the ordinary means of approaching God are not worth your time, then that is the point for taking stock. If you find yourself continually experimenting with this kind of extraordinary piety or that kind of unique religious phenomenon, you need to ask some questions of yourself. . . . Saint Paul reckoned that "the sufferings of this present time are not worth comparing with the glory that is to be revealed to us." And I think the same can be said about our present feelings of religious exhilaration. . . . I rather think the way to get to it

is the way of humble reverence and worship, not the way of striving after emotional experience.[30]

Dubious Studies

Regardless of what Group claims their motives are, those who depend on active-learning games are guilty of following man's ways, not God's. In their own words they admit their reliance on secular research that "shows people remember most of what they do but only a small percentage of what they hear."[31]

Gospel Light concurs, quoting a study "showing that young people retain up to 85 percent of the material when they are *involved* in action-oriented, experiential learning."[32] In other words, young people only retain 5–10 percent of what they hear or read. That admission puts them in direct conflict with the absolute assertion of the Word of God that states, "Faith comes from hearing, and hearing by the word of Christ" (Rom. 10:17). Furthermore, in Revelation it says seven times in the first three chapters, "He who has an ear, let him hear." God would not mislead us. Contrary to what publishers may say, the primary way of receiving spiritual truth is indeed by hearing.

Interactive Learning

Along with active learning, Group also stresses the importance of interactive learning.

> INTERACTIVE LEARNING is what happens when learners purposefully talk together in pairs or small groups. People learn from each other. They share experiences, insights, and concerns. They explore the Bible together, talk to each other, and grow in faith together. Such interdependence builds positive relationships and keeps people coming back for more real-life Bible-learning experiences.[33]

One needs to question whether or not learning from each other is a "real-life Bible-learning experience" as Group claims. The main focus on interactive learning is on peer relationships where teachers don't have to have all the answers. They can learn right along with the students. When such interdependence with peers is encouraged there may be a tendency to accept another's experience as authority instead of God's Word. Human nature tends toward laziness, so it is much easier to listen to what someone else thinks the Bible says than for one to read Scripture, pray, and allow God to do the teaching. One also needs to ask if interactive learning is just another gimmick that gives us the illusion we are somehow in control of our own faith and our understanding of the Bible.

God's Word vs. Experience

Michael Horton expounds upon the importance of preaching doctrinal precepts as opposed to experiences. "The church confesses its faith in what God did in history, not in one's own private experience. By looking outside rather than inside ourselves, we are brought into a saving union with Christ."[34]

"In Christianity," elaborates Horton, "what counts is Christ's crisis experience on a Roman scaffold outside center-city Jerusalem."[35] In reviewing curricula for Christian youth, however, it appears that what is being promoted is an individual's subjective experience, not Christ's well-documented, factual experience upon the cross.

John MacArthur also addresses unscriptural teaching methods and cautions against the teaching and reliance upon experiences in particular. MacArthur quotes 2 Peter 1:16–22, to show the apostle Peter's argument for the authority of Scripture over an authentic spiritual experience. It tells of Peter's eyewitness account of the transfiguration of Christ.

> We did not follow cleverly devised tales when we made known to you the power and coming of our Lord Jesus Christ, but we were eyewitnesses of His majesty. For when He received honor and glory from God the Father, such an utterance as this was made to Him by the Majestic Glory, "This is My beloved Son with whom I am well-pleased"—and we ourselves

heard this utterance made from heaven when we were with Him on the holy mountain.

Peter actually heard the voice of God as he got a glimpse of Christ in His glory. MacArthur then quotes verses 19–21, to show that "even what [Peter] heard with his own ears and saw with his own eyes was not as authoritative as the eternal Word of God contained in Scripture."[36]

> We have more sure word of prophecy; . . . knowing this first, that no prophecy of the scripture is of any private interpretation. For the prophecy came not in old time by the will of man: but holy men of God spake as they were moved by the Holy Ghost. (KJV)

"Peter is *not* saying," explains MacArthur, "that his eyewitness testimony makes the 'prophecy of the Scripture' more sure. He is saying that the written Word of God by its very nature is *more sure* than his own experience." MacArthur adds:

> It is the 'prophecy of Scripture' (v. 20) which is more sure, more reliable, more authoritative than anyone's experiences.
> That surely puts subjective impressions in their proper place. Remember, Peter's experience was *not* subjective. What he saw and heard was real. Others experienced it with him. But Peter knew that the written Word of God is even more authoritative than the shared experience of three apostles.[37]

Scripture is all sufficient and the final authority. Scripture, not emotions resulting from experiences, must be recognized as the indisputable foundation and authority of biblical truth. MacArthur summarizes, "Evangelicals have historically waged their most important battles in defense of truth and sound doctrine—and against undue emphasis on emotion and experience."[38]

Objective vs. Subjective

Michael Horton warns that because "Satan is 'the father of lies' (John 8:44), we are to arm ourselves with truth, not experience. . . . Experience can be easily duplicated by the devil, and its subjectivity renders it vulnerable in battle."[39] God's Word, on the other hand, is objective and external, not subjective and internal. Horton also warns that private spiritual experience is a futile attempt to experience God directly as He is in all of His majesty.[40] Horton adds,

> The Christian is to find God only as he has revealed himself in Scripture, not through direct experience, nor as one deduces things about his nature from that which is visible. Unlike the theology of glory, where the pious and zealous climbers find God through their own experience, "surrender," meditation, and ecstasy, the theology of the cross points to the zeal of God, who descends to sinful humanity by becoming one of us. The cross is a real event in human history. It is not a private spiritual experience. The cross is God's chosen method of saving sinners and bringing them into his family.[41]

It is God's Word, not subjective experiences, which will impact a life for Jesus Christ. Pastor and author James M. Boice emphatically states that we must "regain our confidence in the power of God's Word to change lives."[42] Boice quotes Scripture to show that it is God's Word only that has power. "All Scripture is God-breathed and is useful for teaching, rebuking, correcting and training in righteousness" (2 Tim. 3:16), and, "The word of God is living and active" (Heb. 4:12). Jesus Himself said, "The words I have spoken to you are spirit and they are life" (John 6:63). Boice concludes with the words spoken by God through the prophet Isaiah: "My word that goes out from my mouth: It will not return to me empty, but will accomplish what I desire and achieve the purpose for which I sent it" (Isa. 55:11).

A Reckless Faith

John MacArthur makes the following observation: "In many American churches, reason has been abandoned for something more digestible; faith that *feels* good." MacArthur calls this feel good faith *reckless* for "it leads people away from the one true God."[43]

It appears that the church and parachurch organizations have abandoned truth and sound doctrine for experiences and activities that evoke feelings and emotions—experiences and activities that are patterned after the world and not after God's Word. We have become an emotion-driven people seeking a faith that feels good and that pleases us in accordance with our own desires. God's Word has been exchanged for gimmicks, fads, and mind games devised by major Christian organizations, authors, and publishers who seem to compete with one another to see who can be the most creative using the latest trends and fads to impart biblical truth.

Christians must not rely on research done by secular humanists concerning how people learn (i.e., active learning through experiences) as a way to gain knowledge of biblical principles. Christians must continually remind themselves that God's ways are not man's ways. God does not operate like the world, nor does He take His cues from the world's latest fads or trends.

Church leaders and all believers in the Lord Jesus Christ need to continually ask, when a different interpretation of Scripture is being presented or a new teaching method or technique is introduced: "Where is this biblical truth or teaching method found in the Bible?" We need to have the same motivations that guided Martin Luther, who said, "Unless I am convinced by Scripture and plain reason, my conscience is captive to the Word of God."

Chapter 10

Youth Ministry: A Biblical Model?

Train up a child in the way he should go, Even when he is old he will not depart from it.

—Prov. 22:6

Due to personal experience with our own children in youth groups and the material we have read, we have been forced to ask some hard questions concerning the purpose of youth ministry. We have witnessed spiritual quackery in which secular teaching fads and humanistic philosophies have the potential of creating pseudofaith in young people. Because of all the theological looseness in youth curricula and programs, it is necessary for pastors, elders, teachers, and parents to also ask themselves some hard questions. What is the purpose of youth ministry? Are we fooling ourselves into thinking that playing silly and outrageous games in an attempt to be relevant will produce a personal faith in Jesus Christ? Are youth groups just playgrounds for fun and entertainment, or are they battlegrounds to equip young people to stand for God? But most importantly, the overriding question should be, What does Scripture say concerning a biblical ministry to youth?

Crisis in Youth Ministry

We have heard from youth pastors who are frustrated with the youth ministry experiment. They cite having to deal with all kinds of kids who are attending youth meetings for all the wrong reasons, while at the same time not seeing real spiritual growth in the Christian youth.

It appears that we have put too much emphasis on market-driven curricula and supplemental materials. We have strayed from the Bible and its timeless gospel message. A pastor and the founder of Reformation and Revival Ministries, John H. Armstrong, asks the thought-provoking question, "Has our view of God become so people centered that we are afraid we may lose our opportunity to reach them without a market-based strategy." Armstrong reminds us, "Historically, evangelicals were those who had great confidence in the gospel message. In fact, they believed that their only power was in the message itself—the gospel. It was the gospel that brought life, power, and true growth. . . . Today, we seem to have a sad case of theological amnesia."[1]

In defense of contemporary youth curricula, youth leaders argue that because times have changed, the method for reaching teens for Christ must change also. In fact, the wife of a youth leader rationalized using "cheesy" games found in contemporary youth curricula to draw youth to their meetings. However, we believe that the youth were more than likely drawn to this particular youth group not because of the cheesy games being played, but because of the Christlike love and behavior being modeled by this woman and her husband.

It has become obvious to us that our Bible colleges and seminaries have dropped the ball and are not training biblically discerning youth leaders. An entertainment model, with an emphasis on numbers, appears to have taken center stage in youth ministry. No matter how entertaining our methods may be, they are powerless to affect real transformation of a life. It appears that many youth leaders have mistakenly adopted the contemporary philosophy that they must teach differently in order to be relevant in the 1990s.

Youth Subculture

During our research, we came across a succinct discourse by Christopher Schlect titled *Critique of Modern Youth Ministry,* which was enlightening, thought provoking, and convicting. Schlect, a youth pastor himself and an instructor at Logos School, the nationally acclaimed classical and Christian school in Moscow, Idaho, believes "the church today does not expect what it ought to from children and their parents, and this can be attributed at least in part to a flawed concept of youth ministry."[2] Schlect's booklet discusses the reasons behind this and proposes some biblical solutions.

Schlect traces the development of youth ministry showing that youth ministry is a relatively new concept. According to Schlect, "The segregation of youth struck the church like wildfire in the 1930s with the development of parachurch youth organizations."[3] Parachurch youth ministries were designed to reach teens outside of the traditional church setting. Youth For Christ, a parachurch organization, was a huge success by the mid-1940s, and Young Life, another parachurch organization, was also founded during that time. Schlect adds,

> Witnessing the success of these parachurch ministries, many local churches began youth programs of their own. By the 1950s they were commonplace. Today parachurch youth ministries are flourishing. Seminaries award master's degrees in Youth Ministry. The number of youth summer camps currently in operation boggles the mind, and many full-time itinerants keep very busy schedules[4]

Today, the youth subculture has become a dominant culture in our society, complete with its own music, dress, art, and entertainment; and according to Schlect this youth orientation breeds immaturity. It should come as no surprise, therefore, that youth orientation in the church has the same effect. Schlect points out that "God never patterns his norms after human culture.

Standards are maintained in the church by looking at God's Word, not by looking at the world."[5] Schlect elaborates:

> We have seen that our society's trend toward an emphasis on youth has carried into the church. We saw the source of this phenomenon in our society to be a philosophical commitment to age segregation. . . . Evangelical churches have honored divisions that have existed in our culture for less than a century—divisions which have no basis in either Scripture or common sense. These divisions breed immaturity because they hinder younger people from associating with and learning from their elders.[6]

Schlect goes on to say:

> Regress in maturity happens in the church when we ignore the mandates in Scripture which implore the young and old to interact with one another. With age comes wisdom—wisdom that must be passed on to young people. . . . The so-called "generation gap" has been used as an excuse for age segregation.[7]

Unfortunately, over the last fifty years, parachurch and church youth ministries have experimented with the contemporary segregation model of youth ministry. As a result, teenagers have been isolated from the adult world, sometimes even from their own parents.

The Generation Gap

Social analyst and author Os Guinness talks about tribalism which is the segregation of people into groups according to racial criteria. He illustrates the concept of tribalism promoted by the slogan for Black unity: "It's a Black thing. You wouldn't understand." However, tribalism no longer only refers to racial groups. Guinness elaborates,

> Only those within a group can know what it is like to be a member of that group, . . . so those outside have no right to

comment or criticize. To do so is to be insensitive and show disrespect. In today's setting, many . . . words can be inserted . . . "It's a Jewish/feminist/gay/lesbian/fundamentalist/physically-challenged thing. You wouldn't understand." But recent decades have witnessed the rise of a new kind of tribalism—generational tribalism. . . .[8]

The phenomenon of generational tribalism, better known as *age segregation*, is responsible in large part for the generation gap. The generation gap is a chasm of man's own making between one generation and the next. Schlect also describes the same trend of separation by age. He observes a disturbing consequence, however, resulting from the separation of youth into a group unto themselves. He states, "When young people are allowed to set their own standards as they interact with one another, a 'herd mentality' develops: They follow in the footsteps of one another rather than in those of adults."[9] The question must be raised: Is the Christian church fostering a culture and generation gap that suggests to Christian youth the faith of their parents is not sufficient or relevant for the 1990s? Schlect adds, "The prophets and apostles never prescribed such a state of affairs, but rather assumed that all ages would enjoy fellowship together in the church. The Scripture contain directives which promote cross-generational interaction, and we must avoid cultural patterns that encumber our obedience to them."[10]

The late Dr. Martyn Lloyd-Jones commented about the potential age distinctions in ministry. He stated,

There has been a marked tendency in the last years or so to divide up Christian work according to age groups. I have never been very enthusiastic about these divisions in to age groups— old age, middle age, youth, children, and so on. By that I mean that we must be careful that we do not modify the gospel to suit various age groups. There is no such thing as a special gospel for the young, a special gospel for the middle-aged, and a special gospel for the aged. There is only one gospel, and we must always be careful not to tamper and tinker with the gospel as a result of recognizing these age distinctions.[11]

Tampering with the Gospel

It is disturbing that the writers and major publishers of youth curricula have not heeded Lloyd-Jones warning. They are in fact tampering with the Word of God by presenting a special interpretation of the Bible to youth that is in stark contrast to the message being presented to the adults in the church. This contrast between the two messages is seen, for example, in the description of Stephen from the Book of Acts and the description of Stephen as presented by David C. Cook in the elective course *Extreme: A Real Look at the Forerunners.* The following is the tampered-with profile of Stephen:

> A no-name waiter. Just an Average Joe in a dead-end job destined to watch history unfold from the sidelines. Then it happened . . . Stephen, of all people, took a stand. Up until that point, Stephen's big claim to fame was being one of "the seven." Some claim! All that meant was when the new Christian church started to get too big for the original twelve apostles to manage by themselves, Stephen was one of the people chosen to help wait on tables.[12]

This description of Stephen does not bear any resemblance to the Stephen described in Acts 6. In the authentic biblical account, Stephen was selected by the congregation to serve and minister to widows in the church by managing the distribution of food. He was chosen along with six other men because of his good reputation and wisdom (v. 3) Stephen was also chosen for this ministry because he was a man full of faith and of the Holy Spirit (v. 5). Nowhere in the biblical account is Stephen described as an average Joe in a dead-end job who was destined to watch history unfold from the sidelines!

Scripture has been tampered and tinkered with in a misguided attempt to make personalities from Scripture appear real and relevant to the times. It quickly becomes apparent in the introduction to this mini-course for teens that a different Scripture message will be presented to the youth. For example, youth leaders are told that they "need a curriculum that understands where your teens live." Youth leaders are also being told that "the new generation of youth can't relate to doctored-up, picture-perfect portraits of biblical superheros," for teens live with "depression, loneliness, parents getting divorced, AIDS, suicide, and gangs." In other words, according to the developers of this series, teens need a special gospel because kids are living in a time in which the "stakes are high."[13]

Contrary to those arguments, it is precisely because the stakes are high for our teens that they need the living, inerrant words from Scripture more than ever before. God's Word is always relevant. God's Word does not change with the times.

Demoted to Facilitator

Today, youth leaders who use contemporary youth curricula may be instructed to take on a new role—that of facilitator. Instead of teaching and proclaiming God's Word, they are facilitating (directing) discussion. Instead of preaching the Word as was done in the early church, youth leaders are instructed *not* to preach to teens.[14] This instruction to youth leaders is in direct violation of Scripture which states unequivocally, "I solemnly charge you in the presence of God and of Christ Jesus . . . preach the word" (2 Tim. 4:1–2).

According to one publisher, teens today learn best by doing rather than "sitting quietly in chairs and listening to a speaker expound theories about God—that is passive learning. . . . Active learning is an adventure" where "the kids may learn lessons the teacher never envisioned." The teacher is no longer in the role of a knowledgeable expositor of the Bible of whom insight and wisdom should be sought. Instead, the curricula developers believe that a teacher is someone who trusts students to help create their own learning experiences.[15]

It is tragic that those with knowledge and wisdom of God's Word are being demoted to that of facilitator in group interaction. One curriculum developer gives the following instructions to youth leaders: "Don't try to give students the 'right' or 'best' answers or solutions. In most cases, it's best for leaders to silently participate in the exercises."[16] Youth leaders are even told, "Youth gain a new respect for leaders when the students are allowed to tell the leaders what to do!"[17] Yet another publisher of youth curricula gives the following instructions to youth leaders:

> It is important for you to try to let them see you as a "facilitator"—another member of the group who is helping make the discussion happen. . . . Remember, with teenagers, your opinions will carry more weight the less of an authority figure you appear to be. If you are regarded as an affirming friend, they will pay much more attention to what you have to say. . . . Good discussion leaders know how to listen . . . Keep your mouth shut except when encouraging others to talk."[18]

How sad that those who know the Bible best are asked to remain silent. This method of teaching and learning Scripture is contrary to how the Bible says we are to pass on God's truth. God's people are instructed in Deuteronomy: "You shall love the LORD your God with all your heart and with all your soul and with all your might. And these words, which I am commanding you today, shall be on your heart; and you shall teach them diligently to your sons and shall talk of them when you sit in your house and when you walk by the way and when you lie down and when you rise up" (Deut. 6:5–7). These words are specifically directed to parents, but they are also generally directed to anyone involved in the spiritual training of youth (cf. 2 Tim. 2:2).

Youth leaders are also instructed "to refrain from giving advice. Students need adults who will listen. Indeed, as group members interact and share with one another, they often come up with the same or better solutions than you may have offered as advice."[19] Curricula developers tell youth leaders to remain neutral in order to "discourage the group from thinking of [them] as the 'authority on the subject.'"[20] It appears from these instructions to the youth leaders that these particular youth groups will be more like a nondirective counseling session than a Bible study. Where is the biblical model for teachers who have been gifted and empowered by the Holy Spirit to *facilitate* discussion rather than *teach* God's Word? Teachers who have the spiritual gift to teach must not abdicate their responsibility to teach, since their gift was given to them in order to benefit the Body of Christ (see Eph. 4:12).

Peer Teaching

It is also suggested by one curriculum publisher to relinquish control and "let the students do more teaching? . . . Students can learn from one another, not just from the teacher."[21] Yet another curriculum developer tells youth leaders that "your teens don't want to be told what to think. They learn from relationships."[22]

Inherent in this teaching method is an attitude of rebellion against authority. Youth leaders who consistently use peer teaching are conditioning students to become less dependent on authority figures and more dependent on those of their own age. Why aren't teens being taught to respect the wisdom and knowledge of adults who have lived a life honoring God and who have been trained in His Word? Why are teens being encouraged to believe that they are just as wise and knowledgeable as their adult leaders? Luke 6:40 explicitly states that "a pupil is not above his teacher."

If a young medical student decided to pursue neurosurgery as his specialty, he would expect to be trained by a surgeon who was an expert in that field. He would not expect one of his peers who had no more training than himself to teach the class. Surgery is a serious matter not only for the surgeon, but the patient. The study of God's Word must be taken just as seriously; both endeavors involve life and death. The student engaged in a sincere Bible study should expect to be taught by a mature Christian, someone whose life shows an intimacy and knowledge of the living God.

Christian leaders and parents should be relentlessly asking: Where are the scriptural passages that support peer teaching? If the Bible does not support peer teaching, why is it being used in the church? "Teachers as facilitators" and "peer teaching" have been popularized in the public schools and are responsible in part for the dumbing down of children across this nation. These same teaching methods used in the church will also have the same tragic result of dumbing down our Christian youth.

Amateur Psychologists

Not only are teens acting as teachers for their peers, displacing their youth leader who has biblical knowledge and training, but teens are also being trained in the nondirective counseling techniques of active listening, clarifying questions, and the use of "I" messages. For example, teens are reminded that "listening means more than sitting quietly. . . . Active listening means making eye contact, nodding their heads in agreement, and focusing on what's being said. . . ."[23] Teens are also taught how to ask clarifying questions. The use of "I" statements, a psychotherapy technique used for communication, is also taught. Teens are instructed, "You may not say, 'You never let me do what I want.'" Instead. they are told that they may say, "I understand you want me to do this . . . but I'd rather not because . . ."[24]

It rapidly becomes apparent that young people are being trained in techniques employed in nondirective counseling, rather than being grounded in God's Word so they can encourage one another in the Lord. How does one encourage another in the Lord? The New Testament instructs Christians to "teach, preach, testify, exhort, encourage, come alongside, speak the truth in love, rebuke, identify external sin, correct, comfort, forgive, and pray."[25] It is the Lord in whom we must place our trust, and it is the Lord to whom we must continually point others.

The Role of Youth Pastors and Elders

What did churches do to reach youth before the concept of church youth ministry came into being? Have youth groups proven to be a valid way to promote Christian maturity in our young people? What should the role of a youth pastor be? Are youth pastors necessary to the spiritual maturity of the youth in the church? If youth pastors are necessary, what should be their qualifications? According to Schlect,

> We must reform our view of the qualification for—and even the legitimacy of—a "youth minister." The normative pattern in Scripture implores young people to emulate the values of their elders. They must respect them, be instructed by them and follow their example. . . . Thus, older men in the church bear the first responsibility for training youth; the older women to follow "likewise" in their steps. We must therefore *reject* the appalling notion of the model of youth minister as a recently graduated extrovert who looks and acts just like a high schooler himself. If our youth cannot "relate to" older men, then we are seeing evidence of older men having dropped the ball years ago.[26] (emphasis added)

Schlect bases his admonition on Titus 2:2–3, which instructs older men and women in the church to model and teach behavior to the young people. In other words, the older people in the church should teach the younger people by word and example. This model of teaching supports sound biblical doctrine.

What role should the elders, the spiritual leaders and shepherds in the church, have in ministering to the youth? Interestingly, a recent study by Abilene Christian University researchers Dr. David K. Lewis and Dr. Carley H. Dodd found, "When Dad is not there, the top people who teens turn to are No. 1, mom, and No. 2, youth ministers. Elders are not even in the top ten." The researchers concluded, "There is something about our system that precludes youth contact with the shepherds of the church. We need to look through new glasses at ways to give teens greater exposure to these men with the silver hair who really know about the long haul."[27] It is truly a sad commentary that the spiritual leaders in the church have lost contact with youth to the point that they are not even considered by youth as someone to whom they can turn.

Parental Responsibility

As important as an elder's role is in encouraging, modeling, and teaching, we must remind ourselves that it is ultimately parents who must answer before God for the spiritual training of their children, not an elder or a youth pastor. It is the parents who must recognize and "bear full responsibility for their children."[28] A serious warning is given to parents by C. H. Spurgeon, the renowned nineteeth-century biblical expositor: "But let us never be guilty, as parents, of forgetting the religious training of our children. If we do, we may be guilty of the blood of their souls."[29]

"Let no Christian parents fall," Spurgeon warns, "into the delusion that Sunday school [or youth group] is intended to ease them of their personal duties. The first and most natural condition of things is for Christian parents to train up their own children in the nurture and admonition of the Lord."[30]

Schlect adds:

> The Scriptures couldn't be more clear: the charge for bringing up children in every area is given primarily to *parents* (Deut. 6:7, Eph. 6:4, *passim*). Responsible youth ministry in the church, though perhaps difficult to execute, is simple to understand: It involves teaching and exhorting parents to raise their children biblically.[31]

Schlect continues, "Fathers are responsible for directly overseeing their children in spiritual matters—a responsibility which cannot be delegated to a youth pastor"[32] Schlect stresses that there must be high standards in child rearing, with fathers playing the key role of authority. Since many prospective youth pastors are directly out of seminary and not much older than the teens of whom they have been put in charge, we caution youth pastors to be sensitive to a father who may not be able to spend the time he would like with his own children. A youth pastor should not put himself in the role of father to those in his youth group. If a young youth pastor does not have children of his own, he may not be able to relate to that unique and special relationship between parent and child. Schlect adds, "It is important that the children's dependence upon the youth minister should be transferred back to the parents. . . . The youth minister should also begin deferring to parents whenever possible." Schlect argues, "Deferring to the parents puts healthy pressure on them to attend to their responsibilities, and it teaches youth to honor their mother and father. It is parental counsel that children must seek"[33] (see Prov. 1:8).

We need to rethink the role of contemporary youth pastor. Instead of working entirely with the youth, the youth pastor should be supporting the role of the parents so the parents can successfully fill their God-given role to "train up a child in the way that he should go" (Prov. 22:6). Since youth ministers and youth programs may inadvertently hinder this scriptural directive to fathers, Schlect offers some biblical solutions. Two of the suggested solutions were particularly interesting to us.

One solution is for youth to "attend adult Bible studies and prayer meetings, especially those that their parents attend." This would be an important time together in prayer, reading and studying Scripture, and in fellowship with other believers. By encouraging youth and adults to pray and study together, not only is the opportunity provided for youth to observe adults practicing godly behavior, but it does away with age segregation. After all, Scripture is relevant to all ages, young and old alike. Another of Schlect's solutions is to "organize social events around families." For birthday parties, instead of inviting just those of a particular age, invite entire families. Schlect also recommends including boys and girls in adult functions, however, being careful not to significantly cater to the youth.[34]

A biblical mandate that not only encourages fellowship but also integrates youth into the Body of Christ is that of hospitality.[35] We are told in 1 Peter 4:9 to be "hospitable to one another." Opening up our homes over the holidays to those who are separated from their families or by inviting different families home after church for a meal are ways in which to extend hospitality. Children and youth should not be singled out with special attention, but they should also be included, thus demonstrating to youth that they are an integral part of the Body of Christ.

Feelings of Inadequacy

Many conscientious and dedicated Christian parents desire and diligently strive to raise their children in a manner pleasing to God. In fact, in the public school setting, many parents want to be actively involved in their children's education in order to exercise their God-given responsibility. Public school officials continually say that they want parent involvement, and yet when parents do become involved in their child's education, the not-so-subtle message is "We are the professionals; we know what is best for your kids." Parents have quickly discovered that school officials just give lip service to parental involvement. Is it any wonder that parents have become discouraged and apathetic along with having feelings of inadequacy?

Could it be that the same message is unknowingly given to parents in the church when a youth pastor is hired to be on staff? Have we fallen victim to the erroneous thinking that there truly is a generation gap and that we need someone to relate to our own children in a contemporary, meaningful way? Is the youth pastor unconsciously helping parents to abdicate their God-given responsibility in raising their own children?

Due to feelings of inadequacy, Christian parents may unwittingly buy into the humanist philosophy that public (government) schools are equal partners with parents in the education and raising of children. Parents must not succumb to this lie. Parents are not equal partners! Parents have the sole responsibility for the raising of their own children. Parents may delegate responsibility to the school, but that is totally different than being partners exercising equal authority with those who hold a different worldview. Unfortunately, the term *partners* carries with it the idea of restructuring the social unit of society and is now being used indiscriminately in the church. In one resource book dealing with how to involve parents in youth ministry, there is a chapter titled "Parents as Partners."[36] We must be on guard that the secular mindset portrayed through the use of words does not inadvertently become the mindset of the church.

Undermining Parental Authority

A destructive philosophy also being espoused in public schools is that children should be autonomous from their parents. Children are often encouraged to make decisions independent of the parent's counsel. As a youth minister, Schlect refuses to counsel kids without the matter first being discussed with their own parents. A different attitude prevails in much of the contemporary youth curricula today.

Some contemporary youth material encourages personal dialog about family that has the potential to stir up tension between a teen and his parents. Unfortunately, the lessons often target the home where the parents love their children enough to set standards and rules. One elective study titled "Getting Along with Parents," implied that parents didn't understand their children and that the parents couldn't convey their love. Stated in the curriculum's introduction is the following: "Teenagers don't always like their parents. And parents don't always like their teenagers. Misunderstandings and miscommunication fuel frequent fights. But parents and teenagers *want* to get along with each other. They just don't know how."[37] Unfortunately, a mindset has been established. The concept that parents and teens do not always like each other becomes the norm rather than the exception.

In yet another lesson, the stated aim is "to help teenagers learn to balance their need for independence with their parents needs and desires." The following is the background information based upon Luke 2:41–51 provided for the youth leaders:

> In Judaism, when a boy turns 13 he becomes a full member of the religious community. It wasn't uncommon in Jesus' day for a 12-year-old boy to visit the temple in preparation for his 13th birthday. By staying behind to learn more about God, Jesus made it clear that he knew serving God was the most important priority in life. But by obeying his parents, he also demonstrated he knew how to balance *his own needs with his parents*.[38] (emphasis added)

Something is scripturally amiss, as evidenced by the psychobabble being used. First of all, Jesus was not concerned with balancing his own needs with those of his parents. He was concerned with being obedient to God, which meant being obedient to his earthly parents. Jesus was obedient and subject to his earthly parents until age thirty, at which time he became obedient to God and His business only.[39] Follow-up questions that further undermine respect for parents actually use Jesus as the example to justify disobedience. The questions include: "How did you feel about Jesus' decision to stay at the temple without his parents' permission? How is Jesus' decision to stay at the temple like some of the decisions you make without telling your parents?"[40]

Parental responsibility for children is also undermined in yet another youth ministry resource. Ironically, in a book dealing with trust, the focus is not on building trust between parent and child, or even parent and youth leader, but instead upon building trust within the group. Because the activities in the resource book deal with potent emotions, the youth leaders are warned that "difficult and sensitive issues are bound to surface as you build trust in your group." Parental permission, however, is not recommended before exposing youth to emotional situations. Youth leaders are even instructed to "Be ready to refer students to competent counselors if a key issue such as abuse or depression emerges. Have a list of competent counselors ready and don't be reluctant to refer."[41] Incredibly, there is no mention of consulting with parents. It is presumptuous of a youth leader to think that he can bypass parents and send youth directly to a counselor without parental knowledge or permission. This sounds just like the public schools.

Out of a misguided love and commitment to teens, youth pastors and leaders may unwittingly set themselves up as friend and counselor to youth, thus undermining the rightful role of parents. In some cases, instead of relying upon Scripture to guide their teens, youth leaders are motivated by their teen's approval and applause. It is obvious that church leaders are unaware that they are reasoning the same as the world and by doing so are undermining the family they are trying to protect.

What about Unchurched Kids?

What about those parents who do not take responsibility for the spiritual upbringing of their children for whatever reason? What about those teens who come from unchurched families? A stated purpose of many youth ministries is to be an outreach to unchurched kids.

According to Schlect, "Ministering to children of unbelievers need not be as difficult as it seems. These children should be drawn to associate with Christian *families* rather than Christian *youth ministries*."[42]

We suspect there are many Christian families that are already reaching out to unchurched kids, with the idea to minister not only to the youth, but to the youth's entire family. Parents that love the Lord are already doing what comes naturally. This is not to say that youth do not come to a saving knowledge and acceptance of Jesus Christ as Lord and Savior in youth ministry programs. However, Schlect carefully points out, unchurched teens as well as those who are newly saved from unchurched families must be encouraged to "honor and submit to their ungodly fathers and mothers as God has called them."[43]

A Biblical Model

Parents want and need help from the church to train their children to "walk in a manner worthy of the Lord to please Him in all respects, bearing fruit in every good work and increasing in the knowledge of God" (Eph. 5:15–16). Yes, there are Christian parents who are abdicating their responsibility in the spiritual teaching of their children, but the church will not help the parents or their youth by trying to do the parents' job for them. The church should reinforce and encourage but not take the place of the biblical role of parents in the upbringing of their children.

We are living in turbulent times, and our youth are particularly vulnerable as they are being bombarded by anti-Christian messages and worldly enticements. Our youth must be taught by parents, with the help and support of the church, not to conform to the youth culture's own music, dress, and entertainment, but be willing to stand alone for Christ against the cultural tide. This stand to honor God with their lives is an individual stand, not a group stand. We must all answer individually before the throne of the almighty God. It is our desire that we all be challenged to consider or reconsider God's command to us as parents and spiritual leaders. We need to ask ourselves: Have we as parents and spiritual leaders in the church taken seriously our responsibility to train up children in the way they should go?

Chapter 11

Raising Up Daniels

Therefore, take up the full armor of God, that you may be
able to resist in the evil day, and having done everything, to
stand firm. . . . With all prayer and petition pray at all times
in the Spirit, and . . . be on the alert with all perseverance.

—Eph. 6:13, 18

We are living in a time very much like the Old Testament—a
time when "every man did what was right in his own eyes"
(Judg. 17:6). The Bible, however, gives a strong warning to those
who embrace this false worldly philosophy of a do-it-yourself
religion, "Woe to those who are wise in their own eyes, and
clever in their own sight!" (Isa. 5:21).

Because we are living in a morally corrupt culture, passing
on the faith of our fathers requires all the patience and wisdom
parents, pastors, elders, and Sunday school teachers can gather
in order to raise children with a firm spiritual foundation
grounded in the Word of God. We need to make a conscientious
effort to introduce and emulate the spiritual giants of the Bible
to our children at a young age. As we pray for and with our
children we should challenge them, for example, to be a Daniel.
Using Daniel as a model, we can help our children to stand firm
against a culture that often demonstrates animosity toward God.

Practice, Practice, Practice

Daniel boldly lived his convictions, demonstrating his desire to be obedient to God. If we want to raise up Daniels, we must teach our children to practice obedience in every-day situations with the decision to honor God in their lives. Obedience is not learned by participating in contrived or simulated experiences that stir up emotions, nor is obedience learned by sitting around in a circle and discussing nonjudgmentally what one thinks and feels about a given passage in Scripture.

How does one learn to be obedient to God? How does one learn to do the right thing? William Kilpatrick simply states, "One learns to do the right thing by being trained in it. It isn't enough to know how to play tennis from reading a manual. You practice it."[1] Those who desire to do God's will must not be ignorant of what God's Word says. One must diligently study God's Word, because if one does not know what God's Word says, one cannot do what God's Word says to do. However, even though knowledge of Scripture is vitally important, knowledge is empty and useless unless we put it into practice. Knowledge and conduct must go together. As John MacArthur pointedly asks, "What good is it to know the truth if we fail to act accordingly?"[2] In other words, we must be "doers of the word, and not merely hearers" (James 1:22).

With a fervent dedication, Daniel practiced daily obedience to God. As a result, he was known for his integrity as he served honorably in administrative duties. Deeds of loving and honorable service are evidence of an authentic faith in God. As one pastor observed: "Real faith ministers to the world, but rejects the values of the world."[3]

"Faith is not a passive attitude," explains Martin and Deidre Bobgan, authors of several books exposing the psychoheresy infiltrating the church. "It is steadfast trust. And it is acted on. Some may say one thing, but do another. That is not true faith. True faith in God brings consistency between belief on the inside and action on the outside."[4]

Are Christian youth being trained to put into practice the biblical truth they learn at home and church? Are they being encouraged to practice what they believe so that a right response becomes habitual? Kilpatrick argues that if an individual has been properly trained, he will respond rightly. He uses the example that if a trained boxer is attacked, he will automatically block and counterpunch; but without training, the boxer would more than likely end up flat on his back.[5] Christian teens must be like the boxer who is properly trained so that they can respond reflexively in a manner honoring God when the difficult circumstances of life attack the absolutes they profess. They need to hold up Daniel as an example to follow.

Secular Script

As Christians, we can profess the correct theology but at the same time fail to apply that same theology to our daily lives. Michael Horton articulates the problem. "In theory, we are orthodox; in practice, we are rewriting the Christian religion from a secular script."[6] Christians today, he adds, are "undermining biblical authority by claiming one thing in theory (the authority of an inerrant Bible) while in practice giving priority to secular disciplines and popular culture in defining and shaping the spiritual diet."[7]

A. W. Tozer also observes that "the gulf between theory and practice is so great as to be terrifying. . . . For the gospel is too often preached and accepted without power, and the radical shift which the truth demands is never made. . . . For there is in divine truth an imperious note, there is about the gospel an urgency, a finality which will not be heard or felt except by the enabling of the Spirit."[8] Responsible, at least in part, for this gulf between theory and practice are the developers and publishers of youth curricula who are teaching teens to rely on humanly devised gimmicks to teach and guide.

Christian teens desperately need solid food from God's Word, taught by godly men and women, in order to become mature individuals in Christ. In fact, we are being told by teens and their parents that teens *want* to study God's Word. Hebrews 5:14 states that it is the mature "who because of practice have their senses trained to discern good and evil." Discernment is critical in order to keep from falling victim to the world's foolishness. Theology is important and necessary to know, and appropriately applying what one knows is equally essential. Theology and practice must go hand in hand.

Identify the Counterfeit

Your church may not be using any of the youth curricula or activities mentioned throughout this book, but that does not mean that secular philosophies and methods have not infiltrated your church. For example, unsuspecting youth pastors and parents may use an occasional icebreaker activity that subtly undermines a biblical principle or truth. Remember that even questions may encourage a worldly, materialistic mindset rather than a godly one.

Humanistic philosophies are so pervasive and so commonplace that we may be espousing them without even realizing it. While attending graduate school, one pastor was surprised to learn he had favorably quoted Carl Rogers in a paper that he had written concerning lay ministry in the local church. When asked about the quote, the pastor said that he had selected the quote from pages of quotes given out in class by one of his professors. When the pastor ask his seminary professor about the quote, the professor admitted that he did not know that the quote was by Carl Rogers. The professor had indiscriminately duplicated the pages of quotes given to him by a student who recommended that the quotes might be useful to other students.

In order to stop this infiltration of the secular into the church, we must be diligent students of God's Word. Even seminary students must not let down their guard. They must check everything that their professors teach (or hand out) against Scripture. It has often been said that in order to identify a counterfeit, one must know the real thing. The example is frequently given of the bankteller who is trained to recognize authentic bills and currency. By being able to identify the real thing, the counterfeit is easier to detect. This is equally true of God's Word. We advise parents and church leaders to familiarize themselves with what is going on in the public school. By reading the writings of those individuals who have impacted the secular culture with their philosophies, followers of Jesus Christ will be able to more readily identify the perverse invasion of the secular into the sacred. When Christians identify a philosophy or method that has been used in the public schools for twenty years or more, it would make sense to question the validity of its use in the church, especially since God has been removed from the public school arena. Parents and church leaders should automatically become suspect of anything popularized in and advocated by the public schools, keeping in mind that this is an institution not only void of God, but academic and moral excellence.

Spiritual Nourishment

Teens, as well as all Christians, must be well grounded in God's Word in order to discern false teachings. The importance of studying and meditating on God's Word can be compared to taking in nourishment for our physical needs. Many of us eat three meals each day along with snacks between meals and cannot imagine going even one day without food, let alone several days without it. Yet, Jesus quoted Deuteronomy 8:3 when He was tempted by the devil in the wilderness, "Man shall not live on bread alone, but on every word that proceeds out of the mouth of God" (Matt. 4:4). Are teens being taught that reading, studying, and hearing God's Word are just as important as meeting their physical hunger pangs? Are parents, pastors, and Sunday school teachers teaching that just as the body needs nourishment in order to remain healthy so the spirit needs nourishment in order to be sustained?

Our physical bodies would become weak and malnourished if food was only eaten during Sunday school, worship service on Sunday mornings, and during Bible study or youth group meetings on Wednesday evening. Why do we think that our souls will fare any better with such a scanty spiritual diet? Martyn Lloyd-Jones gives the following advice:

> . . . you must be constant students of the Word of God, you must read it without ceasing. You must read all good books that will assist you to understand it, and the best commentaries you can find on the Bible. You must read . . . biblical theology, the explanation of the great doctrines of the New Testament, so that you may come to understand them more and more clearly, and may therefore be able to present them with ever increasing clarity. . . .[9]

If curricula for Christian youth is any indication, we are indeed experiencing a famine. However, as Amos prophesized to the Israelites, it is "not a famine for bread or a thirst for water, but rather for hearing the words of the Lord" (Amos 8:11). When a people lose the awe of and reverence for their majestic God, sin and rebellion abound; hearts become hardened and unable to understand God's Word. Instead of studying the Bible and allowing the Word of God to penetrate their souls, teens in contemporary youth groups are often playing silly, nonsensical games and participating in psychotherapeutic exercises that encourage a focus on self.

In countries where the people experience the devastating physical effects of famine, an extended abdomen is often indicative of the lack of nourishing food. In countries where people experience the effects of a spiritual famine, an inflated ego is often indicative of a diet of spiritual junk food. Tragically, theology, the study of God, is being subtly replaced with psychology, the study of self. The emphasis in youth groups appears to be on a feel-good faith that tickles the ears rather than on a faith that points to the sinfulness of man and the holiness and grace of an omnipotent God.

Entertainment-Learning Culture

The discipline of studying God's Word has sometimes been replaced with a focus on entertainment. The natural tendencies of teens to seek their own pleasure and enjoyment is being encouraged by curriculum developers who assume that teens will become bored with disciplined study. The primary focus of many of the youth activities, therefore, is often to simply entertain youth. We are not against kids having fun. Games and entertainment, however, should not be the primary focus in a youth group, for the obvious reason that they take away valuable time that could be spent in sincere, disciplined study of God's Word. A constant diet of faddish gimmicks and entertainment will only contribute to the spiritual dumbing down of Christian youth.

According to Group,

> . . . studies reveal that up to 40 percent of the X-er generation and about 25 percent of the Boomer generation are considered functionally illiterate. . . . Also, a very high percentage of the millennial generation (today's young teens) is joining the ranks of the functionally illiterate. . . . Therefore, to successfully minister to people who generally can't read or write, teachers and ministers must deliver the biblical message in a nonthreatening medium that illiterate people use for information and learning—VIDEOS.

In fact, Group not only admits but boasts that their video series as well as all of their curricula is "student friendly to all age groups, learning levels, and functional abilities."

Obviously, in order to teach and minister to all age groups, all learning levels, and all functional abilities, the curricula must be dumbed down to the lowest common denominator: to those who cannot read. This publisher is actually promoting illiteracy in the church by catering to it!

The church must guard against looking like the world. The information accompanying one video series states, "During the past 50 years, America has become an entertainment culture—

which makes video curriculum a successful medium for reaching and teaching within the church."[10]

But should the church mimic the world?

According to the founder and president of Ligonier Ministries, R. C. Sproul, "Too often today, what Christians hear in church is merely a biblical gloss on what they hear every day in popular culture."[11] Just because succeeding generations of Americans are becoming increasingly illiterate and need radio, television, and videos to obtain information, it is being falsely assumed that video curriculum is also the best way to minister to those who are illiterate in the church. Needless to say, extreme care must be taken to make sure that curricula and supplemental material used with youth do not embrace faddish trends from the world. If the church is experiencing an illiteracy problem in reading, then perhaps the church needs to start teaching phonics and raising the standard.

Raising a Standard

Martyn Lloyd-Jones as long ago as the early 1960s made the observation that there were those who believed the Bible "must be put in such simple terms and language that anybody taking it up and reading it is going to understand all about it."

His adamant response: "This is nothing but sheer nonsense!"

> What we must do is to educate the masses of the people *up* to the Bible, not bring the Bible *down* to their level. One of the greatest troubles in life today is that everything is being brought down to the same level; everything is being cheapened. The common man is made the standard and the authority; he decides everything, and everything has got to be brought down to him. . . . Everywhere standards are coming down and down. Are we to do this with the Word of God? I say, No![12]

Power in God's Word: A True Story

We were told this personal, heartwarming story from a youth pastor, reminding us of the power of God's Word to touch and change the life of a teen.

As a fourteen-year-old boy, this youth pastor was asked to baby-sit for his neighbor's two younger children. He eagerly accepted the job because, unlike his own family, his neighbors had a television set and he wanted to watch the preview of *B. J. and the Bears*. However, when he arrived at the scheduled time, he was told, much to his chagrin, that the television set was broken. After playing with the kids and putting them to bed for the night, he wondered what he was going to do to pass the time. The only reading material on the coffee table was a *Good Housekeeping* magazine and a Bible. So he did what any typical fourteen-year-old boy would do: He picked up the magazine to read. Not surprisingly, it did not take him long to go through the magazine's pages, so he picked up the Bible and started reading in Psalms and then turned to the New Testament.

While reading, God convicted him of his sin and need for the Savior. This young teen was tearfully brought down to his knees to pray right there by the coffee table in the home of his neighbor. God touched this young boy's life with the power of His Word. The boy of this story is now a young man in his thirties, married with two children, and serving the Lord in a ministry to youth.

As this true story illustrates, the Bible is supernatural and is not read like any magazine or human book—i.e., *Winnie the Pooh, Gone with the Wind*, or the *Illiad*. Unlike any other human book, the Bible is "living and active" (Heb. 4:12). The Bible teaches that "All scripture is inspired by God" (2 Tim. 3:16), and that "no prophecy of Scripture is a matter of one's own interpretation, for no prophecy was ever made by an act of human will, but men moved by the Holy Spirit spoke from God" (2 Pet. 1:20–21).

Therefore, as C. H. Spurgeon succinctly articulated, "If we keep to holy Scripture, we cannot go wrong. With such a standard, we know that we are right. This Book is the Word of God, and if we teach it, we teach that which the Lord will accept and bless. . . . Let our teaching be more and more scriptural! . . . Teach the holy Scriptures. Let the Scriptures be consulted rather than any human book."[13]

Wordly Relevance

Unfortunately, the wise words of Spurgeon are going unheaded. Dumbing down to the world's standard is becoming increasingly evident in misguided attempts by church leaders to be relevant to the youth of today. Youth leaders and developers of Christian curricula appear to have bought into the lie that the church must be like the world in order to reach the world. However, in an attempt to be relevant, the church runs the risk of becoming so much like the world that one will not be able tell the difference between the two.

Remember that the writers of the *Humanist Manifesto* recognized that in order to destroy the Christian faith, "the distinction between the sacred and the secular can no longer be maintained."[14] Christians must resist the temptation to inappropriately adapt the Bible's message and method in order to appear relevant to the times in which we live. We must make the distinction between the sacred and the secular. James also gives us a solemn warning in the New Testament book after his name: "Whoever wishes to be a friend of the world makes himself an enemy of God" (James 4:4).

John MacArthur pointed out that true Christianity is an offense to the world. Christians "cannot avoid being an offense to the world and still remain faithful to the gospel. The gospel is inherently offensive. Christ Himself is offensive to unbelievers. He is an offense to all in error. He is an offense to all who reject the truth."[15] If the church attempts to be "relevant," then compromise to truth is inevitable.

Back to the Basics

Christian children are faced with many of the same trials and decisions that Daniel faced. The majority of Christian children are being educated in public schools where there is an ongoing assault against the beliefs and values children have been taught at home. Young people are also living in a culture that continually stimulates the desires of the flesh through music, dress, and entertainment. Since these are urgent and critical times—times in which the Christian faith is mocked and frequently under attack—we must adequately prepare our youth to make tough stands for Christ today and in the future.

One cannot help but contrast the Christians of the early church with the young people today involved in youth groups that focus on man's experience and interpersonal relationships (trust in self and others). A. W. Tozer described the first members of the Church of Christ:

> They knew that the Majesty in the heavens was confronting them on earth: they were in the very Presence of God. And the power of that conviction to arrest attention and hold it for a lifetime, to elevate, to transform, to fill with uncontrollable moral happiness, to send men singing to prison and to death, has been one of the wonders of history and a marvel of the world.[16]

Tozer also described the early saints and martyrs as having the fortitude and courage to "stand alone, deserted by every earthly friend, and die for Christ under the universal displeasure of mankind."[17] We cannot help but compare the difference between the early martyrs' courage to stand alone with the emphasis being placed in youth groups on relational activities, group learning, and teamwork. One trembles for our youth. Will Christian young people be able to stand alone during times of persecution if separated from their group, team, or community? Will they be able to be a Daniel? During any type of persecution, the relationship that they have cultivated with the Lord will be more important than the relationship with peers. The rallying motto "Make a commitment to be group builders forever!" rings hollow and irrelevant.[18]

This profound statement was also made by Tozer:

> The church is a body of individuals united in Christ but having separate individual responsibilities. . . . The Holy

Spirit fell at Pentecost on approximately 120 people. But it fell on them individually. . . . Each person is born individually even if he or she is one of a set of triplets. We are born one at a time, and we die one at a time; we face judgment one at a time and, if we as Christians are sick, we will be cured one at a time.[19]

Tozer expounded, "This intercourse with God and the soul is known to us in conscious personal awareness. It is personal: that is, it does not come through the body of believers, as such, but is known to the individual, and to the body through the individuals which compose it."[20] All this contemporary emphasis on groups and team building displaces the emphasis from where it should be, on an individual's personal response to the living God.

The pastor of a large Baptist church in Denver, Colorado, understands the danger. He wrote, "I knew without a shadow of a doubt that it was time to begin the process of getting the church God had given me to pastor *back to the basics*. At that moment, truth became more important than relationships."[21] Back to the basics means back to the Bible. Youth curricula that twists Scripture and embraces psychotherapeutic methods and techniques must be thrown out. We must return our focus back to God and His Holy Word, where Christ alone, Scripture alone, faith alone, and God's glory alone is taught, revered, and loved.

Jude, a half-brother of Christ, wrote the New Testament book after his name and in which he defended the apostolic faith against false teaching. The benediction at the close of his letter is our prayer for all Christians who desire to honor God with their lives as they seek to diligently discern truth from error, and strive to separate that which is holy from that which is unholy:

> Now to Him who is able to keep you from stumbling, and to make you stand in the presence of His glory blameless with great joy, to the only God our Savior, through Jesus Christ our Lord, be glory, majesty, dominion and authority, before all time and now and forever. Amen. (Jude 1:24)

Music for the Sensual or the Sacred?

Sing for joy in the Lord, O you righteous ones;
Praise is becoming to the upright.
Give thanks to the Lord with the lyre;
Sing praises to Him with a harp of ten strings.
Sing to Him a new song;

—Ps. 33:1–3

When we initially started writing and researching about contemporary youth group material, we had no intention of addressing the issue of contemporary Christian music and its impact on Christian youth. However, in our attempt to understand more about the activities used to draw Christian youth to Christ, it became apparent to us that contemporary Christian music also plays a role in the current dumbing down of America's Christian youth. As a result, we found ourselves attending a Christian rock concert to hear one of the nation's most popular Christian bands touring the country under the banner of "The Zombie Tour."[1]

It was very apparent from the onset that, even though we were at a Christian concert, there was something terribly wrong. The first red flag went up when a sponsor of the event came out on stage to lay down the ground rules. He warned that teens were getting hurt every night at these concerts and that some even had to be taken to the hospital for injuries. Therefore, he said, "We will not allow stage diving and crowdsurfing, and anyone caught violating the rules will be kicked out."

Throughout the concert, bouncers were visibly seen roaming the room, keeping any potential problems under control. Yes, we have seen out-of-control secular rock concerts, but we would never have expected the very same spirit to exist at a Christian concert!

In addition, it also became apparent to us that a simulated secular rock concert was intentionally being created. In fact, before the first opening song, a singer enthusiastically shouted out to the kids, "Let's pretend we're at a rock concert!" To those of us who have actually lived through the age of rebellion, drugs, and rock concerts, telling us to pretend we were at a rock concert was the last place on earth we wanted to revisit—simulated or not!

Indeed, there were many similarities between this concert and the rock concerts of the sixties and seventies. First of all, the blaring music was so loud that it was next to impossible to identify if the lyrics of the songs were even Christian. To our surprise, we overheard one teen tell his friend, "I better buy some earplugs. I always get a headache after one of these concerts."

By this point, it was not surprising that teens had caught the spirit of the evening and were dancing in the aisles. After all, what would you expect after one of the singers encouraged them to do so: "Does everyone out there like to dance? OK, let's see everyone moving out there." As we watched the dancing, jumping, and clowning around, it was obvious that this event was not about edifying our holy and righteous God, even though a band member told the crowd of 1,300 that it was.

On the contrary, Christian youth were being subjected to a worldly, party-time mindset subtly desensitizing them away from the reverent and the sacred. Instead of elevating the sacred, the sacred was being cheapened. Instead of teaching Christian youth to separate from the pleasures of the world, they were being subtly taught to copy and conform to them. In the process, Christian teens were being dumbed down to accept a commercialized, reductionist gospel pandering to their emotions and their flesh. In this atmosphere, reference to Scripture was also cheapened by a band member who enthusiastically referred to the Book of James as the book that had "really kicked my butt!"

Unfortunately, the spirit of the concert was intended to live on long after the band's final song. During intermission, in a special meeting for youth leaders, the band's curriculum "Youth Leaders Only" was introduced. Whether the youth leaders realized it or not, this meeting was being used as an outlet to market the band's music directly to teens. Interestingly, the lesson plans were all based on songs from the band's CDs and other contemporaries in the business. By this point, we were not surprised by the curriculum's offer for a free six-foot standup of the popular band to be displayed in your church youth room.

As we looked around this packed room of youth leaders, we also could not help notice the distinct age difference between ourselves and those working with our youth. Many were just coming out of the teen years themselves. Therefore, was it any wonder that they all appeared to see nothing wrong with a Christian rock concert that looked and sounded exactly like the world's? As mothers who have raised our own children through the teen years, we must admit that we questioned what percentage of these youth leaders possessed the necessary maturity, experience, and wisdom required to instruct youth through their teen years.

Also addressing the group of young youth leaders was one of the band's singers. We are not questioning or judging the heart of this young man, who shared how God rescued him from a life of drugs and despair, but we do question placing him in the capacity of a role model to the youth of the church. We couldn't help but wonder how many Christian parents would approve of their sons mimicking the dress of this band member, complete with his blue sparkle fingernail polish and his long scraggly hair. We wondered how many Christian fathers would want their daughters to be courted by a young man who fashions his dress and his music after the world? We seriously doubt if many would approve. Nevertheless, Christian parents can expect their Christian sons and daughters to do so if we don't think twice about the kind of role models we parade before our youth.

Spirit of the Age, or the Spirit of Christ?

Contemporary Christian artist Steve Camp has courageously called for a reformation in the Christian music industry, writing in his *107 Theses* that they had "gone too far down the wide road of worldliness. . . ."

Camp warns, ". . . when Christian artists today take the old song of the world and dress it up, modify it, and say it now represents the person of Jesus Christ, a Christian message, or describes the character of God, they fortuitously assault the gospel and diminish the gift that has been entrusted to them. This is inappropriate at best and sacrilegious at worst. We cannot pour new wine into old wine skins."

What will be the fruits of a generation of Christian youth whose role models and youth leaders think nothing is wrong with telling them to pretend they are at a rock concert? Are we unwittingly allowing the creation of a Christian youth culture, a generation gap, in the church where adults and youth will eventually speak a different language? Are we creating a mindset in our youth that subtly implies that Mom and Dad, Grandma and Grandpa are old-fashioned?

To be sure, we can hear those who will say, "But if we want to reach the kids of today, we have to make Christianity relevant to their world by giving them what they want." On the contrary, in their effort to reach kids for Christ, they must guard against giving them the world's model along with all of its "trivial messages that devalue Deity and raise 'felt need' affairs above eternal 'real need' concerns," which is tantamount to "playing marbles with diamonds." [2]

When introducing someone to Christ, the Lord must be presented as different from the world. Scripture teaches that we are not to "love the world, nor the things of the world" (1 John

2:15) and that "whoever wishes to be a friend of the world makes himself an enemy of God" (James 4:4).

The Character of Christian Music

> When we are saved by grace, we become "new creatures" in Him; "Old things are passed away; behold all things become new" (2 Cor. 5:17). From then on we "walk in newness of life" (Rom. 6:4). We are alive in Him, alive for Him, "alive unto God through Christ our Lord."[3] (Rom. 6:11)

Therefore, as Leonard Seidel wrote in his book *God's New Song*, "The new life in Christ Jesus is accompanied by (new standards, including) new standards in music."[4]

> God never takes away without giving something better. As *new* creatures in Christ, He gives us a new song. A song that glorifies Him, that brings true peace and joy that makes molehills out of mountains—and mountains of victory out of molehills of defeat. And, since our internal is to manifest itself in the external, our music should now be in harmony with God's word and Christian principles.[5]

Yes, unlike the world, Christian music is inspired by the Holy Spirit and inspires the musician, the singer, and the listener. Thus, this new song of the redeemed people of God is "a different and distinct song, a more glorious song, a purer, truer, and more beautiful song than the world can ever sing."[6]

The Gospel According to St. Bernard?

Beware lest any man spoil you through philosophy or vain deceit, after the tradition of men, after the rudiments of the world, and not after Christ.

—Col. 2:8 (KJV)

The following is a complete critique of the activities and philosophies taken from "Bernie and his gospel." *Disturbing, irreverent, and shocking* are just a few words to describe this curriculum, so hang on!

An Angel Disguised as a Dog

Christian Video Enterprises, Inc., and the Zig Ziglar Corporation have joined efforts in the development and marketing of a character-building curriculum to the churches of America called *The Gospel According to Saint Bernard*. This curriculum demonstrates the depth and magnitude of the secularization and the dumbing down of the church. Because of the high national profile of Zig Ziglar, a Christian motivational speaker and author, we cannot ignore or underestimate the far-reaching impact of the ideas used in the curriculum. *The Gospel According to St. Bernard* is an example that just because something is labeled *Christian* does not mean that it is based on biblical truth.

The main character of the curriculum is Bernie, an angel disguised as a dog, sent to earth by God on a special assignment to teach two children, Daniel and Jennifer Sullivan, how to solve their daily problems by applying God's Word to their lives. Teachers and parents are told in an introductory letter, "Don't be surprised if . . . Bernie becomes part of your family." However, it is our contention that no discerning Christian parent would ever invite this angel to be part of their family!

This character-building series is advertised as "one of the most comprehensive theological and practical Christian courses available to churches."[1] But in reality, the Bernie curriculum falls far short from teaching real character to Christian youth. In fact, upon close scrutiny, Bernie could not possibly be an angel sent from God. Would an angel sent from God dishonor and question the commands of his God? Would an angel sent from God tempt children to disobey their parents or ignore the rules of the house? Would an angel sent from God use hocus-pocus or give a child New Age–type experience involving a mystical state of consciousness? Would an angel sent from God sin?

This extensive multimedia curriculum consists of 12 lessons, each accompanied by a video featuring real actors rather than animated caricatures. To everyone except Daniel and Jennifer, Bernie appears to be an ordinary St. Bernard, but to the Sullivan children, the Bernie angel appears as a make-believe dog. In addition to the videos, there is a teacher's manual containing a synopsis of each video, the main Bible truth and themes for each lesson, questions for discussion, and suggestions for follow-up activities. Two workbooks are also included, one for ages 4–6 and the other for ages 7–12. Promoters have marketed this curriculum for easy use, giving it tremendous buying appeal for busy teachers. Hopefully, however, teachers will look beyond the outward packaging and look closely at the content.

Bernie's Gospel?

The name alone of this curriculum should put up a red flag. The title, *The Gospel According to St. Bernard*, carries an aura of authority and subtly implies that Bernie is on par with the apostles of the Bible. Unless a child has committed the books of the Bible to memory, it would be easy to see how a child could become confused and assume that Bernie is not only an angel, but Bernie has his own book in the Bible.

One of today's respected Christian thinkers, Os Guinness, talks about the importance of words. He says, "Created by a word-speaking God, human beings are word-speaking people. Unless words have meaning, everything becomes chaos. Unless words have power, everything becomes barren."[2] Since the words *gospel* and *saint* refers to apostolic authority, the logical conclusion for children would be that Bernie is an apostle.

Discerning Christians, however, would recognize the title of this curriculum as an assault on truth. Guinness points out that we are experiencing "a barrage of words." He elaborates, "Words in a wordy world have lost their power. . . . They no longer communicate, convey truth and understanding, . . . or provide the common ground on which people can meet and build society. Noisy but empty, words have a Babel capacity for confusion and division that is stronger than ever."[3] The title should be immediately offensive to Christians because it does not convey truth. After all, there is no such book of the Bible.

Throughout this series, Bernie continually distorts and twists Scripture. Is this the action of an angel sent from God or that of an apostle of God? On the surface, Bernie appears to be a cuddly dog who wants to help his newfound friends, but Bernie hardly meets the qualifications of either an angel or an apostle. Church leaders may be inclined to let down their guard and mistakenly think that nothing could be so wrong with this cute, make-believe dog/angel.

A generation of children are being raised who cannot articulate the basics of their faith, and curricula like Bernie are in part responsible for this Bible illiteracy. Bernie takes valuable time away from legitimate Bible study. Without time in God's Word, which "is living and active and sharper than any two-edged sword" (Heb. 4:12), there will be no changed lives, spiritual growth, or training in discernment. The fact that Bernie is found in Sunday school classrooms across this nation is a strong indication that we are already losing our ability to discern.

Dumbed Down Role Models

How many times has it been said that kids need more positive role models? Christians are fortunate. Unlike the world, Christians have no shortage of positive role models. The Bible is full of men and women of character who did great things because of what God did in and through them. As a result, they have made a profound, positive impact on boys and girls throughout the ages. Would it not, therefore, only make sense that if the Christian church wants to instill life-changing character traits within the hearts of small children that we would use the characters of the Bible? What will make the biggest impact on a child's life? Will it be teaching the values and faith of a make-believe dog, or will it be introducing them to real characters like David?

David is known as having a heart after God. Perhaps one of the most inspiring and best-loved stories in the Bible is David's defeat of Goliath. Even as a young boy, David had strong convictions and great courage. While all of Israel retreated in fear, David stood alone before the Philistine's giant warrior. David, equipped with only a sling and five smooth pebbles, refused to tremble before his enemy. Whose words would you take more seriously: the words of David, a real person from the Bible who demonstrated true courage, or Bernie, a make-believe talking dog?

Spiritual Quackery

Much to our dismay, Bernie proves himself to be a dumbed-down angel. It quickly becomes apparent that he is a shallow, superficial representation of an angel. In fact, Bernie blatantly dishonors the holy character of angels. Angels are spiritual beings created by God who help carry out God's work on earth. As messengers from God, they act and speak with dignity and authority. God's powerful, majestic, celestial beings do not call attention to themselves, but rather point heavenward to the exalted God of the universe.

The Gospel According to St. Bernard contradicts biblical teaching about angels. The Bible reveals that angels are spiritual messengers, not teachers (Heb. 1:14). Contrary to Scripture, Bernie is cast in the role of a teacher as he attempts to teach Daniel and Jennifer biblical truths. Angels, however, do not understand the gospel as presented in the Bible. Bill Deckard, Christian writer and editor, explains, "The gospel has to do with redeeming a creature made in God's image. Angels are not made in God's image, and that is why they can't quite understand [the Bible]."[4] Since angels do not understand the gospel as presented in the Bible (1 Pet. 1:12), then they would not or could not be teachers to teach something which they do not understand. *The Gospel According to St. Bernard,* therefore, revolves around a false premise concerning the role of angels.

Tragically, however, even if angels were teachers, Bernie does not model in his own behavior the biblical truths he is trying to teach. For example, when Bernie was sent by God to Earth on a special assignment to help Daniel and Jennifer, Bernie grumbles, "A special assignment, are you sure I can handle it? . . . Listen, I don't mean to be ungrateful, but what if I can't do it."[5] Bernie does not like his special assignment and plans on using the escape clause, which says that if after twenty-four hours he does not want to be a part of the special assignment, he does not have to be. Amazingly, Bernie disrespectfully questions his earthly assignment made by God. It is incomprehensible that one of God's angels would not immediately be obedient with the intense desire to fulfill his mission for God.

Children learn in Sunday school to "do all things without grumbling or disputing" (Phil. 2:4). What message is Bernie subtly sending to children? Is it the message that angels do not have to obey God? Or is it the message that it is OK to grumble? If Bernie was the exemplary role model that an angel should be, he would not act contrary to Scripture. He would not grumble. However, Bernie even continues to grumble once he has been placed on earth.

> I'm supposed to be on a special assignment and look where He's put me! Where am I? In a forest? Hey! What happened to my voice? . . . No food and I'm hungry! . . .Oh, my heavens, I just had a terrible thought. Dogs don't get to have pizza. That's my most favorite food and I may never get to have it again. Oh, no! I've got to calm down so I can think rationally. . . . I think I'll just lay down and close my eyes for a minute. Maybe if I rest I'll be able to figure out what to do next about the mess I'm in.[6]

In Titus 2:7–8, we are told, "In all things show yourself to be an example of good deeds, with purity in doctrine, dignified, sound in speech, which is beyond reproach." In contrast to the Scripture's standards for good character, Bernie's speech is anything but dignified—*argumentative* and *whiny* might be better descriptions. Bernie's good deed to fulfill a special mission on earth for God is also undermined by an uncooperative, belligerent attitude.

Bernie's biggest concern about his earthly assignment appears to be that he will not be able to eat pizza. It quickly becomes apparent that pizza is more important to Bernie than fulfilling God's mission. Unlike Bernie, God's holy angels do not dwell on the trivial. They reverently worship and serve their ever-present, all-knowing, all-powerful Creator. Tragically, after viewing this video and the ones to follow, children will be grossly misinformed about angels. The authors' portrayal of a dog-angel's obsession for pizza is probably meant to be funny, but in an attempt to entertain and amuse, reverence for our holy God and His angels is sacrificed. This is too high a price to pay.

Angelmania

Because of renewed interest in the spiritual, TV programs, books on angels, and angel paraphernalia have become increasingly popular. Unfortunately, much of the programming, information, and paraphernalia do not accurately portray God's angelic beings.

Due to an increased interest in angels, Christians should take seriously the words of Paul Little, author of *Know What You Believe*. He warns that a Christian "is well advised to understand who and what they [angels] are. Otherwise he may be in danger of being victimized by popular ideas that are totally erroneous and harmful."[7] The Church should be taking every opportunity to accurately teach about angels.

An Angel Using Magic?

The authors of *Seduction of Christianity* wrote, "There can be little doubt that we are in the midst of an unprecedented rival of sorcery worldwide that is deeply affecting not only every level and sector of modern society, but the church as well."[8] Evidence that this statement is more true than we would probably like to admit is that *The Gospel According to St. Bernard* uses magic and visualization.

Bernie unashamedly uses his mystical powers in several different situations in the curriculum. In the first video, Daniel falls and breaks his arm, necessitating a rushed trip to the doctor's office where his arm is put in a cast. That evening, much to the amazement of Daniel and Jennifer, Bernie signs Daniel's cast with his paw. When Bernie lays his paw on Daniel's casted arm, a luminous glow radiates as Bernie burns his paw print into the cast.[9]

Bernie uses his mystical powers again when he and Daniel are being threatened by two mischievous boys who called themselves the "Green Monsters." When one of the boys was going to strike Bernie with a baseball bat, Bernie turned the bat into a teddy bear. When the other boy held a screwdriver to Daniel's throat, Bernie turned the screwdriver into a large sucker. The boys, rather shaken up, ask, "What is going on here? What kind of dog is that?"[10] Not surprisingly, we are asking ourselves the same question.

Bernie does yet another act of mysticism at the end of the video series. As the Sullivans are preparing for Christmas, they decide to make their gifts to one another. Mr. Sullivan is not especially talented with his hands so everyone is wondering if Mr. Sullivan's homemade gifts will be as bad as they think. The gifts do turn out as bad as everyone thinks, but an unexpected surprise awaits when Bernie decides to become "Santa's little helper."[11] After everyone has gone to bed, and the homemade gifts have been placed under the tree, Bernie sneaks inside to put his homemade gifts under the tree. He sees all the gifts made with love by each member of the Sullivan family and says, "Yuk! Looks like they could use some help?"[12] Bernie does a little heavenly hocus-pocus, and the gifts are all wonderful.

Close Your Eyes and Visualize

Bernie further demonstrates his mystical power on Jennifer's birthday. Her family wanted to surprise her with a party later that day, so they made her think that they had forgotten her birthday. Jennifer was deeply hurt. In fact, she was so hurt that she thought her family really did not love her. Bernie, however, attempted to show Jennifer that her family really did love her with a "close your eyes and visualize" New Age technique.

> BERNIE: Would you like to see what it would be like if they really didn't love you?
> JENNIFER: I don't know. What are you talking about?
> BERNIE: Close your eyes. (Bernie and Jennifer rub noses.)
> JENNIFER: Where are we? It looks like my room, but where is everything? Where are my toys? Where are my clothes?
> BERNIE: Well, since you're mom and dad don't love you, they don't care to buy you anything.

JENNIFER: Look at me. I look awful!

BERNIE: You're parents don't care so they never remind you to take a bath or brush your teeth.

MRS. SULLIVAN (crossly): Jennifer, if you want something to eat, you better get out here right this minute. I'm not going to call you again.

JENNIFER: Mom's never talked to me that way before.

BERNIE: You better go. She sounds serious.

MRS. SULLIVAN (crossly): What took you so long? Why are you sitting there? Take your food to the corner where you belong.

DANIEL: Yah. We don't want to look at your face.

MR. SULLIVAN: She's just in the way around here.

JENNIFER: But today is my birthday.

DANIEL: Big deal!

JENNIFER: Don't any of you care?

MRS. SULLIVAN: No, we don't care. Now go to your room. . . .

JENNIFER: Bernie, this is awful.

BERNIE: Let's get out of here.[13]

It appears that after Bernie and Jennifer rub noses, Bernie and Jennifer are transported into some sort of a mystical state of consciousness. As Bernie guides Jennifer, she visualizes herself in her bedroom that has been replaced with crude and sparse furnishings. Jennifer, scraggly and hungry, is scolded and harshly treated by her brother, mother, and father.

The reader may be asking, Is not Jennifer just using her imagination about what it would be like if her parents did not love her? If that were the case, why didn't Bernie just tell Jennifer what it would be like. Why was it necessary for Jennifer to close her eyes and rub noses with Bernie? Why are both Jennifer and Bernie talking as if all of this was really happening? Significantly, Bernie is with Jennifer and speaking to her during this entire traumatic experience, an experience that caused Jennifer such mental anguish that she was in tears. Could it be that Bernie is acting in the role of spiritual guide in some sort of guided visualization?

Seeds of Apostasy

In *Thieves of Innocence*, John Ankerberg, John Weldon, and Craig Branch, respected authorities on the New Age and the occult, state,

> It is important to realize that in visualization, guided imagery, and hypnosis we are not merely dealing with the natural or even innocent use of imagination. In normal use of the imagination, we find a discriminating use of internal thoughts. The person is in control of how he uses these thoughts whether it is visualizing winning a race or what it would be like to marry another person. This natural use of the imagination is not what we find in New Age visualization, guided imagery, or hypnosis. . . .
>
> In essence, it is the particular characteristics of visualization, guided imagery, and hypnosis which distinguish them from a normal use of imagination. These may include: relaxation, suggestion, the creation of a new reality, an altered state of consciousness, being directed by another person so that the participant is not ultimately in control, and having to be brought out of the internal condition into which one has been placed. Further, visualization, guided imagery, and hypnosis can all be powerful methods for introducing children to the occult. . . .[14]

This incident with Bernie and Jennifer has definite New Age overtones. It certainly is not scriptural. Angels in the Bible do not come to people and have them visualize or imagine what it would be like if things were different. Angels do not encourage people to imagine a different reality! Angels acting as messengers often point to future events but never to possible or imagined ones.

Even though Bernie used this mystical technique in an attempt to show Jennifer that her parents really did love her, he used a practice that is contrary to what God would have us use. Deuteronomy 18:10–12, states, "There shall not be found among you anyone . . . who uses divination, one who practices witchcraft, or one who interprets omens, or a sorcerer, or one who casts a spell, or a medium, or a spiritist, or one who calls up the

dead. For whoever does these things is detestable to the LORD."
It is alarming that Bernie is opening up the door and dabbling in
practices that are forbidden by God.

We would like to believe that the authors of *The Gospel According to St. Bernard* do not realize that they are promoting practices contrary to Scripture. However, young children exposed to
such unscriptural teaching may not be able to escape the consequences of the authors' ignorance. Children may develop an attitude of tolerance for mysticism as they become desensitized to
practices forbidden by God; after all these practices are being
presented in the church. Hunt and McMahon warn, "Uncritical
acceptance of whatever Christian leaders teach, instead of check-
ing it carefully against the Word of God . . . is one of the seeds
of apostasy. This is how visualization and other forms of sorcery
are entering the church."[15]

God's Character Attacked

Not only must we be on guard against New Age practices
infiltrating the church, we must be on guard to protect the character of, and reverence for, our God by not using a curriculum
that attacks the true character of God. In the first lesson, which
sets the tone for the entire series, after Daniel has fallen and
broken his arm, Bernie tells the children that "God can't stop
bad things from happening."[16]

This is a lie!

God is all powerful. Tell the Israelites who witnessed the
parting of the Red Sea as God protected His people from Pharaoh's
army (see Exod. 14:13–22) that God cannot stop bad things
from happening. Tell the men who brought their paralyzed friend
to Jesus who healed him (see Luke 5:18–25), that God is not all
powerful. There is story after story from the Bible that demon-
strate the awesome power of our God.

Jeremiah, the prophet, also affirmed the greatness and power
of our God as he prayed, "Ah Lord God! Behold, Thou has made
the heavens and the earth by Thy great power and by Thine outstretched arm! Nothing is too difficult for Thee" (Jer. 32:17). It is

unconscionable that Bernie, representing an angel of God, does not believe God is all powerful. If Bernie does not believe that God is omnipotent, why should the children watching the video?

Bernie is guilty of having little faith in our great God. Since God is the same yesterday, today, and forever (see Heb. 13:8), He has the same power today that He demonstrated in the Old and New Testaments. As the Lord says of Himself in Malachi 3: 6, "I the LORD, do not change."

Perhaps one the greatest affirmations of faith in God and His power was made by Shadrach, Meshach, and Abed-nego:

> If it be so, our God whom we serve is able to deliver us from the furnace of blazing fire; and He will deliver us out of your hand, O king. But even if He does not, let it be known to you, O king, that we are not going to serve your gods or worship the golden image that you have set up. (Dan. 3:17–18)

Shadrach, Meshach, and Abed-nego knew the consequences of not bowing before false gods and worshipping the golden image. They knew that to disobey the king could cost them their lives, but they trusted God. They did not doubt God's power to deliver them, if it be His will. The faith of Shadrach, Meshach, and Abed-nego was succinctly articulated by one pastor who said, "God is God. We cannot presume that God will do anything, but we have faith that God can do everything."[17]

It is obvious that lesson 1 missed the mark. Instead of learning a priceless truth from the Bible, children are more likely to learn that Bernie is an angel obsessed with pizza and God is not all powerful. This is nothing less than a blatant assault on the character of God.

Jesus Replaced

Perhaps one of the most disturbing features of this curriculum is that a make-believe dog-angel replaces Jesus. It is through Bernie that the children learn God's Word, albeit often distorted, and how to apply it to their daily situations. The emphasis of the entire curriculum is wrong! This is just another example of how children are being dumbed down in their knowledge about the Bible. It is only Jesus who can say, "I am the way, and the truth, and the life; no one comes to the Father, but through Me" (John 14:6). It is through Jesus we come to God, not through Bernie the St. Bernard.

At the conclusion of each lesson there are activities and worksheets that center around Bernie. For example, in lesson 1 the children are to draw a picture of Bernie and color it. Then they are to hang it in their room or somewhere they can see it to remind them of God's love and protection.[18] If we are going to stoop to this level of teaching, then why not also write the word *dog* under Bernie's picture so kids can read it backward to remind them of God.

There is even "Bernie's Theme Song" which introduces each video and is listed as an activity for each lesson.

> BERNIE'S THEME SONG The questions of life are tough to figure/But we found a friend, like us, but bigger/He helps when we're caught off guard/Here comes the Gospel According to Saint Bernard./Bernie loves kids like you and me/His doghouse is Florida by the sea./He helps us follow God's plan/When we listen to Bernie/It's never very hard/To love him, he's Bernie/The Saint Bernard.[19]

This song with its catchy little tune points to Bernie as the one children should go to when life gets tough. It is Bernie who loves them and whom the children love. The entire focus is on Bernie. It is a travesty that so much time will be spent learning about Bernie rather than about Jesus, for "No man can lay a foundation other than the one which is laid, which is Jesus Christ" (1 Cor. 3:11). The majority of parents who have children in a Sunday school class want their children to learn about Jesus rather than a make-believe dog-angel. In fact, the emphasis placed on Bernie is idolatry and a violation of the first and second commandment!

Jesus, a Sinner?

Jesus' name is seldom mentioned throughout the entire curriculum. One of those times, however, is in context of questions asked of the children in lesson 5, "The Devil and Macaroni Pizza." The questions are, "Is everyone tempted by the devil? Are your parents? Your minister? Do you think Jesus was ever tempted by the devil?" The suggested teacher's response is, "Yes. Everyone has a time when he hears a little voice that makes him want to do wrong."[20]

According to the teacher's suggested answer, Jesus is placed in the same category as all sinners. The problem with the teacher's answer is that Jesus was perfect and without sin; therefore, He must not be placed in the same category as all sinners. Luke 4:5–8 tells how Jesus was tempted by the devil, but Jesus resisted the devil's temptation to sin. Another critical distinction needs to be made between Jesus and sinners. Jesus never *wanted* to do wrong as implied by the authors. "This would suggest an evil desire or a lustful thought of which He was never guilty."[21] His desire was to be obedient to His Father's will, even unto death (See Phil. 2:8).

In a recent pole taken by George Barna, 28 percent of those claiming to be born-again Christians believe that Jesus, while on earth, committed sins.[22] We cannot help but wonder what they do with the verse, "He made Him who knew no sin to be sin on our behalf" (2 Cor. 5:21). This is the heart of the gospel. Jesus, who was sinless, died for our sins so that all who believe and acknowledge Jesus as their Lord and Savior may be declared righteous and stand holy and blameless before God. The name of Jesus had no business being listed among sinners. One cannot help but speculate why the name of Jesus was not used throughout the curriculum. Bernie continuously referred to God, even though sometimes irreverently. Why did not Bernie also continuously refer to Jesus?

An Angel That Sins

Christians today tend to play down the seriousness of sin. But to a holy, righteous God, sin is an abomination. Bernie, who supposedly was sent by God to help Daniel and Jennifer learn and apply God's Word to their lives, does the unthinkable: Bernie sins.

On one such occasion, Bernie tempts Jennifer to disobey her parents by allowing him to come into the house. It is Jennifer's birthday and Bernie has written her a poem that he wants to read to her. When Bernie asks to come in, Jennifer responds, "You know Mom and Dad don't like you inside. . . . Let me see if Mom and Dad are around." After discovering that her parents are not around, Jennifer lets Bernie in. Bernie shows even more disrespect for house rules when he asks Jennifer, "Do you mind if I sit on the bed?"

Jennifer emphatically answers, "No, I don't mind, but Mom sure would!"[23] Bernie gets on the bed anyway. What a blatant disrespect for authority! How can the child who is viewing this program possibly be expected to obey his parents with an example such as this!

Bernie disregards the house rules established by Mr. and Mrs. Sullivan on other occasions. One of those times is when his doghouse springs a leak during a heavy rainstorm and he sneaks into Daniel's bedroom. The other time is when Daniel, who tricked his mother into letting him stay home from church by feigning illness, goes into the kitchen after everyone leaves and finds Bernie at the table. Bernie, surprised to see Daniel, exclaims, "You're supposed to be in church!"

To which Daniel responds, "And you're supposed to be in the doghouse!"[24]

If there is anything children will understand, it is: Obey your mother and father. It is through learning to obey parents that children learn to obey God. The not-so-subtle message is that if an angel can disobey parents and authority, so can children. Another word for *disobey* is *sin*. By sinning, Bernie has set the stage for moral dilemmas in the hearts and minds of the children who have become card-carrying Bernie Club members.

Tattling on Parents

Yet another example of a moral dilemma used in the curriculum can be found in lesson 7. The suggested activity reads: "Have the children draw someone who didn't tell them the truth. It will probably be a friend or perhaps a parent. Have the children tell why that person probably didn't tell the truth."

This activity puts the child in the difficult position of deciding what to tell the class about whom. A child should never be asked to publicly disclose intimate information about a parent, family member, or friend, particularly in front of their peers. The child's answer to why a parent or a friend did not tell the truth will be purely subjective. A Christian teacher should throw out any question or activity that could damage the bonds of allegiance children have for their parents.

Encouraging children to reveal personal information about their parents is a form of child and family abuse. Putting children in the position of tattling on parents is unconscionable. Evidence indicates that programs and questions that encourage the disclosure of private and sensitive family information may jeopardize a child's respect and loyalty to family members, not unlike the former social climate in the Soviet Union and Nazi Germany. One must ask why such an offensive technique to elicit personal information is being used in the public schools, but more importantly, why is this same technique being used in the church?

Running Away from Home

Throughout *The Gospel According to St. Bernard* there is a subtle, and sometimes not-so-subtle, message that undermines respect for parents and authority in general. In lesson 9 the teacher is instructed to say, "All children want to run away at some time or another or 'want a new family' when things don't go their way. Ask [the children] if they have ever felt this way and what was happening at home."

The stated theme of lesson 9 is for children to obey their parents, but in reality, through the lesson's introduction and following question, the idea is planted in a children's minds to rebel against their parents' authority. Implied is that *all* children have thoughts of running away from home or of wanting a new family because parents are unreasonable, perhaps even unloving. If children have not had those thoughts, the subtle implication is that they are not normal. To ask the question about what was happening at home to make them feel like running away or wanting a new family shows the authors' disrespectful attitude toward the parents of the children in the class. It is irresponsible of the authors to have children entertain negative ideas about their family.

The authors do not stop at planting and entertaining disrespectful thoughts in children's minds about their family, but the authors also list an activity in which the children role-play negative behavior. The activity reads: "Children love to pretend that they are . . . on their own. If possible, set up a tent and have the children imagine that they have run away from home."[25] It is unconscionable for anyone, let alone a Sunday school teacher, to give the false impression that running away from home is fun and games! Not only could this activity have devastating effects on the unity of a family, but it also may put children who act on the idea of running away in grave physical and emotional danger. The world is not a safe place for young children without the love and protection of their parents or guardians.

The Boss

The curriculum authors' position on authority can be found in their own words under "Important Information":

> You will find that children view the Series differently than adults. As an example, adults expect the voice of Bernie to be deep and resonate, but children want to hear a friendly voice that speaks to them on their level, not a voice of authority.[26]

Something is wrong here! How can children be taught to obey their parents if respect for authority is not also being taught? And why should children care what the Bible says and desire to live by its teachings if the Bible is not God's voice of authority?

In the Bernie curriculum, God is referred to as "The Boss" and as "Sir." These words do not command the respect we should have for God. These words are cutesy and an attempt to reflect a sense of humor, but no where in the Bible are they used to address the one true, living God. Should we not be teaching children how to reverently address their Creator, Lord, and Savior? Speech often reflects the attitude of the heart, so we must be careful to guard what kind of ideas and concepts are transmitted by words, because words do have an impact on young impressionable minds.

Role-Play the Devil?

Role-playing was developed in 1948 by Dr. J. L. Moreno, to be used as a technique for the mentally ill. Today, however, this technique is being used on normal, well-adjusted children when they unsuspectingly participate in many of the nonacademic courses promoted in the public school. Incredibly role-playing has now hit the church!

Our first exposure to role-playing introduced us to a book called *Therapeutic Psychology: Fundamentals of Counseling and Psychotherapy.* It states, "Role-playing is a counseling technique often used to help a client gain a better perspective of himself and others. . . . Even when used in a group situation by qualified workers, emphasis should be placed on the fact that many complications can arise if it is not used properly. There can be possible traumatic effects of premature externalizing of threatening material through role-playing."

We also discovered that even B. F. Skinner, the behavioral scientist who studied the effects of positive and negative reinforcement, acknowledged that one should not put people in roles where their positive behavior is not reinforced. Negative role-playing reinforces negative behavior. Therefore, you can imagine how utterly amazed we were to read the following activity in *The Gospel According to St. Bernard*:

> Have each child write down on a piece of paper something that he was really tempted to do. Then put the children in pairs and have one person from each pair draw one of the pieces of paper. Role-play the devil tempting the other person to do what is written on the piece of paper. Discuss how that child "handled" the devil.[27]

It is not difficult to imagine the possible traumatic effects on a child pretending to be the devil.

In Philippians 4:8, we are instructed to focus and discipline our minds to think on whatsoever things are true, honest, pure, lovely, and good. We find it alarming that a "Christian" curriculum would so carelessly expose children to role-play the devil! We cannot imagine a worse character to role-play. Satan is deceitful, arrogant, and rebellious against God. No loving parent would want their child to imitate the devil enticing another child to succumb to a temptation!

The Devil Made Me Do It

Another one of the lesson's suggested activities is to have each child write down on a piece of paper what the word *temptation* means and the slogan "The devil made me do it." Although we should never underestimate the power and the deception of the devil, for he is a formidable enemy, the implication is that the devil is the one who always tempts us to do wrong. Yes, the devil may tempt us, but James 1:4 says, "But each one is tempted when he is carried away and enticed by his own lust." In other words, children must be taught that they cannot always blame the devil when they do something they should not have done. They must be taught to take responsibility for their own disobedience and sin. Once that responsibility has been acknowledged, the sin can be confessed before God; and God, who is faithful, will forgive.

The devil, one of God's fallen angels, is also portrayed as having attributes that neither good or bad angels actually possess. One of the characteristics falsely attributed to the devil is the ability to read a person's thoughts. The following "thought" conversation takes place between Jennifer and the devil as the devil tempts Jennifer to cheat on a test:

JENNIFER: I'm tired of studying.

DEVIL: There's no need to study. Take the easy way. All you have to do is look over Cheryl's shoulder. She's got all the answers, and no one will ever know. Now, go out and play.

JENNIFER: This math is turning my brain into mush.

DEVIL: Why don't you go out to play?

JENNIFER: Because, I'm stuck here studying math. That's why.

DEVIL: Don't be silly. You know you would rather be playing. Besides, I've already told you how to pass that test. You even could get to go to goofy golf.

JENNIFER: But that would be cheating.

DEVIL: No, it wouldn't. It would just be borrowing. Besides, it won't make any difference because no one will know. Now, go on out to play and have a great time.

JENNIFER: Yeah, it would just be borrowing.[28]

The devil cannot read a person's thoughts. Only God knows the thoughts and intentions of the heart (see Heb. 4:12). Only God is omniscient. The devil can place a thought in a person's mind, but he cannot dialog with another person through thoughts. The above episode implies that the devil has more power than he really has. How ironic! This curriculum portrays God as having less power than He actually has and the devil as having more.

Busybody Questions

As mentioned earlier, the public school's "new basics" deal with attitudes, feelings, beliefs, and behavior. The teacher is often put in the role of amateur psychologist when open-ended questions elicit personal information from a child.

A privacy-invading question from the curriculum found in lesson 1 reads, "Tell about something 'bad' that has happened to you." This is an inappropriate question. Children listening will be exposed and subjected to the bad experiences of others. What happens if the bad that happened to one child causes that child or another child to elicit a response of fear or anger? Is the teacher prepared for the extreme range of emotions that may surface? This is clearly outside the role of a Sunday school teacher. Parents do not send their children to Sunday school to have their children exposed to questions and responses that may illicit strong emotions or to hear about the "bad" experiences of other children. Parents also do not expect to have their children answer questions that reveal personal information about themselves or their family.

In lesson 4, other privacy-invasion questions read, "Has anyone ever called you names or said things about you that weren't true? How did you feel?" These are loaded questions. The child is asked to open up and recall unpleasant experiences in front of his peers. These questions are designed to stir up negative emotions and feelings. Needless to say, a typical Sunday school teacher is not trained or prepared to handle the problems that will inevitably surface. Questions may be asked of a child for him to answer privately in his own mind to get him thinking, but, personal questions should not require a public response in front of peers.

Questions can be asked to reinforce a Bible lesson without delving into children's personal beliefs, feelings, and values or eliciting personal information about themselves or other family members. What a child thinks or feels is really irrelevant to the lesson. In fact, if there is a wide range of answers, the lesson will actually be weakened.

It is imperative that parents, Sunday school teachers, pastors, and church leaders learn the difference between an academic question that has a right and wrong answer, and a belief or feeling question that reveals personal information about an individual and his or her family. Then they need to teach children the difference between these two types of questions so children can protect themselves from being emotionally manipulated and exploited by unscrupulous or well-meaning but unknowledgeable individuals. Children need to be instructed not to answer privacy-invasion questions, whether they be in a public school classroom or a Sunday school class.

Twisted Scripture

Perhaps one of the most disturbing lessons in the entire series is lesson 2, "Judge Not!" This is a potentially dangerous lesson because it has taken a biblical truth out of context and wrongly applied a politically correct solution to the situation. The lesson is about the new kids at school, Jason and Amanda. Jason and Amanda are being called dweebs because Amanda, who the kids at school said was fat and ugly, didn't talk to them and Jason showed a marijuana joint around school to the boys to impress them.

The stated Bible truth for this lesson is that "we should not judge other people." The focus of the lesson states, " Children can more easily put aside differences if they learn early to not judge people and to accept them as they are." One has to question the intent of the authors for putting together two very different scenarios to "judge not." To equate a girl who is quiet and unattractive with a boy showing an illegal drug around is not only confusing, but is an example of distorted and twisted reasoning.

As parents, we teach our children not to be critical of or judge another child based upon physical appearance—i.e., weight, color of hair, skin color, etc. On the other hand, we do teach our children not to associate with another child, or anyone for that matter, involved with drugs because drugs are harmful and illegal. We tell our children to judge illegal behavior as wrong! The Bible even takes this idea of judging one step further by commanding us to reprove or correct that which is wrong (see Eph. 5:11).

As moms, we would be upset if someone, especially a Sunday school teacher, told our children that they were to associate with another child of questionable character and that they were not to judge this child's behavior? It is our responsibility as parents to protect our children from harm, and we would hope that Christian curricula and Sunday school teachers would help and support us do the same in this often difficult task

If a classmate showed our twelve-year-old child a marijuana joint on school premises, we would expect our child to avoid that child until adults can take care of the matter. According to Bernie, it is "stupid" to have a marijuana joint, but it is not something to run away from. Bernie's advice goes against Scripture, which says to "abstain from all appearances of evil" (1 Thes. 5:22 KJV). If our children learned Bernie's lesson, our children would think nothing of befriending a kid who was showing marijuana joints around school.

As parents, we tell our children to pick their friends carefully. We want our children to associate with friends who have high standards and live according to biblical principles. Christians are told repeatedly throughout Proverbs to avoid bad company. Proverbs 4:13 states, "Do not enter the path of the wicked, and do not proceed in the way of evil men." Please note, this proverb is not referring to a young girl who is quiet and overweight, but it does refer to a boy would is in possession of an illegal drug. In 1 Corinthians 15:33, we are told, "Do not be deceived: 'Bad company corrupts good morals'"; and 2 Thessalonians 3:6 commands, "Keep aloof from every brother who leads an unruly life."

Toward the end of the video we are told that Jason showed the marijuana joint around because his cousin had told him it would impress the kids. Both the cousin and Jason sound like trouble. They both appear to be followers, who desire the acceptance of their peers over doing the right thing. Distressingly, Daniel and Jennifer were never told by Bernie to tell their parents about the marijuana. Doesn't such a serious matter merit encouraging children to confide in their parents?

It is true that only God can judge the thoughts and intentions of the heart, but we must teach our children to judge truth from error, good from bad, and right from wrong.

Our children must learn to judge bad behavior. We must also teach our children to identify Scripture taken out of context.

New Creatures in Christ

Sometimes a curriculum can look appealing. It is novel and something different. Public schoolteachers have admitted to experimenting with new curriculum because they get bored doing the same thing day after day, year after year. But Sunday school teachers and others must remember that they cannot improve upon the gospel. God's words are life giving and life changing, "for the word of God is living and active" (Heb. 4:12). There are many children who have never heard the gospel's message, so lessons must be consistent Sunday after Sunday, year after year. According to C. H. Spurgeon, those who teach Sunday school are possibly in a more responsible situation than even that of a mininster.

> [The minister] preaches to grown-up people, to men of judgment, who, if they do not like what he preaches, can go somewhere else. But [Sunday school teachers] teach children who have no option of going elsewhere. If you teach the child wrongly, he believes you. If you teach him heresies, he will receive them. What you teach him now, he will never forget.[29]

Even after being befriended and personally taught by a dog-angel, it is interesting to note that Daniel and Jennifer's attitudes and behavior did not improve. They were just as disrespectful at the end of the video series as they were at the beginning. A visit from an authentic angel should have increased Daniel and Jennifer's spiritual longing to seek God with the desire to be obedient to His word. Since they were supposed to have been in the presence of a holy angel, we would have expected their behavior to have become more holy. Such was not the case. But is it any surprise? How can any character-education program have life-changing results without the gospel message and plan of salvation?

It is the change that takes place on the inside once a person has recognized his own sinful nature and the need for a Savior that results in an outward change that can be observed by others. We cannot save ourselves. It is only through the shed blood of Jesus on the cross that we are saved. How can this character curriculum be Christian if there is no confrontation that leads to the conviction of the sinfulness of one's own nature? Teachers must be careful not to imply that morality is the way to salvation, but rather that good behavior and good works are to no avail unless there is a new nature, unless one has become a new creature in Christ.

We are told in Scripture that "God so loved the world, that He gave His only begotten Son, that whoever believes in Him should not perish, but have eternal life" (John 3:16). We are also told that if any man is in Christ, he is a new creature (see 2 Cor. 5:17). Scripture explains that once we become a new creature, Christ lives in us (see Gal. 2:20). This is probably the greatest miracle of all. Jesus Christ is the most important name in all the world. It is Jesus Christ, our Lord and Savior, not Bernie the St. Bernard, who will help us live lives pleasing to God. It is the name of Jesus that saves (see Acts 4:12), not the name of Bernie.

A Formidable Warning

Through the years, we have either personally critiqued or read about many of the controversial, public school curricula currently being used in school districts across America, but we have never read a curriculum more disheartening than *The Gospel According to Saint Bernard*. We reiterate that it is distressing to us that the parties involved in the development and promotion of this curriculum would advertise the Bernie curriculum as "one of the most comprehensive theological and practical Christian courses available to the churches." We shudder to think that Bernies' gospel is the standard we raise to teach Christian character to children in the church!

One cannot help but wonder if our society is already so dumbed down that curriculum developers would actually think Christian parents would accept this dog as part of their family. We also wonder what Jesus would say to the writers of a curriculum who would tell impressionable children to hang a picture of a dog on their wall to remind them of their God?

If we want to raise a generation of children who will worship and respect the God of the universe, we need to keep remembering that we have comparatively little time with our own children and others. How can we expect to impart biblical truth to a child when we depend on the foolishness of the world to inspire character development?

We realize that we have spent considerable time on this character called Bernie, but it is Bernie himself who exposes to us the extent of the deception going on in the name of Christian youth curricula. It is apparent that we live in a time when we can no longer assume that curricula is based on sound doctrine even though it comes with a big name or a Christian label. At least in public school classrooms Christian parents and their children know to be on guard, but in Sunday school classes parents don't expect that their children will also be confronted with ideas that will subtly attack their child's faith.

Parents need to be concerned and alarmed. They can no longer just send their kids off to Sunday school class and trust that the teacher's lesson is based on truth. It is a travesty that this program would be marketed to the churches of America. To a Christian, real character is the result of a real conversion and relationship with Jesus Christ. To imply or to teach children otherwise is to completely miss the mark.

If we continue down the path of today's popular Sunday school curricula it will eventually result in an abandonment of Bible knowledge and Bible truth, ultimately setting up our youth for false teachings and doctrines. John Ankerberg and Craig Branch, *Thieves of Innocence*, also acknowledge that, "When we distance students from the truth, they become more subject to manipulation or false doctrine."[30]

Now more than ever, our children at a young age need to be grounded in the Word of God. Instead, the contemporary church is giving our children a watered-down version of Christianity and following "after the tradition of men, and the rudiments of the world and not after Christ" (Col. 2:8). If we want to correct this dumbing-down trend in Christian youth curricula, then we must get back to the basics—with Jesus as the cornerstone. Jesus inspires real character in children, not a make-believe dog called Bernie. A solid foundation must be built upon God's Word if we want our children to withstand the temptation and deception of the world. Jesus compares withstanding temptation and deception to a house built upon the rock. "I will liken him unto a wise man, which built his house upon a rock. And the rain descended, and the floods came, and the winds blew, and beat upon the house; and it fell not; for it was founded upon the rock" (Matt. 7:24–25).

The *Gospel According to Saint Bernard* cheapens and demeans the God of all creation. This curriculum dishonors God. Rather than modeling godly character traits, a confusing scriptural message is presented. Anyone who writes Christian curricula or teaches little children in church needs to recall the sobering and formidable words of our Lord and Savior, Jesus Christ: "And whoever causes one of these little ones who believe to stumble, it would be better for him if, with a heavy millstone hung around his neck, he had been cast into the sea" (Mark 9:42).

Evaluating Curricula Used in the Church

Examine everything carefully; hold fast to that which is good.
—1 Thess. 5:21

This first checklist is taken from *Child Abuse in the Classroom*. It was designed to help parents evaluate elementary and secondary public school programs and material. Since we have seen the infiltration of the secular into the sacred, these questions are equally valid for programs and material used in the church. The *it* in the following questions represents a curriculum, a teacher's manual, a film, a workbook, or extra-curricular activities.

1. Is it antiparent? Does it lead the child to believe that parents are ignorant, old-fashioned, or out of touch with the modern world?
2. Does it suggest that the child not tell his parent what he is taught in class?
3. Does it encourage the child to seek advice from organizations or adults other than his parents (such as Planned Parenthood or a teen clinic)?

4. Does it present information that depresses the child, leads him to a negative view of himself, his family, his country, or his future? Does it produce fear, guilt, and despair in the child?

5. Is it preoccupied with death and tragedy? Does it encourage the child to dwell on unhappy or tragic events, or foster bad feelings such as hate, anger, and revenge? Does it require the child to write morbid exercises, such as his own epitaph or a description of the last death in the child's family?

6. Is it antiparent and antireligion by leading the child to reject the moral standards and values he has been taught in home and church? Does it lead the child to believe that there are no absolute moral standards, but that the morality of an act depends on the situation?

7. Does it present courses about sex, suicide, alcohol, or illegal drugs in such a way as to encourage experimentation? Does it desensitize the child to the use of gutter language?

8. Does it use pre- and posttesting to measure attitudinal change?

9. Does it lead the child to believe that religion is unimportant or out of date?

10. Does it affirmatively teach the ideology of secular humanism or that all religions are equally valid? Does it constantly question values, standards, and authority and teach that all moral decisions and lifestyles are equally to be respected?

11. Does it attack the child's religious faith by ridiculing the belief that God created the earth? Does it spend class time on such antireligious elements as the occult, witchcraft, or astrology?

12. Does it force the child to make choices in hypothetical situations that require him to decide if it is all right to lie, cheat, steal, kill, have sex outside of marriage, have an abortion, or commit suicide. Does it pose hypotheti-

cal dilemmas that upset the child's moral values taught in the home and induce him to seek the approval of his peers?

13. Does it spend class time on lessons, exercises, and questions about feelings and attitudes, rather than teaching knowledge, facts, and traditional basic skills?

14. Does it force the child to play psychological games in class (such as Survival, Magic Circle, or Dungeons and Dragons)?

15. Does it force the child to answer questionnaires or surveys that probe into the child's or his family's attitudes, feelings, behavior, customs, or political preferences—all of which invade the family's privacy and are none of the school's business?

16. Does it force the child to engage in role-playing of sociopolitical situations or unhappy personal problems caused by divorce, premarital sex, pregnancy, or VD?

17. Does it force the child to write journals, diaries, or compositions that require the child to reveal private family information or relive unhappy events?

18. Does it require classroom discussion of personal and private matters that embarrass the child in front of his peers?

19. Does it force the child to confront adult problems that are too complex and unsuitable for his tender years, such as nuclear war?

20. Does it blur traditional concepts of gender identity and force the child to accept the radical notion of a gender-free society in which there are no differences in attitudes and occupations between men and women? Does it induce role reversals by showing women in hard physical-labor jobs and men as house-husbands?

To the preceding checklist we have included additional questions to help parents, Sunday school teachers, youth pastors, and anyone involved in ministry to youth, evaluate curricula for its biblical content and methods. Once again, the *it* in the following questions represent a curriculum, a teacher's manual, a film, a workbook, or suggested activities. The following list is not conclusive.

1. Does it teach that the Bible is the inerrant Word of God, or does it subtly undermine that Scripture must be added to in order to be relevant in meeting an individual's deep and personal needs.

2. Does it teach that God is sovereign—all powerful, all knowing, and ever present—or does it subtly imply that God is weak and unable to intervene in the lives of His people?

3. Does it teach children to reverently address their Creator, Lord, and Savior? Does it cause teens to seek fellowship with God in awe and holy reverence and not casual familiarity?

4. Does it teach children to honor and obey their parents, or does it subtly attack a parent's God-ordained right to act as the authority over the lives of their children?

5. Does it promote truth as an absolute for all people for all time, or does it promote a relativistic mindset in which any belief and opinion is accepted or tolerated? Is there a clear demarcation between truth and error and right and wrong, or is every value, belief, or opinion acknowledged as equally valid and authoritative? Does the teacher's instructions imply that teachers are not to correct wrong answers given during class time?

6. Is it Christ-centered or self-centered?

7. Does it teach that we are all sinners and in need of a savior, or does it assume that human nature is intrinsically good? Is there a clear presentation of the gospel message?

8. Does it teach and encourage youth to diligently seek God and His righteousness? Does it encourage a pursuit for holiness, or does it emphasize relationships with others

and a nonjudgmental acceptance regardless of behavior and attitudes?

9. Is Scripture accurately presented or is Scripture "tweaked" in an attempt to be clever or relevant? Is there a tendency to modify the gospel to suit various age groups?

10. Does it teach the sufficiency of Scripture, or does it imply that contrived, simulated experiences are a viable medium to impart biblical truth and understand God?

11. Is active learning (teaching through experiences) considered by the author to be life changing and more relevant to the student than the Word of God?

12. Does it teach that feelings and personal experiences are subjective and unreliable and therefore cannot be trusted, or does it subtly teach that one *can* rely on his emotions and experiences to grow in his faith?

13. Does it teach individual responsibility before God, or is it fostering a group mentality? Does it imply directly or indirectly that growth in Christ is contingent upon the cohesiveness of the group? Are buzzwords such as *community building, bond building, group dynamics,* and *team building* being used?

14. Is humility taught as a virtue and its practice encouraged, or is self-esteem motivated through exercises that elicit praise from peers and public recognition?

15. Is there importance placed upon Scripture memorization, or is learning Scripture replaced with "learning from relationships"?

16. Does it attempt to entertain and amuse at the expense of pursuing knowledge of, and reverence for, our holy God?

17. Is the youth leader instructed to view himself as the facilitator of youth group discussion rather than an authoritative teacher who imparts biblical truth to his students? Does the youth leader depend upon peer teaching, under the false premise that teens learn best from other teens.

18. Does it rely on the teaching methods and techniques of secular nonacademic curricula (i.e., drug and sex education), such as values clarification, sensitivity training, moral dilemmas training, and negative role-playing?
19. Does it teach respect and submission to authority, or does it encourage the child to become his own authority? Is personal interpretation of Scripture encouraged through "I think" and "I feel" questions?
20. Does it encourage authentic fellowship centered around the Word of God, or does it manipulate a climate in which self-disclosure is coerced?

Endnotes

Preface
1. *The Humanist Manifesto* (Buffalo, NY: Prometheus Books, 1973), 9.
2. D. M. Lloyd-Jones, *Knowing the Times* (Carlisle, PA: Banner of Trust, 1989), 60.

Chapter 1: *But I Don't Like Licorice!*
1. Thomas Sowell, *Inside American Education: The Decline, the Deception, the Dogmas* (New York: The Free Press, 1993), 34.
2. *Child Abuse in the Classroom,* Phyllis Schlafy, ed., excerpts from Official Transcript of Proceedings before the US Department of Education (Westchester, IL: Crossway Books, 1985), 13.
3. John MacArthur Jr., *Our Sufficiency in Christ* (Dallas: Word Publishing, 1991), front cover.
4. Youth Specialties, *High School Talk Sheets: 50 Creative Discussions for High School Youth Groups* (Grand Rapids, MI: Zondervan Publishing House, 1987), 9.
5. Ibid.
6. Thom and Joani Schultz, *Why Nobody Learns Much of Anything at Church: And How to Fix It* (Loveland, CO: Group Publishing, Inc., 1993), 111.
7. Ibid., 108.
8. *The Word on the New Testament: Youth Builders Group Bible Studies,* Jim Burns, ed. (Cincinnati, OH: Gospel Light, 1977), 12.
9. Ibid., 65.
10. *Case Studies, Talk Sheets and Discussion Starters,* Jim Burns, gen. ed. (Cincinnati, OH: Gospel Light, 1977), 103.
11. *The Word on the New Testament,* 161.
12. Denny Rydberg, *Trust Builders: 71 Activities to Develop Community in Your Youth Group* (Loveland, CO: Group Publishing, Inc., 1993), 78.

13. Sidney B. Simon and others, *Values Clarification: A Handbook of Practical Strategies for Teachers and Students* (New York: Hart Publishing, 1972), 311–13.

14. Rick Wesselhoff, *Extreme: A Real, Live Look at the Forerunners* (Colorado Springs, CO: David C. Cook Publishing, 1996), 6.

15. Lois Keffer, *Sunday School Specials: Quick and Easy Bible Lessons for Combined Ages* (Loveland, CO: Group Publishing, Inc., 1992) 65–67.

16. Ibid., 8.

17. Ibid., 7; *Case Studies, Talk Sheets and Discussion Starters,* back cover.

18. Lois Keffer, *Sunday School Specials: Quick and Easy Bible Lessons for Combined Ages* (Loveland, CO: Group Publishing, Inc., 1992), 93.

19. The Covenant Syndicate, *The Deweese Report* (Herndon, VA: July 1998), 6. Used by permission.

20. *Angels Sent on Assignment* video series (Loveland, CO: Group Publishing, Inc.), information labeled "Important: Read This," 3.

21. *Jesus: The Main Attraction* (Loveland, CO: Group Publishing, Inc., 1997), 27.

22. Ibid., 28.

23. *Why Nobody Learns Much of Anything at Church,* 12.

Chapter 2: *Gimmicks, Fads, and Mind Games*

1. Martin and Deidre Bobgan, *Psycho Heresy: The Psychological Seduction of Christianity* (Santa Barbara, CA: Eastgate Publishers, 1987), 77.

2. According to Dr. W. R. Coulson, founder of the Research Council on Ethnopsychology, Maslow used quotation marks around the word *higher,* suggesting not only a social scientist's timidity about value-laden terms, but also the tentative nature of his hierarchical theory of needs. The theory remained tentative and subject to revision the rest of his life, but many educators have taken it as an absolute.

3. *Psycho Heresy,* 77.

4. Jay E. Adams, *The Biblical View of Self-Esteem, Self-Love, Self-Image* (Eugene, OR: Harvest House Publishers, 1986), 32.

5. Ibid., 34.

6. Jay E. Adams, *Competent to Counsel* (Grand Rapids, MI: Zondervan Publishing House, 1970), 82–83.

7. Testimony of Malcom Lawrence, *Child Abuse in the Classroom,* Phyllis Schlafy, ed. (Westchester, IL: Crossway Books, 1985), 389.

8. W. R. Coulson, excerpts from the manuscript *Psychology of a Very Bad Dream* (San Diego, CA: Center for Enterprising Families, 1989), 2d ed., 7.

9. W. R. Coulson, excerpts from the manuscript *Memorandum to the Federal Drug Education Curricula Panel,* April 23, 1988; 3.

10. W. R. Coulson, "Focus: Classroom Courses Promote Drugs and Sex," *Education Reporter,* June 1988, 3.

11. *Memorandum to Federal Drug Education Curricula Panel,* 2.

12. Reported in the newsletter of the Association for Humanistic Psychology, special issue, Fall 1981, 11.
13. Roberts, Fitzmahan, and associates, *Here's Looking at You Two* (Seattle, WA: 1985) 39–42. A version of this secular activity can be found in *The Word on the New Testament* (Gospel Light, 1977), 102.
14. Johnson and Johnson, *Basic Elements of Cooperative Learning*, information page.
15. John Dewey as quoted by John A. Stormer, *None Dare Call It Education* (Florissant, MO: Liberty Bell Press, 1998), 36.
16. Thom and Joani Schultz, *Why Nobody Learns Much of Anything at Church: And How to Fix It* (Loveland, CO: Group Publishing, Inc., 1993), 151.
17. Ibid., 141.
18. Denny Rydberg, *Building Community in Youth Groups* (Loveland, CO: Group Publishing, Inc., 1985), 22.
19. Denny Rydberg, *Trust Builders: 71 Activities to Develop Community in Your Youth Group* (Loveland, CO: Group Publishing, Inc., 1993), 116.
20. *Building Community in Youth Groups*, 134.
21. Ibid., 135.
22. Jeffrey Shrank, *Teaching Human Beings: 101 Subversive Activities for the Classroom* (Boston: Beacon Press, 1972), 153.
23. *Sensitivity Training and Group Encounter: An Introduction*, Robert W. Siroka, Ellen K. Siroka, and Gilbert A. Schloss, eds. (New York: Grosset & Dunlap, 1971), synopsis on back cover.
24. Ibid., vii.
25. Carl Rogers, quoted by W. R. Coulson in the manuscript *Psychology of a Very Bad Dream*, 4.
26. *Carl Rogers on Encounter Groups* (New York: Harper & Row, 1970), 5.
27. William K. Kilpatrick, *Psychological Seduction: The Failure of Modern Psychology* (Nashville, TN: Thomas Nelson Publishers, 1983), 23.
28. C. H. Spurgeon, *Spiritual Parenting* (Springdale, PA: Whitaker House, 1995), 37.
29. Ibid., 113.
30. Scott Ardavanis, sermon on the Epistle to Titus: Titus, 2:6–8 (Wheaton, IL: Grace Ministries, May 31, 1998).

Chapter 3: It Is a Duck

1. *Carl Rogers on Encounter Groups* (New York: Harper & Row, 1970), 7.
2. Carl Rogers, *On Becoming a Person: A Therapist's View of Psychotherapy* (Boston: Houghton Mifflin Company, 1961), 114.
3. W. R. Coulson, *Principled Morality vs. Consequentialism* (San Diego, CA: Research Council on Ethnopsychology, 1987), 1.
4. *Carl Rogers on Encounter Groups*, 8–9.
5. Lyman Coleman, *Hassles: Problems That Hit Home* (Littleton, CO: Serendipity House, 1994), 46.

6. Denny Rydberg, *Trust Builders: 71 Activities to Develop Community in Your Youth Group* (Loveland, CO: Group Publishing, Inc., 1993), 9, 13.

7. Youth Specialties, *High School Talksheets: 50 Creative Discussions for High School Youth Groups* (Grand Rapids, MI: Zondervan Publishing House, 1987), 9.

8. *Trust Builders,* 11.

9. *Youth Elective Sampler* (Colorado Springs, CO: David C. Cook Publishing, 1994), 78.

10. *Carl Rogers on Encounter Groups,* 11.

11. *Trust Builders,* 12–13.

12. *High School Talksheets,* 8–11.

13. *Hassles,* back cover.

14. *On Becoming a Person,* 34.

15. Ibid., 21.

16. *Trust Builders,* 12.

17. Ibid., 56.

18. *Hassles,* 46.

19. *High School Talksheets,* 9.

20. *Carl Rogers on Encounter Groups,* 29.

21. *Trust Builders,* 96.

22. *High School Talksheets,* 8–9.

23. *On Becoming a Person,* 23–24.

24. Ibid., 27.

25. *Why Jesus Christ Matters,* Core Belief Series (Loveland, CO: Group Publishing, Inc., 1997), 57.

26. Ibid., 59.

27. *Hassles,* 46.

28. *The Encyclopedia of Education,* Lee C. Deighton, ed. (The MacMillan Co. and the Free Press, 1971), vol. 3, 199.

29. *Handbook of Educational Psychology,* David C. Berliner and Rodbert C. Calfee, eds. (New York: Macmillan Library Reference USA, Simon & Schuster Macmillan; London: Prentice Hall International, 1996), 3.

30. *Carl Rogers on Encounter Groups,* 6.

31. *Hassles,* 6.

32. D. M. Lloyd-Jones, *Knowing the Times* (Carlisle, PA: The Banner of Truth, 1989), 321.

33. Ibid., 320.

34. W. R. Coulson, "Let's Go Roller-Skating for Christ! An Article on Group Dynamics" in *The Living Light: A Christian Education Review,* Mary Perkins Ryan, ed.; vol. 5, no. 2, Summer 1968.

35. *Knowing the Times,* 28.

36. Martin and Deidre Bobgan, *Psycho Heresy Awareness Letter,* November/December 1997, vol. 5, no. 6, p. 1.

37. Martin and Deidre Bobgan, *Competent to Minister: The Biblical Care of Souls* (Santa Barbara, CA: Eastgate Publishers, 1996), 19–20. They quote

P. Sutherland and P. Poelstra from their paper entitled "Aspects of Integration" presented at the meeting of the Christian Association for Psychological Studies, Santa Barbara, CA, June 1976.

38. *Trust Builders*, 7.

39. W. R. Coulson, "Does Therapy Belong in the Classroom?" *Education Reporter* (Alton, IL: Eagle Forum Education & Defense Fund, November 1987), 3.

40. W. R. Coulson, personal communication, November 2, 1994.

41. Carl Rogers, tape recorded in La Jolla, CA, on July 19, 1976.

42. Ibid.

43. W. R. Coulson, personal communication, November 2, 1994.

44. Carl Rogers, quoted by Pearl Evans in *Hidden Danger in the Classroom* (Petsluma, CA: Small Helm Press, 1990), 44.

45. William K. Kilpatrick, *Psychological Seduction: The Failure of Modern Psychology* (Nashville, TN: Thomas Nelson Publishers, 1983), 100.

46. Ibid., 15.

47. Ibid., 100–01.

48. Michael S. Horton, *In the Face of God: The Dangers and Delights of Spiritual Intimacy* (Dallas: Word Publishing, 1996), 134.

Chapter 4: *More Child Abuse in the Classroom*

1. W. R. Coulson, personal communication, November 2, 1994.

2. Paul Kelly, *Psalms*, Active Bible Curriculum series (Loveland, CO: Group Publishing, Inc., 1993), 13.

3. A. W. Tozer, *Tragedy in the Church: The Missing Gifts*, Gerald B. Smith, ed. (Camp Hill, PA: Christian Publications, 1990), 32.

4. John Ankerberg with John Weldon and Craig Branch, *Thieves of Innocence* (Eugene, OR: Harvest House, 1993), 187. *Newsweek* cover article, February 17, 1992; 46–47.

5. *U.S. News & World Report*, April 1, 1990; 16.

6. Denny Rydberg, *Trust Builders: 71 Activities to Develop Community in Your Youth Group* (Loveland, CO: Group Publishing, Inc. 1993), 87.

7. William K. Kilpatrick, *Psychological Seduction: The Failure of Modern Psychology* (Nashville, TN: Thomas Nelson Publishers, 1983), 58.

8. *Trust Builders*, 63.

9. Thomas P. Miller, quoted by Mel and Norma Gabler, *Educational Research Analyst's Handbook* (Longview, TX: The Mel Gablers, 1985).

10. Carl Rogers, quoted by Mel and Norma Gabler, *Educational Research Analyst's Handbook*, B-5, 1.

11. Lyman Coleman, *Hassles: Problems That Hit Home* (Littleton, CO: Serendipity House, 1994), 4.

12. *Psalms*, Active Bible Curriculum series, 7.

13. *Trust Builders*, 60.

14. Sidney B. Simon, Sally Wendkos Olds, *Helping Your Child Learn Right from Wrong: A Guide to Values Clarification* (New York: Simon and Schuster,

1976), 32–33.

15. *Trust Builders*, 61.

16. *Educational Research Analysis Handbook*, B-5, 2.

17. Beth Copeland, "Fitting In," *Why the Church Matters* (Loveland, CO: Group Publishing, Inc., 1998), 27–29.

18. *Hassles*, 6.

19. Rick Wesselhoff, *Extreme: A Real Live Look at the Forerunners*, Bring 'em Back Alive! series (Colorado Springs, CO: David C. Cook Publishing, 1996), 4.

20. Pearson and Campbell, *Just Look at You!* (Colorado Springs, CO: David C. Cook Publishing, 1994), 38.

21. William K. Kilpatrick, *Psychological Seduction: The Failure of Modern Psychology* (Nashville, TN: Thomas Nelson Publishers, 1983), 113.

22. *Trust Builders*, 135.

23. *Youth Elective Sampler* (Colorado Springs, CO: David C. Cook Publishing, 1994), 58.

24. *Psychological Seduction*, 111.

25. Thomas Sowell, *Inside American Education* (New York: The Free Press, 1993), 65–66.

26. *Youth Elective Sampler*, 58.

27. *Youth Elective Sampler*, 60.

28. W. R. Coulson, *Groups, Gimmicks and Instant Gurus* (New York: Harper & Row, 1972), 53.

29. *Youth Elective Sampler*, 55.

30. Kurt Bickel, *Getting Along with Parents* (Loveland, CO: Group Publishing, Inc., 1990), 11.

31. Ibid., 24.

32. Ibid., 33, 15, 20.

33. Ibid., 35.

34. Paul S. Beck, pastor of Calvary Bible Church, Huntsville, AL; personal communication, June 1998.

35. *Psychological Seduction*, 27.

36. *Psychological Seduction*, 127.

37. *Getting Along with Parents*, 17.

38. W. R. Coulson, *Memorandum to Federal Drug Education Panel*; April 23, 1988; 12.

39. Ibid.

40. *Youth Elective Sampler*, 59.

41. Ravi Zacharias, *Deliver Us from Evil: Restoring the Soul in a Disintegrating Culture* (USA: Word), 66.

42. Martin Luther as quoted by Michael S. Horton, "Recovering the Plumb Line" in *The Coming Evangelical Crisis: Current Challenges to the Authority of Scripture and the Gospel*, John H. Armstrong, ed. (Chicago: Moody, 1996), 247.

43. "Recovering the Plumb Line," 247.

44. See A. H. Maslow; Journal entry of January 6, 1969, in *The Journals of A. H. Maslow*, Richard J. Lowry, ed. (Monterey, CA: Brooks/Cole Publishing Company, 1979), 1158.
45. W. R. Coulson, radio interview on *Help for Life*, KNTR, Bellington, WA, October 26, 1989.
46. *Youth Elective Sampler*, 61.
47. Jeffrey Schrank, *Teaching Human Beings: 101 Subversive Activities for the Classroom* (Boston: Beacon Press, 1972), 46.
48. Gil Rugh, *Psychology: The Trojan Horse* (Lincoln, NE: Indian Hills Community Church, 1995), 8.
49. *Tragedy in the Church*, 74.

Chapter 5: *Judge Not! Tolerating Tolerance*

1. Paul S. Beck, pastor of Calvary Bible Church, Huntsville, AL; personal communication.
2. D. M. Lloyd-Jones, *Knowing the Times* (Carlisle, PA: Banner of Trust, 1989), 39.
3. Denny Rydberg, *Trust Builders: 71 Activities to Develop Community in Your Youth Group* (Loveland, CO: Group Publishing, Inc., 1993), 56.
4. Denny Rydberg, *Building Community in Youth Groups* (Loveland, CO: Group Publishing, Inc., 1985), 23.
5. W. R. Coulson, Memorandum to the Federal Drug Education Curricula Panel, April 23, 1988; 1.
6. Ibid.
7. Lyman Coleman, *Hassles: Problems That Hit Home* (Littleton, CO: Serendipity House, 1994), 46.
8. Richard A. Bauer Jr., quoted by Carl Sommer, *Schools in Crisis: Training for Success or Failure* (Houston, TX: Cahill Publishing Co., 1984), 212.
9. Thomas Sowell, *Inside American Education: The Decline, the Deception, the Dogmas* (New York: The Free Press, 1993), 65.
10. *Hassles*, 6.
11. Paul C. Vitz, *Psychology as Religion: The Cult of Self-Worship*, 2d ed. (Grand Rapids, MI: William B. Eerdmans Publishing Co., 1994), 77.
12. Dave Hunt & T. A. McMahon, *The Seduction of Christianity: Spiritual Discernment in the Last Days* (Eugene, OR: Harvest House Publishers, 1985), 85.
13. W. R. Coulson, remarks prepared for a conference on love, life, and the family; 1.
14. *Why Jesus Christ Matters*, Core Belief Series (Loveland, CO: Group Publishing, Inc., 1997), 59.
15. Youth Specialties, *High School Talksheets: 50 Creative Discussions for High School Youth Groups* (Grand Rapids, MI: Zondervan Publishing House, 1987), 9.
16. Sidney B. Simon and Sally Wendkos Olds, *Helping Your Child Learn Right from Wrong: A Guide to Values Clarification* (New York: Simon and Schuster,

1976), 43–44.

17. Ibid., 17.

18. Richard A. Baer Jr., "Parents, Schools and Values Clarification," *The Wall Street Journal*, April, 12, 1982.

19. Sidney B. Simon and others, *Values Clarification: A Handbook of Practical Strategies for Teachers and Students* (New York: Hart Publishing, 1972), 16.

20. W. R. Coulson, *Principled Morality vs. Consequentialism* (San Diego, CA: Research Council on Ethnopsychology, 1987), 2.

21. *High School Talksheets*, 7–8.

22. *Helping Your Child Learn Right from Wrong*, 45.

23. Ibid., 197–98.

24. William K. Kilpatrick, *Psychological Seduction: The Failure of Modern Psychology* (Nashville, TN: Thomas Nelson Publishers, 1993), 178.

25. *The Gospel According to St. Bernard,* compiled and edited by the Zig Ziglar Corporation (Plantation, FL: Christian Video Enterprises, Inc. 1992), lesson 2, "Judge Not!"

26. Carl Rogers, *On Becoming a Person: A Therapist's View of Psychotherapy* (Boston: Houghton Mifflin Company, 1961), 115.

27. *Helping Your Child Learn Right from Wrong*, 59.

28. John Dutshall and Mikal Keefer, *Why God's Church Matters* (Loveland, CO: Group Publishing, Inc., 1998), 21.

29. Ibid., 19.

30. Jane Vogel, *Why God's Justice Matters,* "For His Eyes Only" (Loveland, CO: Group Publishing, Inc., 1997), 35.

31. John F. MacArthur, *Reckless Faith: When the Church Loses Its Will to Discern* (Wheaton, IL: Crossway Books, 1994), 51.

32. Ibid., 22.

33. Os Guinness, *Fit Bodies, Fat Minds: Why Evangelicals Don't Think and What to do about It* (Grand Rapids, MI: Baker Books, 1994), 52.

34. G. K. Chesterton, quoted by Os Guinness, *Fit Bodies, Fat Minds,* 52.

35. *Knowing the Times*, 43.

36. Paul S. Beck, personal communication.

37. Gary L. Johnson, "Does Theology Still Matter?" in *The Coming Evangelical Crisis,* John H. Armstrong, ed. (Chicago: Moody Press, 1996), 66–67

38. William Secker as quoted by R. C. Sproul, "Only One Gospel" in *The Coming Evangelical Crisis,* John H. Armstrong, ed., 113.

39. *Reckless Faith*, 82–83.

40. Ibid., 52.

Chapter 6: *A Pseudo and Reckless Faith*

1. The trust walk is found in (1) David C. Cook's *Youth Selective Sampler,* taken from SNAP Sessions, 43; (2) David C. Cook's Bring 'em Back Alive series *Extreme: A Real Live Look at the Forerunners,* 10; (3) Group Publishing's Core Belief Series *Why Jesus Christ Matters,* 58; (4) Group

Publishing's Active Bible Curriculum *Getting Along with Parents*, 28; (5) Group Publishing's VBS curriculum *Wild Frontier Park and Bible Theme Park: Leaders Guide for Rides and Games*, day 3; (6) Denny Rydberg's *Trust Builders*, 32; *Building Community in Youth Groups*, 54; (7) David Lynn, *Talk Sheets* (Grand Rapids, MI: Zondervan Publishing House, 1987), 76; (8) *The Word on the New Testament: Youth Builders Group Bible Studies*, (Gospel Light, 1996), 61; (9) Wayne Rice and others, *New Directions for Youth Ministry* (Loveland, CO: Group Publishing, Inc., 1998), 37.

2. Jeffrey Schrank, *Teaching Human Beings: 101 Subversive Activities for the Classroom* (Boston: Beacon Press, 1972), xii.

3. Ibid.

4. *Teaching Human Beings*, 156.

5. Quoted in *Carl Rogers on Encounter Groups* (New York: Harper & Row, 1970), 61.

6. Questions were taken from a personal communication from a Christian youth leader who asked these questions of her youth group following the trust-walk exercise. These questions parallel those from secular texts.

7. *Carl Rogers on Encounter Groups*, 8.

8. Personal communication with a Christian youth group leader.

9. Dr. W. R. Coulson, personal communication, February 1997.

10. Lesson plan for trust walk from Christian youth leader.

11. Dr. W. R. Coulson, personal communication, March 1997.

12. Lesson plan for trust walk from Christian youth leader.

13. Dr. W. R. Coulson, personal communication, March 1997.

14. D. M. Lloyd-Jones, *Knowing the Times* (Carlisle, PA: Banner of Trust, 1989), 3.

15. Ibid.

16. Ibid., 6.

17. RTS, "Williams Reaches Out in Reconciliation," *Reformed Quarterly*, Summer 1997, 16. Article featured games played at a Young Life Camp at Lake Champion, NY.

18. Denny Rydberg, *Building Community in Youth Groups* (Loveland, CO: Group Publishing, Inc., 1985), 17.

19. Dr. W. R. Coulson, personal communication, March 1997.

20. Carl Rogers, quoted by Dr. W. R. Coulson, *The Active Listening Hoax: Affective Education and the Decline of Literacy* (San Diego, CA: A Publication of the Research Council on Ethnopsychology, 1990), 10.

21. Paul Kelly, *Psalms* (Loveland, CO: Group Publishing, Inc.), 27. A variation of this exercise is also found in Denny Rydberg's *Building Community in Youth Groups*, 87.

22. Stephen Parolini, *Why Jesus Christ Matters* (Loveland, CO: Group Publishing, Inc., 1997), 28.

23. Denny Rydberg, *Trust Builders: 71 Activities to Develop Community in Your Youth Group* (Loveland, CO: Group Publishing, Inc., 1993), 20.

24. *Building Community in Youth Groups*, 42.

25. Lyman Coleman, *Hassles: Problems That Hit Home* (Littleton, CO: Serendipity House, 1994), 39. This activity is also promoted by secular humanist Jeffrey Shrank in *Teaching Human Being*. Looking face to face is a common component of sense education.

26. W. R. Coulson, *Groups, Gimmicks and Instant Gurus* (New York: Harper & Row, 1972), 55.

27. W. R. Coulson, personal communication, March 1997.

28. *Groups, Gimmicks and Instant Gurus*, 49.

29. Ibid., 51.

30. Ibid., 53.

31. *Knowing the Times*, 25.

32. Andrew Murray, *A Heritage of Great Evangelical Teaching*, "All You Who Have Come to Him," (Nashville, TN: Thomas Nelson Publishers, 1988), 653.

33. *Psychological Seduction*, 180.

34. Paul S. Beck, "The Just Shall Live by Faith," sermon on the Book of Habakkuk given at Rome Community Bible Church, Bellingham, WA, July 12, 1994.

35. *Trust Builders*, 13.

36. John F. MacArthur, *Reckless Faith: When the Church Loses Its Will to Discern* (Wheaton, IL: Crossway Books, 1994), xiii.

37. Paul Little, *Know Why You Believe: A Clear Affirmation of the Reasonableness of the Christian Faith* (Wheaton, IL: Victor Books, 1987), 19.

38. David Barton, *The Myth of Separation* (Aledo, TX: WallBuilder Press, 1992), 32.

39. Reachout Expeditions, brochure, 7.

40. Ibid.

41. Personal correspondence with a mother whose son participated in this activity.

42. Personal communication with Gary Small, pastor, Liberty Fundamental Baptist Church, Lynden, WA, March 30, 1998.

43. A. W. Tozer, *The Divine Conquest: God's Pursuit of Man* (Camp Hill, PA: Christian Publications, 1950), 79.

44. A. W. Tozer, *Whatever Happened to Worship?* (Camp Hill: PA: Christian Publications, 1985), 86.

45. A. W. Tozer, *This World: Playground or Battlefield*, Harry Verploegh, ed. (Camp Hill, PA: Christian Publications, 1989), 104.

Chapter 7: Idolatry of Self-Worship

1. Jay E. Adams, *The Biblical View of Self-Esteem, Self-Love, Self-Image* (Eugene, OR: Harvest House Publishers, 1986), 28.

2. Darrell Pearson and Stan Campbell, *Just Look at You* (Elgin, IL: David C. Cook Publishing, 1994), 9.

3. Ibid., 21.

4. A. W. Tozer, *The Divine Conquest: God's Pursuit of Man* (Camp Hill, PA: Christian Publications, 1950; renewed 1978, Lowell Tozer), 39.
5. Paul C. Vitz, *Psychology as Religion: The Cult of Self-Worship*, 2d ed. (Grand Rapids, MI: William B. Eerdmans Publishing Co., 1994), 91.
6. *Just Look at You!*, 29.
7. Ibid., 28.
8. Ibid., 36.
9. Ibid., 9.
10. Paul S. Beck, pastor of Calvary Bible Church, Huntsville, AL, personal communication, June 1998.
11. Dave Hunt and T. A. McMahon, *The Seduction of Christianity: Spiritual Discernment in the Last Days* (Eugene, OR: Harvest House Publishers, 1985), 200.
12. David Powlison and others, *Power Religion: The Selling Out of the Evangelical Church*, Michael S. Horton, ed. (Chicago: Moody Press, 1992), "Integration or Inundation?" 209.
13. Ibid.
14. A. W. Tozer, *This World: Playground or Battleground?* Harry Verploegh, ed. (Camp Hill, PA: Christian Publications, 1989), 34–35.
15. Ibid., 35.
16. *Just Look at You!*, 24.
17. Paul S. Beck, personal communication, June 1998.
18. *The Biblical View of Self-Esteem*, 104.
19. Ibid., 104–05.
20. William K. Kilpatrick, *Psychological Seduction: The Failure of Modern Psychology* (Nashville, TN: Thomas Nelson Publishers, 1983), 43.
21. Michael S. Horton, *In the Face of God: The Dangers and Delights of Spiritual Intimacy* (Dallas: Word Publishing, 1996), 26.
22. A. W. Tozer, quoted by Paul E. Little in *Know What You Believe: A Practical Discussion of the Fundamentals of the Christian Faith* (Wheaton, IL: Victor Books, 1989), 22.
23. Ibid.
24. John F. MacArthur, *Reckless Faith: When the Church Loses Its Will to Discern* (Wheaton, IL: Crossway Books, 1994), 82.
25. Carl Rogers, *On Becoming a Person: A Therapist's View of Psychotherapy* (Boston: Houghton Mifflin Company, 1961), 111–13.
26. Carl Rogers, *A Way of Being* (Boston: Houghton Mifflin Company, 1980), 177.
27. Denny Rydberg, *Trust Builders: 71 Activities to Develop Community in Your Youth Group* (Loveland, CO: Group Publishing, Inc. 1993),, 18.
28. *Psychological Seduction*, 146.
29. Denny Rydberg, *Building Community in Youth Groups* (Loveland, CO: Group Publishing, Inc., 1985), 80.
30. Martin and Deidre Bobgan, *Psycho Heresy: the Psychological Seduction of Christianity* (Santa Barbara, CA: Eastgate Publishers, 1987), 61.

31. *The Divine Conquest*, 36.
32. *Psychological Seduction*, 39.
33. Andrew Murray, *Humility* (Springdale, PA: Whitaker House, 1982), 12.
34. Ibid., 59.
35. Ibid., 69.
36. Charles H. Spurgeon, *Morning and Evening* (USA: Hendrickson Publishers, Inc., 1995), 360.
37. *Power Religion*, 209.
38. *The Biblical View of Self-Esteem, Self-Love, Self-Image*, 90–91.
39. Ibid., 101.
40. Ibid., 94.
41. *Humility*, 19.
42. *In the Face of God*
43. Charles H. Spurgeon, *Morning and Evening* (USA: Hendrickson Publishers, 1995), 458.
44. Dr. Paul Brand, *Fearfully and Wonderfully Made* (Grand Rapids, MI: Zondervan), 187.
45. Sermon by Paul S. Beck, pastor of Calvary Bible Church, Huntsville, AL, February 16, 1997.
46. *Psychology as a Religion*, 72.
47. *The Divine Conquest*, 120.

Chapter 8: *Encounter in the Trees*

1. RTS, "Williams Reaches Out in Reconciliation," *Reformed Quarterly*, Summer 1997, 16. This activity is used in Young Life camps across the nation.
2. Reachout Expeditions, brochure, 11.
3. Ibid.
4. Ibid., 1.
5. Letter from Tony Campolo, national chairperson for WAKE UP AMERICA!
6. WAKE UP AMERICA! philosophy of ministry statement.
7. Ibid.
8. Promotional material from World Game Institute.
9. Thomas Sowell, *Inside American Education: The Decline, The Deception, The Dogmas* (New York: The Free Press, 1993), 36.
10. *Inside American Education*, 41.
11. Letter from Tony Campolo, national chairperson of WAKE UP AMERICA!
12. *Inside American Education*, 37.
13. Letter from teacher to parents concerning WAKE UP AMERICA's 18-Hour Encounter.
14. WAKE UP AMERICA's 18-Hour Encounter, "Money Talks."
15. Ibid., "Encounter Guidelines for Students."
16. Ibid., "Hour Two." All students get pizza later, even though they don't know at this time that they will.
17. Ibid., "Encounter Guidelines for Students."

18. The ideas and methods presented in the 18-Hour Encounter are also found in Denny Rydberg's *Building Community in Youth Groups* (Loveland, CO: Group Publishing, Inc., 1985), 99–105.
19. W. R. Coulson, quoted by Pearl Evans, *Hidden Dangers in the Classroom: Disclosure Based on Ideas of William Coulson* (Petsluma, CA: Small Helm Press, 1990), 56–57.
20. Carl Rogers, quoted by Pearl Evans, *Hidden Dangers in the Classroom*, 56.
21. Teen Mania's 1997 Acquire the Fire brochure, 4.
22. Rick Wesselhoff, *Extreme: A Real Live Look at the Forerunners*, from the Bring 'em Back Alive! series (Colorado Springs: David C. Cook Publishing, 1996), 4.
23. Promotional by Ron Luce, president and CEO of Teen Mania.
24. Reachout Expeditions, brochure, 1.
25. Ibid., 3.
26. *Reach Out and Embrace the Challenge,* brochure from Reachout Expeditions, Washington Branch, 1.
27. Ibid., 3–4.
28. Ibid., 8.
29. Letter from Bernie Waterhouse, executive director of Waterhouse Center, Inc., Lynnwood, WA, to parent/guardian of students from a local high school.
30. John MacArthur, *Reckless Faith: When the Church Loses Its Will to Discern* (Wheaton, IL: Crossway Books, 1994), 155.
31. George Gallup as quoted by Michael S. Horton, "Recovering the Plumb Line" in *The Coming Evangelical Crisis*, John Armstrong, ed. (Chicago: Moody, 1996), 259.
32. *Reckless Faith,* 154–55.
33. William K. Kilpatrick, *Psychological Seduction: The Failure of Modern Psychology* (Nashville, TN: Thomas Nelson Publishers, 1983), 167.
34. Ravi Zacharias, *Deliver Us from Evil: Restoring the Soul in a Disintegrating Culture* (Dallas: Word Publishing, 1996), 189.
35. D. M. Lloyd-Jones, *Knowing the Times* (Carlisle, PA: Banner of Trust, 1989), 86–88.

Chapter 9: *Tweaking Scripture*

1. *Carl Rogers on Encounter Groups* (New York: Harper & Row, 1970), 113–16.
2. Sidney B. Simon and others, *Values Clarification: A Handbook of Practical Strategies for Teachers and Students* (New York: Hart Publishing, 1972), 117.
3. Thomas Sowell, *Inside American Education: The Decline, the Deception, the Dogmas* (New York: The Free Press, 1993), 55.
4. Ibid., 56.
5. Denny Rydberg, *Trust Builders: 71 Activities to Develop Community in Your Youth Group* (Loveland, CO: Group Publishing, Inc., 1993), 11.

6. Denny Rydberg, *Building Community in Youth Groups* (Loveland, CO: Group Publishing, Inc. 1985), 59.
7. *Trust Builders*, 133.
8. Rick Wesselhoff, *Extreme: A Real Live Look at the Forerunners*, from the Bring 'em Back Alive! series (Colorado Springs, CO: David C. Cook Publishing, 1996), 4.
9. Ibid., 7.
10. Carl Rogers, *A Way of Being* (Boston: Houghton Mifflin Company, 1980), 89.
11. Carl Rogers, quoted by W. R. Coulson, from the manuscript of *Psychology of a Very Bad Dream*, Rogers and Coulson, eds., 5.
12. Jackie Perseghetti, *Dangerous Devotions* (Colorado Springs, CO: Chariot Books, a division of Cook Communications, 1995), back cover.
13. Adam Clarke, *Clarke's Commentary*, (Albany, OR: Books for the Ages, 1997) NT, vol. 5A; 860.
14. Ravi Zacharias, *Can Man Live without God* (Dallas: Word Publishing, 1994), 11.
15. *Why Jesus Christ Matters*, Core Belief Series (Loveland, CO: Group Publishing, Inc., 1997), 7.
16. Ibid., 21.
17. *Trust Builders*, 101–02.
18. Ibid., 102.
19. Ellen Graham, "Dewey Disciple: A conversation with the most ardent backer of active learning," *The Wall Street Journal*, September 11, 1992.
20. Kurt Bickel, *Getting Along with Parents*, Active Bible Curriculum (Loveland, CO: Group Publishing, Inc., 1990), 6.
21. Lois Keffer, *Sunday School Specials: Quick and Easy Bible Lessons for Combined Ages* (Loveland, CO: Group Publishing, Inc., 1992), 7.
22. *Building Communities in Youth Groups*, 11.
23. *Trust Builders*, 17.
24. *Why Jesus Christ Matters*, 58.
25. William K. Kilpatrick, *Psychological Seduction: The Failure of Modern Psychology* (Nashville, TN: Thomas Nelson Publishers, 1993), 179.
26. *Why Jesus Christ Matters*, 21.
27. Ibid., 58.
28. *Values Clarification*, 268.
29. *Trust Builders*, 97.
30. *Psychological Seduction*, 167–68.
31. *Sunday School Specials*, 7.
32. *Case Studies, Talk Sheets and Discussion Starters*, Jim Burns, gen. ed. (Cincinnati, OH: Gospel Light, 1977), 11.
33. *Angels Sent on Assignment*, Video Curriculum Series (Loveland, CO: Group Publishing, Inc., 1996), pages labeled "Important," 4.
34. Michael S. Horton, *In the Face of God: The Dangers and Delights of Spiritual Intimacy* (Dallas: Word Publishing, 1996), 53.
35. Ibid., 40.

36. John F. MacArthur, *Reckless Faith: When the Church Loses Its Will to Discern* (Wheaton, IL: Crossway Books, 1994), 196.
37. Ibid., 197.
38. Ibid., 153.
39. Michael S. Horton, "What This Book Is and Is Not" in *Power Religion: The Selling Out of the Evangelical Church?* (Chicago: Moody Press, 1992), 17.
40. *In the Face of God,* 79.
41. Ibid., 78–80.
42. James M. Boice, "A Better Way: The Power of the Word and the Spirit" in *Power Religion: The Selling Out of the Evangelical Church?* Michael S. Horton, ed. (Chicago: Moody Press, 1992), 130.
43. *Reckless Faith,* back cover of book.

Chapter 10: *Youth Ministry: A Biblical Model?*

1. John H. Armstrong, "Introduction: Two Vital Truths" in *The Coming Evangelical Crisis: Current Challenges to the Authority of Scripture and the Gospel* (Chicago: Moody Press, 1996), 24.
2. Christopher Schlect, *Critique of Modern Youth Ministry* (Moscow, Idaho: Canon Press, 1995), 3.
3. Ibid., 8.
4. Ibid., 9.
5. Ibid., 18.
6. Ibid., 11.
7. Ibid., 12.
8. Os Guinness, *Fit Bodies, Fat Minds: Why Evangelicals Don't Think and What to do about It* (Grand Rapids, MI: Baker Books, 1994), 120.
9. *Critique of Modern Youth Ministry,* 12.
10. Ibid.
11. D. M. Lloyd-Jones, *Knowing the Times* (Carlisle, PA: Banner of Trust, 1989), 2.
12. Rick Wesselhoff, *Extreme: A Real, Live Look at the Forerunners,* from the Bring 'em Back Alive! series (Colorado Springs, CO: David C. Cook Publishing, 1996), 5.
13. Ibid., 4.
14. Ibid., 4.
15. *Why Jesus Christ Matters,* Core Belief Series (Loveland, CO: Group Publishing, Inc., 1997), 57–58.
16. Denny Rydberg, *Trust Builders: 71 Activities to Develop Community in Your Youth Group* (Loveland, CO: Group Publishing, Inc., 1993), 17.
17. Denny Rydberg, *Building Community in Youth Groups* (Loveland, CO: Group Publishing, Inc. 1985), 30.
18. Youth Specialties, *High School Talksheets: 50 Creative Discussions for High School Youth Groups* (Grand Rapids, MI: Zondervan Publishing House, 1987), 9.
19. *Trust Builders,* 18–19.

20. *High School Talksheets,* 9.
21. *Why Jesus Christ Matters,* 60.
22. *Extreme,* 4.
23. *Trust Builders,* 55.
24. Kurt Bickel, *Getting Along with Parents* (Loveland, CO: Group Publishing, Inc., 1990), 14.
25. Martin and Deidre Bobgan, *Competent to Minister: The Biblical Care of Souls* (Santa Barbara, CA: Eastgate Publishers, 1996), 85.
26. *Critique of Modern Youth Ministry,* 15.
27. The Pastor's Weekly Briefing, a publication of Focus on the Family, Dan Davidson, editor June 13, 1997.
28. Schlect, 15.
29. C. H. Spurgeon, *Spiritual Parenting* (Springdale, PA: Whitaker House, 1995), 16.
30. *Spiritual Parenting,* 70.
31. *Critique of Modern Youth Ministry,* 15.
32. Ibid., 20.
33. Ibid., 20–21.
34. Ibid., 19.
35. Personal communication with Christopher Schlect, May 1998.
36. *130 Ways to Involve Parents in Youth Ministry* (Loveland, CO: Group Publishing, Inc., 1994), 3.
37. *Getting Along with Parents,* 5.
38. Ibid., 18
39. Paul S. Beck, pastor of Calvary Bible Church, Huntsville, AL.
40. *Getting Along with Parents,* 22.
41. *Trust Builders,* 15.
42. *Critique of Modern Youth Ministry,* 22.
43. Ibid., 22.

Chapter 11: *Raising Up Daniels*

1. William K. Kilpatrick, *Psychological Seduction: The Failure of Modern Psychology* (Nashville, TN: Thomas Nelson Publishers, 1983), 105.
2. John MacArthur, *Reckless Faith: When the Church Loses Its Will to Discern* (Wheaton, IL: Crossway Books, 1994), 85.
3. Paul S. Beck, while Pastor of Rome Community Bible Church, Bellingham, WA.
4. Martin and Deidre Bobgan, *Competent to Minister: The Biblical Care of Souls* (Santa Barbara, CA: Eastgate Publishers, 1996), 136.
5. *Psychological Seduction,* 106.
6. Michael S. Horton, "Recovering the Plumb Line" in *The Coming of the Evangelical Crisis: Current Challenges to the Authority of Scripture and the Gospel,* John H. Armstrong, ed. (Chicago: Moody Press, 1996), 225.
7. Ibid., 253.

8. A. W. Tozer, *The Divine Conquest: God's Pursuit of Man* (Camp Hill, PA: Christian Publications, 1950), 34.
9. D. M. Lloyd-Jones, *Knowing the Times* (Carlisle, PA: Banner of Trust, 1989), 12.
10. *Angels Sent on Assignment* (Loveland, CO: Group Publishing, Inc., 1996), Information labeled "Important," 3.
11. R. C. Sproul, "The Object of Contemporary Relevance" in *Power Religion: The Selling Out of the Evangelical Church?* Michael S. Horton, ed. (Chicago: Moody Press, 1992), 321.
12. *Knowing the Times,* 112.
13. C. H. Spurgeon, *Spiritual Parenting* (Springdale, PA: Whitaker House, 1995), 73–75.
14. *The Humanist Manifesto* (Buffalo, NY: Prometheus Books, 1973), 9.
15. *Reckless Faith,* 54.
16. *The Divine Conquest,* 24.
17. Ibid., 42.
18. Denny Rydberg, *Building Community in Youth Groups* (Loveland, CO: Group Publishing, Inc., 1985), epilogue.
19. A. W. Tozer, *Rut, Rot or Revival: The Condition of the Church* (Camp Hill, PA: Christian Publications, 1992), 4.
20. A. W. Tozer, *The Pursuit of God* (Harrisburg, PA: Christian Publications, 1948), 14.
21. Tom Stipe, foreword to *Counterfeit Revival: Looking for God in All the Wrong Places* by Hank Hanegraaff (Dallas: Word Publishing, 1997), xvi.

Appendix A: *Music for the Sensual or the Sacred?*

1. According to *Webster's International Dictionary* (2d ed.) a zombie is a soulless human corpse, still dead, but taken from the grave and endowed by sorcery with a mechanical semblance of life—it is a dead body which is made to walk and act and move as if it were alive (W. B. Seabrook).
2. Steve Camp, *107 Theses* (Nashville, TN: Steve Camp Ministries), poster.
3. Russ Walton, *Biblical Principles: Concerning Issues of Importance to Godly Christians* (Plymouth, MA: Plymouth Rock Foundation, 1984), 219.
4. Leonard Seidel, quoted by Russ Walton in *Biblical Principles,* 219.
5. *Biblical Principles,* 219–20.
6. *107 Theses.*

Appendix B: *The Gospel According to St. Bernard?*

1. Promotional distributed by Christian Video Enterprises, Inc., and the Zig Ziglar Corporation for *The Gospel According to St. Bernard.*
2. Os Guinness, *Fit Bodies, Fat Minds: Why Evangelicals Don't Think and What to Do about It* (Grand Rapids, MI: Baker Books, 1994), 97.
3. Ibid., 94.
4. Bill Deckard, "Angels We Have Heard?" *Moody,* April 1995; 46.

5. *The Gospel According to St. Bernard,* text compiled and edited by the Zig Ziglar Corporation (Plantation, FL: Christian Video Enterprises, Inc., 1992), video 1.
6. Ibid..
7. Paul Little, *Know What You Believe: A Practical Discussion of the Fundamentals of the Christian Faith* (Wheaton, IL: Victor Books, 1989), 101.
8. Dave Hunt and T. A. MacMahon, *The Seduction of Christianity: Spiritual Discernment in the Last Days* (Eugene, OR: Harvest House Publishers, 1995), 213.
9. *The Gospel According to St. Bernard,* video 1.
10. Ibid., video 6.
11. Ibid., A teacher and parent guide found inside video box for lesson 12.
12. Ibid., video 12.
13. Ibid., video 3.
14. John Ankerberg with John Weldon and Craig Branch, *Thieves of Innocence* (Eugene, OR: Harvest House, 1993), 18.
15. *The Seduction of Christianity,* 144.
16. *The Gospel According to St. Bernard,* video 1.
17. Sermon notes of Paul Beck, pastor of Calvary Bible Church in Huntsville, AL.
18. *The Gospel According to St. Bernard,* activity in lesson 1.
19. Ibid., theme song, verses 1 and 4.
20. *The Gospel According to St. Bernard,* lesson 5.
21. Paul S. Beck, personal communication, June 1998.
22. "Poll Reveals Biblical Ignorance: Angels Hot, Holy Spirit Not," *Northwest Christian Journal,* June 1997.
23. *The Gospel According to St. Bernard,* video 3.
24. Ibid., video 6.
25. Ibid., lesson 9.
26. Promotional material with the heading "Important Information."
27. *The Gospel According to St. Bernard,* lesson 5.
28. Ibid.
29. C. H. Spurgeon, *Spiritual Parenting* (Springdale, PA: Whitaker House, 1995), 111–12.
30. *Thieves of Innocence.*

Index

acceptance, 35, 41, 45, 80, 81, 91
active learning, 47, 51, 60, 154, 155, 156, 158, 162
active listening, 34, 172
Adams, Jay E., 32, 33, 111, 118, 125
affective education, 17
affirmation, 42, 45, 48, 55, 57, 60, 91, 117, 118, 121
Ankerberg, John, 208, 224
angel, 200, 201, 202, 203, 204, 210, 211, 212, 218
Armstrong, John H., 164
attitudes, 16, 42, 45, 46, 50, 71, 84, 90, 141
authority, 46, 48, 71–74, 85, 111, 114, 118, 119, 159, 171, 201, 215, 228, 232
    of Scripture, 87, 90, 131, 160
    undermining of, 19, 96, 177
autonomous, 33, 96
Bobgan, Martin and Deidre, 32, 52, 122, 182
brainwashing 135
Branch, Craig, 208, 224
Campolo, Tony, 133
Chesterton, G. K., 92
choice, 85, 86, 87
Christian Video Enterprises, 199

Coleman, Lyman, 44, 48, 51, 81, 149
collectivist, 36
community, 36, 37, 43, 48, 53, 57, 133
confidentiality, 44,
Coulson, W. R., 34, 49, 60 69, 72, 74, 81, 82, 85, 98, 103, 104, 138
critical thinking, xii, 60, 75
David C. Cook Publishing Co., 22, 140, 149, 168
death, xi, 22, 59, 228
decision making, xii, 17, 60, 72,
Dewey, John, 24, 36, 85
discernment, 79, 91, 93
drug, 80, 81
edge moments, 141
encounter group, 32, 41, 42, 48, 53, 57, 134, 144
    18-Hour Encounter, 133–35, 138, 145
    questions, 26
emotion, 18, 93, 120, 121, 131, 132, 133, 138, 154, 160, 162
entertainment, 27, 187
experience, 22, 46, 47, 50, 51, 52, 60, 108, 132, 133, 135, 144, 155, 160, 161, 162
facilitator, 19, 33, 39, 169, 172

feedback, 42, 46, 55

feelings, 32, 42, 43, 47, 62, 84, 97, 102, 103, 105, 106, 111, 120, 121, 218, 229

fellowship, 49, 50, 57, 58, 127, 230

Fuller, Buckminster, 134

Gospel According to St. Bernard, 16, 88, 199, 200, 205, 209, 214, 223, 225

Gospel Light, 20, 21, 51, 158

group
dynamics, 38, 54, 231
think, 34, 38

Group Publishing, Inc., 19, 25, 26, 27, 36, 51, 166, 154, 155, 156, 158, 187

Guinness, Os, 91, 166, 201

Hatch Amendment, 55

heresy, 17, 19, 45

hierarchy of needs, 32

Horton, Michael, 58, 74, 119, 127, 159, 161, 183

human potential, 68

Humanist Manifesto, xii, 36, 135, 190

humility, 119, 124, 129

Hunt, Dave, 82, 115, 116, 209

idolatry, 122, 211

"I" messages, 34, 172

individualism, 36

interactive learning, 51, 158

interdependence, 36

James, William, 107

Johnson, Gary L., 92

judgment, 80, 81, 84, 90, 91, 144

Kilpatrick, William K., 39, 56, 62, 67, 68, 71, 87, 118, 121, 123, 144, 155, 157

Kuyper, Abraham, xiv

Little, Paul, 107, 119

Lloyd-Jones, Dr. Martyn, xiv, 49, 50, 79, 92, 100, 101, 104, 145, 167, 168, 186, 188

Luther, Martin, 74, 162

MacArthur, John, 18, 91, 93, 106, 119, 143, 144, 159, 160, 161, 190

Maslow, Abraham, 31–34, 52, 55, 134

Maslow's Pyramid, 31, 32

McMahon, T. S., 82, 115, 116, 209

memorization, 26, 28, 66

moral dilemmas, 16, 21, 60, 67, 68, 89, 412

Murray, Andrew, 105, 124

new basics, xii, 218

Newton, Isaac, 128

nondirective, 32, 34, 171, 172

old basics, xii

opening up, 36, 42, 43, 55

pantheism, 25

parachurch, 143, 154, 162, 165, 166

passive learning, 20, 47

peer
pressure, 85
relationships, 158, 171
teaching, xii, 171, 172

Powlison, David, 115, 116, 125

psychological climate, 41, 42, 48, 57, 78

psychotherapy, 32–34, 38, 39, 51, 53

questions
open ended, 83
privacy invading, 16, 60, 65, 219, 220
think/feel, 83, 97, 113, 118, 219

Reachout Expeditions, 132, 141, 142, 149

rebel, 152, 153

rebellion, 60, 114, 152, 153, 171

relationships, 43, 44, 53, 54, 56, 62, 127, 142

relativism, 57, 59, 69, 76, 82, 89, 92, 93

revolution, 27, 154

risk, risktaking, 44, 51, 138, 147, 148, 149, 150, 151, 153, 156

risktaker, 81, 149

Rogers, Carl, 15, 31–34, 41, 44–46, 52–54, 89, 95, 97, 120, 134, 138, 147, 184

role-play, xii, 16, 18, 20, 67, 216, 217, 232

rope course, 132
Rydberg, Denny, 21, 36, 37, 44, 51, 80, 81, 101, 148, 155, 157
Schlafly, Phyllis, 17
Schrank, Jeffrey, 37, 95, 96, 105
Schlect, Christopher, 165, 166, 167, 173, 174, 175, 179
Schultz, Thom, 27, 36
segregation, age, 166
self-actualization, 34, 32
self-concept, 80, 115, 116
self-disclosure, 39, 42, 232
self-esteem, xi, xii, 16, 32, 61, 62, 111, 112, 115–18, 124, 126, 231
sensitivity/diversity training, 60, 62, 63, 134
sex education, xi, 32, 59, 68, 74
Simon, Sidney, 65, 83, 85, 86, 87, 89, 147, 156
simulated therapy, 98
simulation, 20, 24, 137
sin, 27, 33, 56, 123, 127, 212, 213, 217
situational ethics, 16, 60, 89
Sizer, Ted, 154
Sowell, Thomas, 17, 69, 135, 147, 148
Sproul, R. C., 188
Spurgeon, Charles H., 39, 40, 124, 125, 174, 189, 190, 222
standards, 84, 166, 228
team building, 38, 44
Teen Mania, 139–41
Tolerance, xii, 59, 79, 80, 89, 91, 92
touch, 102, 103, 104
therapy, 69
Tozer, A. W., 61, 77, 110, 113, 116, 119, 123, 129, 183, 191, 192
tribalism, see *segregation*
trust, 48, 49, 52, 53, 56, 60, 62, 81, 96–103, 110, 132, 139, 147
mutual, 41, 43, 55
trust fall, 101, 102
trust walk, 15, 95, 96, 97, 139, 155
values clarification, xii, 16, 17, 60, 67–69, 76, 82, 83, 85, 86, 87, 89
"Christian," 81, 82

visualization, 207, 208
Vitz, Paul C., 82, 113, 128
World Concern, 133, 136
Young Life, 21, 36, 132, 165
Youth Specialties/Zondervan, 18–20, 44, 51, 83, 86
Zacharias, Ravi, 73, 153, 144, 152
Zig Ziglar, 199
Zombie Tour, 193

About the Authors

Cathy Mickels is the Washington state president of Phyllis Schlafly's national conservative organization, Eagle Forum. She has been an effective voice on behalf of many pro-family and education issues, such as strong opposition to outcome-based education.

She was also appointed to Governor Booth Gardner's Task Force on AIDS. Because of Cathy's intense lobbying efforts, legislation was passed in Washington state that requires sexual abstinence outside lawful marriage to be taught in all public school AIDS education.

In addition, Cathy was elected to represent Washington state on the National Platform Committee at the 1992 Republican National Convention in Houston.

Cathy and her husband, Stan, are associates of Hillsdale College in Michigan. They reside in Lynden, Washington.

Audrey McKeever has a Bachelor of Arts from Western Washington State University and has taught in both public and private schools.

As regional director of Eagle Forum in Washington state, Audrey has focused on the radical transformation taking place in public education. She has written many articles on the subject, including an article for Phyllis Schlafly's national newspaper, *The Education Reporter.* As a guest on local radio, Audrey has alerted parents to the dangers of controversial public school curricula.

Now her efforts are turned toward the church, alerting parents to the increasing problem of secular worldviews and humanistic teaching methods appearing in Christian youth curricula.

Audrey and her husband, Doug, reside in Bellingham, Washington.

To order additional copies of

Spiritual
Junk
Food

send $12.99 plus $3.95 shipping and handling to

Books Etc.
PO Box 1406
Mukilteo, WA 98275

or have your credit card ready and call

(800) 917-BOOK